The ultimate
Goddess

The ultimate Goddess

Be the woman
you want to be

Elisabeth Wilson

Acknowledgements

Infinite Ideas would like to thank Tania Ahsan, Nicholas Bate, Linda Bird, Paul Blake, Darren Bridger, Sally Brown, Eve Cameron, Kate Cook, Peter Cross, Sabina Dosani, Barbara Griggs, Lisa Helmanis, Lynn Huggins-Cooper, Ken Langdon, Maggie Loughran, Natalia Marshall, Victoria Perrett, Colin Salter, Steve Shipside, Alexander Gordon Smith, Cathy Struthers and Elisabeth Wilson for their contributions to this book.

The right of the contributors to be identified as the author of this book has been asserted in accordance with the Copyright, Designs and Patents Act 1988.

First published in 2008 by
The Infinite Ideas Company Limited
36 St Giles
Oxford, OX1 3LD
United Kingdom
www.infideas.com

A CIP catalogue record for this book is available from the British Library

ISBN 978-1-905940-90-5

Text designed and typeset by Baseline Arts Ltd, Oxford
Cover designed by Cylinder
Printed in Singapore

Brilliant ideas

2   LOOK GORGEOUS

4   BE HEALTHY AND ENERGISED

5   WORK SMARTER

6   GREEN GODDESS

7   ME TIME

Introduction

Welcome to *The Ultimate Goddess* – sequel to the highly successful *Goddess: Be the woman you want to be.*

We think the first *Goddess* volume struck a chord with so many readers because it recognised that for twenty-first century women the choices are endless – and although that can be exhilarating, it can also be confusing and exhausting. Sometimes we need a map, and just like the original *Goddess, The Ultimate Goddess* is just that, packed with even more brilliant solutions for taking control of your future with the minimum of effort.

There are an awful lot of ideas here. So where should you start? First, recognise which goddess you are manifesting right now. This changes throughout our lives reflecting the many choices we face. Recognising which female archetype (goddess) we are resonating with during any particular period in our lives can be liberating – we can either harness the energy to make the most of it, or work out how to move away from it if we want to achieve something different.

Which thumbnail character sketch most resonates with you right now?

Character 1
- ❁ I am absorbed with my personal relationships.
- ❁ I am living a lot in my head right now.
- ❁ How I look and how I am perceived is important to me.

Character 2
✿ I like challenges that allow me to show how resourceful I am.
✿ I get recognition for my achievements and I suppose that is important to me.
✿ I am quite private and don't show my vulnerabilities easily.

Character 3
✿ I am fascinated by the idea of reaching my full potential.
✿ I'd rather be on my own than in a bad relationship, and people have complained that I can shut them out.
✿ I am self-reliant.

Character 4
✿ I am seen as nurturing, strong and kind.
✿ I often put others' needs before my own.
✿ I have a lot of inner strength but sometimes feel others don't realise I need support, too.

If **character 1** is most like you, right now you are exhibiting your inner Aphrodite, the Goddess of love and desire. You feel bold, passionate, charismatic and throw yourself into sensual pleasures. You will find more ways to express this wild energy in ideas 45–64. **Ready to move on?** If you feel a little restless, you could benefit from unleashing your inner Artemis, stepping back from personal relationships, building boundaries and demonstrating your abundant creativity in more ways than developing a killer wardrobe. Turn to ideas 1–19 and 90–113 for some inspiration.

If **character 2** is most like you, right now you are exhibiting your inner Athena, the Goddess of wisdom. Your career or ambitions for yourself are probably important to you, your relationships less so. You inspire other people with your cleverness and resourcefulness and are idealistic, believing you need to give more back. You will find more ways to do this in ideas 90–130. **Ready to move on?** If you feel a little restless, you could benefit from unleashing your inner Aphrodite, moving towards sensual pleasure and indulging yourself. Turn to ideas 20–32 for some inspiration.

If **character 3** is most like you, right now you are manifesting your inner Artemis, the Goddess of hunting. You are independent, creative and a little wild. You can be a loner – you hate to feel tied down and you love the feeling that you don't know what is round the next corner. You will find more ideas for building the life you want in ideas 1–19. **Ready to move on?** If you feel a little restless, you could benefit from unleashing your inner Demeter, doing more for others, recognising we're all connected and harnessing your energy for the good of us all. Turn to ideas 114–130 for some inspiration that will let you maintain your own space.

If **character 4** is most like you, currently your inner Demeter, the Goddess of harvest and motherhood, is to the fore. You are loving and nurturing, putting others before yourself as a matter of course. This selflessness can drift into self-neglect, however. You will find more inspiration for looking after yourself in ideas 131–147. **Ready to move on?** If you feel a little restless, you could benefit from unleashing your inner Athena, moving towards fulfilling your own ambitions. Turn to ideas 1–19 for some inspiration.

No matter which goddess you are manifesting at the moment you will be able to find ideas in all sections that will make you think, make you smile and inspire you to act. Quizzes at the start of each section will suggest where you might like to begin or dip in and out as you please and begin to unleash the ultimate goddess in you!

1. Sort out your life and get what you want

You want so much from life, you just don't know where to start. This section will help you work out your priorities, form goals, make plans to achieve those goals. Then, do it! There are also some expert tips on overcoming the obstacles that can get in our way.

What's holding you back?

Ever get the feeling that no matter how hard you work at it, life is difficult? Could you be the problem? Sometimes we can't see clearly what is getting in our way of succeeding. This quiz could help.

1. You start the day:
- ☐ a. In a perfectly clear work environment – but you never seem to get everything done.
- ☐ b. Invariably looking for something important that you've mislaid.
- ☐ c. Catching up on something you should have done yesterday.

2. A friend calls you for a chat. You:
- ☐ a. Chat – you deserve a break.
- ☐ b. Chat but let her know that you're really busy.
- ☐ c. Let the phone pick up the call – you've got way too much to do.

3. When it comes to booking your summer holidays, you tend to:
- ☐ a. Leave it to the last minute – you never have time to research it.
- ☐ b. Leave it to the last minute because you're never sure if you're going to be able to take the time off.
- ☐ c. Leave it to the last minute because it takes longer than you thought to find somewhere nice.

4. Simple jobs always take longer than they should. Agree?
- ☐ a. Yes, because I get distracted while I'm doing them.
- ☐ b. Yes, because I keep putting them off as something important has come up.
- ☐ c. Yes, because they seem to grow when I focus on them.

5. I'm often late to meet friends because:
- ☐ a. I get caught up with someone or something else.
- ☐ b. I forget my purse, lose directions, get the time wrong.
- ☐ c. I've always got a million things to do.

Mostly 'a's. You are a procrastinator, putting jobs off until the last minute. This means that jobs build up so there are days when you have nothing but grim tasks to complete and all at breakneck speed – and there's absolutely no room for fun. Look at idea 10 and idea 11.

Mostly 'b's. You are a muddler, spending too much of your time chasing your tail . But you probably don't realise the problem lies with you – you think you are overburdened, hard done by and incredibly busy. We know it's dull but losing a little of the arty chaos might help. Look at idea 19 as a first step.

Mostly 'c's. You are an underestimator. There is so much you want to achieve that you pack it all in, assuming you can do in an hour what in reality will take you a day. Ideas 1 and 7 may help you remember that you have to decide on your priority, set your own agenda – and stick to it. Because sadly, you really can't do it all!

1. You're the boss of you

Taking responsibility for your own life may be the toughest thing you do in your quest for inner peace. But the sooner you realise that you're your own knight in shining armour the better.

The President of the United States is the highest office in that country for the same reason that you hold the highest office in your life; the buck stops with you.

The life you lead is the result of decisions that you have made and are constantly making. This is not to say that the outside world doesn't have any influence – of course it does – but ultimately you're running the show. You must not cave in to feeling powerless to make changes in your own life. While you may only have limited control over what you do, you can exercise full control over what you feel and how you react to those limitations.

Here's a typical example: your boss decides to give you a report to do last thing on a Friday night and wants it first thing on Monday morning. It is probably not a practical response for you to jack in your job (though if you have to miss your wedding or a relative's funeral to do it and your boss doesn't cut you some slack, you may do well to start looking at the jobs ads). However, how you deal with a) the feelings this invokes in you and b) the actual task ahead can be vital to your sense of inner peace.

A bad way to respond would be to stomp off home with the work, be in a bad mood all weekend and do it angrily and reluctantly, regularly sighing loudly and bemoaning your fate, while snapping at any poor family member silly enough to pass within a few feet of you.

> **Here's an idea for you...**
>
> **Do you know what your income and expenditure is? List all your income in one column and all your outgoings in the next and then create a budget that ensures you're not exceeding your income. It's not boring... well OK, it is a bit boring, but boring is better than the serious distress of insolvency.**

A better way would be to accept that you've decided to do the work. And you have, because you didn't resign at the point that you were told about it. So you had the power to leave but you didn't. So, having made a decision to do something, do it well. Put on your favourite music, fix yourself something tasty to snack on while you work and maybe even get your partner to work in the same room so you can have a sense of camaraderie. Take regular breaks but, instead of breaking your flow by going to the TV room, go for a short walk instead or have a boogie round the room.

Society is organised in a very complex way and one of the side effects of this organisation is to make you feel very small and insignificant. If we want to buy a house, most of us have to get a mortgage. To get a mortgage you need a job – a very well-paying job if the house is to be in a nice area. To get the partner you want, you have to be attractive to him or her – be it in looks or behaviour. You have to continue to attract if you want to retain your partner. Let's not even start on the demands of the children. In short, it can very quickly seem as if everyone has got a

vested interest in your life – except you. You can feel trapped by all of these social restrictions you put on yourself.

The real revolution happens when you realise that this is your own construct. You have made this. You have decided you want this house or that job. Your choice of partner is determined by you. The way you raise your kids is partly determined by you. As such, if you're feeling unhappy and conflicted by any aspect of your life, YOU can change it. Feel that power coursing through your veins – doesn't it feel fantastic? Now get back out there and go 'Grrrrr!' at the world.

Defining idea...

'Man is condemned to be free; because once thrown into the world, he is responsible for everything he does.'
JEAN-PAUL SARTRE, being his ever-cheery but highly-perceptive self. Think not of it as being 'condemned' but more 'blessed'.

2. Far out, man

You can achieve an altered state without needing to find your nearest drug dealer – honestly, you can. You just need to start engaging with the world again.

If you're stuck in a rut, it can feel as though nothing is new or special. When that feeling of stagnation hits you, you need to find ways to achieve a new state of being.

Meditation doesn't work for me. Being a mind, body and spirit editor that's a bit of shameful admission as we're all supposed to be meditation adepts who can hightail it to a higher state of awareness quicker than you can say 'Ooooommmmmm'. But altered states can be achieved in ways other than sitting around in pristine white clothes chanting with our eyes closed.

For example, I don't need pot. I have a friend called Nish who has the exact same effects as those that potheads crave. She makes you feel relaxed and the longer you spend in her company, the more you're likely to start giggling. She also makes you not want to get up and leave to start your day. You just want to stay there and get high on her. However, she has none of the side effects. You're unlikely to receive a police caution (well, at least as long as she's not driving). You're also unlikely to be sold Nish cut with bad things that will make you ill. Nish is the perfect recreational drug.

Do you have anyone like that in your life? Someone who is so engaged with everything and so interested in you that they make you think that, hey, perhaps I am interesting after all! If you don't, you need to begin a quest to find someone like that. Perhaps you had someone like that but you lost touch? If so, find them again.

For others, music is the path to a drug-free high. I have had more spiritual moments listening to the Counting Crows than I have meditating. I know some folks who devote vast tracts of time, money and energy to music. They're not musicians but they've found a way to reach a state of joy and engagement through appreciating the music made by others.

> Here's an idea for you...
>
> **Try spinning around in the garden, like you used to when you were little and then when you stop, lie down on the grass and look at the sky. This gives you a sensation like the earth is moving beneath you. Well, it certainly moved for me anyway.**

Engagement is the word you're looking for. Not the big diamond ring kind but the 'can't take my eyes off this' kind. Now, here's an exercise. Close your eyes. Take three deep breaths. Don't worry, I'm not going to ask you to mediate. You can open your eyes again. Now, think really hard of where and when you last felt completely joyous. Properly joyous. It could be when you last laughed so hard, you cried. Or it could be something more wacky.

My personal one is from last Christmas when I got invited as a 'plus one' to someone's office Christmas party. I'm not a corporate person so the thought of an evening making small talk with people I didn't know wasn't filling me with hope and excitement. However, I wanted to see the friend who had invited me and I figured we could chat the night away, even if it was a bit of a chore to be with others. The party was a surprise one as no-one had been told where we were being taken. A bunch of cabs had been booked to take all the guests to a secret location.

When we got there, the place was just a black door with a doorman outside. It was in middle of somewhere random like Kennington. Once we stepped through the door though, it was completely different. We were in an enchanted garden, all themed in a 'horror' style with dry ice acting as fog and moving mechanical creatures in the garden. Through the garden was Simon Drake's House of Magic! There followed the best evening of magic and cabaret I have ever seen and it created a memory like no other. I felt like I was five again and seeing the world anew. That sense of wonder is what you should be aiming for.

Defining idea...

**'He does not need opium.
He has the gift of reverie.'**
ANAIS NIN, diarist and author

3. Retox for life

Bring on the booze and fags – you know you want to. Try this weekend retox and see whether a lot of what you fancy does you any good.

Frightening health reports have us regarding our food and drink with suspicion. You never know what is going to be found to be lethal for us next.

Everything is terrible for you. Meat? Awful. Dairy products? Forget it. White bread? Bad idea. Actually, all wheat comes to your bread bin via Satan's inner sanctum. It is baked in the fires of hell and is there simply to cause you to put on weight and then have a heart attack before your time. Vitamins aren't that great for you either because you never know what the capsules they're contained in are made of. And you could be overdoing them anyway.

No, the best thing for you to do is not eat. Or drink. Except pure water triple-filtered and served at room temperature. Aaargggh! When did we become so LA? Not wanting to offend readers in LA but I personally love going there just to eat juicy, succulent steaks and thick cut fries. Simply because it's considered on a par with mugging pensioners in that crazy city. You can always tell the tourist or the out-of-towner there as they'll be the ones with bad teeth who actually eat, rather than push food around their plates, as if they were examining particularly revolting slugs.

Here's an idea for you...

Go for a traditional cream tea or to an ice cream parlour and enjoy a big treat. If you can't afford that, make your own sundae at home. Ensure you get as many toppings as possible and relish every bite. You are banned from making comments like 'the diet starts tomorrow' or 'this'll go straight to my hips'.

People, this is no way to live. I know, I've been there. I've tried every diet and healthy eating plan under the sun. You name it, I've denied myself it. It got so I couldn't actually see what was being offered to me, all I could see was calorific content. It didn't matter if my taste buds zinged at the idea of eating what was put in front of me, I had to first ascertain if it was 'safe' for me to eat. I no longer enjoyed food. It was all just a mathematical equation and not particularly exciting math either.

One day I popped out to the supermarket to get some lunch and I returned an hour later, on the verge of tears. I had been unable to decide on my lunch as I had picked up one sandwich after another, calculating the calorie value and then putting it down again. I was so determined to pick a meal that was healthy and non-fattening that I had no idea what I was doing. I didn't pick up anything because it looked appealing but only because it looked low fat.

I stopped dieting and started remembering what I really enjoyed eating. I love Cornish ice cream, meringues, carrot cake, seafood, medium-rare steak with new potatoes, Yorkshire puddings, rocket and parmesan salad with balsamic vinegar, cheeses, pasties, ooooh chocolate, and sushi. I began a litany of all my favourite foods, some of which were good for me and some of which weren't. Then that weekend, I had a massive feast with several of the dishes I named there for me. I didn't just wolf them down. I ate with all my senses. Before I get all Nigella on you, it was a sensuous delight. Best of all, I didn't once think 'I wonder what the calorie content of that is?'

We tend to save treats for special occasions like Christmas or birthdays but have some champagne this weekend to start off your retox and then maybe make yourself some canapés to have before supper. Yes, it's indulgent (especially if you're dining alone) but you deserve a treat as much as those guests you would normally slave over a hot stove for. By the end of the weekend, you'll have restored your sense of serenity through mindful eating of all that gives you 'happy mouth'.

> Defining idea...
>
> **'When choosing between two evils, I always like to pick the one I never tried before.'**
> MAE WEST, actress and supreme Queen of wit

4. Me, myself and I

Don't compare or compete with anyone but yourself. You're not a carbon copy of anyone – not even your identical twin, if you have one.

Each person on the planet is unique and we should celebrate that uniqueness by not constantly trying to measure up to somebody else.

The worst people for comparing themselves to others are overachievers. Instead of enjoying the successes and blessings they have had, they're too busy looking at the next target and this mindless dash to some imaginary finishing line that never comes. Will they be happy being the next Richard Branson? Hell, no! They don't want to be the 'next' anybody – they want to be the original, the one that people quote in business or reference books; the epitome of success.

The problem with being that sort of a person is that when life throws you a curve ball, you can be hit a lot harder than you'd expect. Redundancies happen, the business doesn't do as well as you thought it would, your loved one leaves and your supposedly 'perfect' marriage falls apart. Any manner of unexpected and unwelcome changes can happen. If you've spent your life living up to someone else's idea of success, it can be a terrible blow when that is taken away from you.

I know someone who always brings up the subject of salaries whenever we meet. She seems to want to confirm, every time we meet, that she is earning more than any of our other friends. Now I know from where this stems; she had a very unhappy childhood whereby she was the poorest kid in school and she was often mocked for having a modest home and never having the latest things. Instead of rising above the psychological wounds of her childhood, she is attempting to repair them by achieving material success and then by comparing herself to her peer group to satisfy herself that she is not the 'poor kid' any more. For those in our circle who don't know her very well, her questions are starting to grate and they now avoid her because it feels like she's lording it over them. This is very sad as it is the exact opposite to her desired outcome – acceptance.

We all have benchmarks by which we measure success. It may be money, it may be how handsome and charming our lovers are or by how good we look. Since all of these things have no intrinsic value in themselves, we only learn of their value through comparison. I once had the unenviable task of choosing between two men. Both were gorgeous, both rich and both very clever. In the end I chose neither. Why? Because when I thought about them, I thought about the fact that they were rich and handsome rather than that I really loved them. I intuitively knew that those value judgements would go out the

> *Here's an idea for you...*
>
> **Channel your future self. This is an exercise you can do simply for fun. Relax your body and close your eyes for a minute, imagine that you're about 65 years old and about to retire (if you are that age then take it another 20 years forward). Then write down some questions about your life that you'd like answered by your future self. A typical question might be 'Did I live abroad at all?' and then try to see your future self answering that question for you. You don't have to put much store by it but it does open you up to the way you would like things to pan out.**

Defining idea...

'**Envy consists in seeing things never in themselves, but only in their relations. If you desire glory, you may envy Napoleon, but Napoleon envied Caesar, Caesar envied Alexander, and Alexander, I daresay, envied Hercules, who never existed.'**
BERTRAND RUSSELL, philosopher and Nobel Laureate

window when I met the right guy. I'd no longer be thinking whether my guy would impress my friends but whether I enjoyed his company and whether he made me laugh.

In the same way, you should measure your success not by whether it meets the criteria of others or society but by whether you're happy with it. Happiness for you could be a small doughnut shop in a busy part of town while for the guy down the road it may be a baked goods empire, providing doughnuts to supermarkets across the world. You be the judge.

5. Less is more

Having a clearout is great for the soul and even better for your pocket so get sorting through all your possessions, remembering to only keep what's useful or beautiful.

It's not just Stepford wives that need a neat, tidy home – we all need to come back from the chaos of the world outside to a haven of beauty and order.

I have this fantasy. No, not the one where I'm a mermaid and Josh Holloway (the actor who plays Sawyer in *Lost* and who's in the Davidoff Cool Water ads) dives into the sea, accidentally startling me in the middle of a bath… 'Oh, Mr Holloway! But I am naked!'… ahem. Anyway, moving on, I have this fantasy that I will come home one day and everything will be pristine and orderly. It will be as if Jeeves came by on his leave from Bertie Wooster and cleaned and tidied the house from top to bottom. Clothes would be neatly pressed and put away. Paperwork would be in files convenient to locate. Surfaces would have very little on them and so be easy to dust and keep clean. Beautiful objets d'art and frames would adorn the house.

It's a fantasy because I'm a hoarder. I never think 'this is junk', I think 'I could use that for Christmas wrapping decoration' or 'this might be useful one day'. Of course that one day is never, ever likely to come. Unless of course you throw away said bit of junk, in which case, you'll find a need for it the very next day.

Sue Kay, author and professional declutterer, once had a session with me. She called a lot of my concerns 'negative thinking'. I assumed bad things would happen if I let go of my junk. I'd not be able to prove my existence without my hundreds of scraps of paper. Except why would anyone be trying to eradicate my existence? After all, I'm not a top spy. I kept two copies of everything I'd ever written, just in case one of the copies went missing, had coffee split on it or was burned to a cinder. My logical mind can grasp that if I have stuff piled up everywhere, it is much more likely to go missing or have coffee split on it. Plus I keep the two copies together and can't think of one occasion on which one would be burnt to a cinder while the other remained unscathed.

> *Here's an idea for you...*
>
> **Pick an area of your house you have been avoiding decluttering, play one of your favourite albums and just begin. If it's not beautiful or useful, it gets the heave-ho. Most albums are under an hour long and you can stop as soon as the music stops. If at the end of the album, you want to keep going, pop on another album and carry on.**

Sue did a two-hour session with me and cleared masses of things. We had a charity bag, a keep bag and a throw away bag. Sue seems to have a morbid terror of moths and, given the amount of silk I've lost to the little blighters over the years, I share her concerns. She explained that the more stuff I had, the less likely I could keep it all clean and the more likely things like moths would get at it.

By the end of the session, my room felt lighter, I had got rid of loads of unnecessary stuff and I had found some earrings to wear that I had forgotten I had. It was a lot like treasure hunting. Her cool, calm approach made everything go fast and I didn't

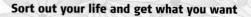
linger over every little thing, paralysed by fear that I might throw away something useful. Reading is also a big problem for me when decluttering as I tend to get caught up reading some clipping I've kept or a magazine that must be read before it is donated to the doctor's surgery. Having Sue there meant I couldn't indulge this real 'time bandit' when it comes to decluttering. Find a 'tough love' friend who'll sit drinking coffee while you declutter. Ask him or her to stop you if it looks like you're about to start reading something instead of getting on with it.

> Defining idea...
>
> **'No person who can read is ever successful at cleaning out an attic.'**
> ANN LANDERS, American advice columnist

19

6. Soul rage

How to deal with anger (without getting 25-to-life). Take a deep breath before you blow your top – remember you're a person, not a firework.

We wouldn't be human if we didn't sometimes feel angry but how you deal with that anger is what separates the peaceful at heart from the raging at heart.

My mate Simon trained as a Buddhist monk for several years in Thailand. This gives him a very calm and collected exterior and I have only ever heard him raise his voice once or twice in the whole time I've known him. His way of dealing with things is to laugh at the absurdity and then go get a mug of coffee. He rarely went into an all-out strop and rage about anything.

I used to vampire energy off him whenever I could. It was like sidling up to a fire and warming your hands. When you're naturally highly strung, meeting someone who's not is a revelation. You have a blood vessel pounding in your forehead because of something someone's said while your calm contemporary will simply say 'that's not really true, is it?' at the person talking nonsense. It is disarming.

Now please don't confuse Simon's composure with bottling things up. I am the expert on bottling things up. I used to go for years carrying rages in my stomach that I hadn't expressed. When I was 14 years old, I chased down a boy with a tennis racket with the intention of bludgeoning him to death with it because I had had enough of seven previous years of younger kids being cheeky at school. All that pent-up rage exploded and I'm pretty certain that if I hadn't been so bad at running, I would have swiftly ended my school career in a very newsworthy murder.

Anger in and of itself is not bad. If it was then you'd never have had the civil rights movement, women would never have got the vote, we would not have been able to remove corrupt leaders from our governments; quite a few good things have resulted from a well-placed sense of righteous anger. What's bad is when you hurt someone else – either emotionally or physically – because you're unable to express your anger appropriately.

We have tongues and lips to speak out our rage and to kiss and make up after having expressed it. When we feel angry with our partners, it is particularly difficult as they are the people we expect to spend the rest of our lives with. Just remember that an argument does not a break-up make. You can feel angry and you can row

> *Here's an idea for you...*
>
> **Experiment with your food intake by keeping a food/emotion diary. Many people find their tempers calm down if they cut out red meat, and alkaline dairy products are also calming foods. If your diary shows you have a row whenever you have that medium-rare steak, it might be worth keeping it to special occasions when rows are less likely. Always, always drink a glass of water if you feel you're going to blow your top.**

without it needing to reach critical levels. Your partner knows how to press your buttons better than anyone else so remember that before you fly off the handle.

Also, when you feel angry about something, consider first if there is anything constructive you can do about it. Write to your MP? Write a letter of complaint? Ask to see a manager? Go to marriage or career counselling? Once you've exhausted the constructive 'dealing with the problem' options, look at dealing with the emotion. Physical exercise tends to drain away anger like nothing else. So perhaps you could go for a swim or a walk? Above all, don't take your anger out on your friends and family. They are your support network and you should be kind to them. You know it makes sense.

Defining idea...

Get mad, then get over it.'
COLIN POWELL, retired General and former US Secretary of State

7. List lustre

Lists can bring order into your life and mind – but only if you use them wisely, young Padwan.

The beauty of writing a list is that you can tick it off and have a visual reminder of how much you have achieved in the day.

My friend Alex could probably sort out world peace if she was given a pad, a pen, a bit of time and a free hand. She is the list genius. I once made the mistake of telling her how overwhelmed by work I felt.

'Right,' she announced, in the manner of one about to go to war. 'Get me my pad and start telling me what you have to do.' She sat there and made a list of everything I had to do over the course of that month. She then went through and prioritised it. I tend to do a lot of favours for my ex – probably in the hope that he'll fall back in love with me. His bits and pieces were the first to be chopped from Alex's master list. 'Only do that which you have a good reason to do. If you're struggling to find time to do the tasks that earn you your money, you do not have time to do tasks that are just about emotional unfinished business'. Of course, she was right and her red pen is a great deal more lethal than any sword and several boys had been beheaded metaphorically by the end of the list-making.

While we were working on this 'master list', Alex told me about one of her friends who was very like me. She had a beautiful mahogany dining table that she never got to eat at or even see properly because it was groaning under the weight of all her paperwork, magazines and projects. Alex sorted it out for her by refusing to let her handle one piece of paper more than once. Like me, her friend was used to picking things up, going 'oh I must do that' and then putting it down again and going onto the next thing. By the end she was left with everything still undone but Alex changed all that.

If a piece of paper had a phone number or address on it that she needed, it was to be copied down into her contacts book straight away and the paper could go in the recycling bin. Old newspapers went straight to the recycling bank because it was old news and not worth reading. If a paper reminded her friend of something she had to do, it was written down on the master list. Anything to be filed had to be filed then and there, with a new filing system created to deal with the bits of paper. By the end, she had a clear, beautifully polished table and one list containing all the information about what she had to do.

Here's an idea for you...

Right before you go to bed, make a wish list. During the day we are so busy with work lists that we forget that you can use the power of the list to manifest lovely, fun things too. Choose something enjoyable like beach holidays or books or restaurants you'd like to visit and make a list of the top ten you'd really like to have or do. Then when each happens, cross it off your list. When the last is done, make a new list!

Alex then told her friend (and me) to go through each thing, in priority order, and just do it. Once done, tick it off. At the end of the day, we had to transfer any unfinished tasks onto the next day's list. It was a very satisfying thing and, since I've started doing this, I get through so much more and have such a great sense of achievement and – yes, you've guessed it – inner peace.

Defining idea...

'Nothing is so fatiguing as the eternal hanging on of an uncompleted task.'
WILLIAM JAMES, American psychologist and philosopher

8. Clever, not cheap

When society pressurises you to spend, spend, spend, gain the confidence to just say no.

Frugality doesn't need to turn you into a joyless cheapskate.
Get financially savvy and no longer dread the dull thud of your credit card bill on the mat.

How much money do you have in your purse or pocket? Those who respect money could probably tell you almost to the penny how much they have. Those, like me, who have a more complicated relationship with it, will probably get it quite wrong. The problem with money is that it is rarely what it truly is: simply a medium of exchange. No, money is often a way of expressing your beliefs about your status, class and even worth as a human being. Your attitude to money can enslave you or set you free.

Economical living can make you feel deprived and miserable or it can fill you with a sense of achievement and excitement. Take the task of living well within your means as an enjoyable challenge rather than something to be feared or resented.

First things first: make your monthly budget. List your income and your expenditure and see what you have got left each month to play with. For the first couple of days of the month, don't buy anything; just keep some money in your pocket. If you're a spendaholic, this will be quite difficult but try to see how liberating it is to have money you could spend if you wanted to but then not spend it. The decision is yours and you don't have to bow to pressure to buy.

Clothes can be a heavy expenditure, especially if you need to look smart for work. Since retro clothing became more popular, more and more people are hunting out second-hand and vintage shops to stock up on bygone fashions. This is great for the wardrobe and for the pocket as you can really pick up some superb bargains. Avoid the dedicated vintage stores as they overprice and look for second-hand/charity shops in areas with an older population as they are more likely to donate originals that will be in excellent condition. I once found a gorgeous Biba coat for just £3. You will get a frisson of excitement at finding a designer item at a fraction of the cost.

Another major expense is the monthly grocery shopping bill. Take a look at where you can make savings. Have you tried some of the supermarket generic brands for taste and quality? Some things you'll find are awful but a lot of others are very good and a fraction of the price of big name brands. Start gently and try substituting something you always buy like washing powder or pasta with a supermarket own brand and see if your family notice the difference. If not, then swap to it and save loads of wonga.

Here's an idea for you...

Challenge yourself to find, make or acquire very cheaply a present for a friend whose birthday is coming up. The rule is that your friend must love the gift and you can't spend more than a fiver on it. Funnily enough the secret to doing this one well is to listen to your friends carefully as we often learn about their preferences through careful listening. My friend once made me bergamot bath salts as I had mentioned in two separate conversations my love of bergamot and of baths.

Get your family and friends in on the act and share tips for saving money and still living well. Perhaps you can revert to barter for some things? If your cousin is great at gardening and you're brilliant at dress-making, barter and use your respective skills to help each other out. You'll save money and have the satisfaction of a job well done.

During the Second World War, pamphlets were distributed to housewives encouraging them to 'make do and mend'. This meant that when clothing got worn, they'd be mended rather than chucked out. Leftovers were made into fresh meals. Very little was thrown away. While we're now in a period of rampant consumerism, there is a quiet revolution happening, led by those who can see the logic of a 'waste not, want not' attitude. It is a simpler, happier way of living that contributes significantly to a sense of inner peace.

Defining idea...

'I've been rich and I've been poor. Believe me, rich is better.'
MAE WEST, ACTRESS AND WIT

9. Advertising is evil

Logos, posters, labels; we are drowning in advertising. Learn how to fight back.

Yell 'I am not a consumer, I am a free man!' and see if you can't beat the advertisers at their own game.

Obviously all advertising isn't evil as we need some advertising to find out what's happening in the world. An advertisement for a concert we want to see is the very opposite of evil as it gives us the means to go and have a moving experience. If you are promoting a product or an experience, you need to be able to communicate with your audience to ensure it is a success. I appreciate that and I'm not calling for a ban on all advertising.

The problem is not with an unobtrusive poster or a billboard; it's with the sneaky ways that advertising tries to get in on every aspect of human endeavour. Sports events are sponsored by companies who flash their logos over everything, including the players. TV advertisements force us to watch if we don't want to miss the next bit of our TV show. Cinema audiences are forced to sit through adverts instead of just trailers at the cinema now. The advertisers are now even trying desperately to find a way to use the popularity of social networking websites to their advantage.

None of this would be very sinister if it didn't work. No advertiser would bother us if he thought his adverts were falling on deaf ears. No, the reason advertising has gone crazy is that it works. American economist, Juliet Schor, estimated almost a

Here's an idea for you...

Pick out all the labels from your clothes. Not only will they hang better and you'll have no itching around the neck or back, you will also not have to see a brand name each time you get dressed. You already paid for your clothes; why should you have to give the company free subliminal advertising to you each time you get dressed?

decade ago that the average American's annual spend is increased by $200 for every hour of TV (above the national average) he or she watches each week.

Ads make us more stressed because they constantly assault us on subconscious and conscious levels. They are a constant visual 'noise' that we simply can't shut up, no matter how hard we try. Our daily commute is plastered with poster ads and even digital moving ads on buses and some billboards. We are constantly taking in that there are millions of products out there for us to consume. It is spiritually and physically draining.

It is pretty hard to avoid TV ads (though several people I know lead very happy lives without a TV) but there are other ways you can strike back at the corrosive influence of advertising in your life. Try to get rid of branded packs of things in your home. So buy un-branded ceramic containers for things like flour, sugar, coffee, etc. Unfortunately we seem to be swamped with packaging nowadays – very useful for the advertiser who wants to stick their logo right where you can see it as much as possible – and the days of things wrapped in plain paper are long gone. However, you can return to a slower pace of life by getting rid of a lot of packaging and storing things in pretty, air-tight containers.

The next act of anti-advertising you can do is to ensure you tick the right box on forms to avoid direct mail advertising. You know all that junk mail that gets through anyway? How about writing 'Take me off your mailing list,' onto their order forms and posting it back to them using the pre-paid envelope they provide. This costs you nothing and should start to get your message across to them. You can also contact the mailing preference service to be removed from the mailing lists companies buy in (www.mpsonline.org.uk). It is now not uncommon for marketing, aka advertising calls, to come to your home on a Sunday. My dad usually yells at them but I saw a brilliant wind-up whereby the person being called pretended he was an inspector at the scene of a crime and that the telemarketer was under suspicion of murder because he called at that number. Probably going a bit far but a good indication of what you can do with a little imagination.

> Defining idea...
>
> *'History will see advertising as one of the real evil things of our time. It is stimulating people constantly to want things, want this, want that.'*
> MALCOLM MUGGERIDGE, JOURNALIST AND BROADCASTER

10. A change is as good as a rest

Are you selling some sort of service? Here are some pointers about how you can get the best rate of pay for your services.

When you're stuck in a rut, start misbehaving until you find you manage to get yourself chucked out of it.

Every time you do something you build a neural pathway. The more times you repeat a particular behaviour, the stronger that pathway becomes. Eventually you'll do it almost on auto-pilot. This is great for saving time when doing things like driving or typing as who would want to learn those skills over and over again each time we needed them. The problem arises when things that shouldn't feel automatic become so. A good example is that of addictions. If your response to stress is to reach for the bottle or a cigarette, apart from the addictive qualities of the substance in question, you're conditioning yourself to drink or smoke to alleviate stress. If every time you felt stressed, you reached for your yoga mat instead, you'd build up a conditioning process that would link yoga with what to do if you get stressed. It would certainly be a huge benefit to your body and mind for you to build those associations.

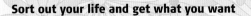

Today, make a list of areas in your life where you'd like some changes to occur. Would you like to lose some weight? Be healthier? Spend less money? Get more time for hobbies? Make a big list and put everything you'd like to change in your life on there. Then pick just one thing that is bothering you. Forget the rest and put the list away until you have tackled that one thing. Having chosen one thing to deal with, make a new list of 10 things that you can do to tackle this problem. Suppose mine is to lose weight (actually that is one of mine – wow, this book is like a reality show!). My 10 things could be:

1   Drink 2 litres of water a day
2   Give up fizzy drinks
3   Eat at least five portions of fruit and vegetables a day
4   Join a weight-loss programme
5   Get half an hour of exercise three times a week
6   Walk an hour a day
7   Join a dance class
8   Go swimming
9   Not have seconds at meals
10 Switch to skimmed milk in tea

Here's an idea for you...

If you use an electric toothbrush, buy a manual one. If you have a manual one, buy an electric one. Then alternate the two for a week. It will feel really weird to begin with and, while dentists the length and breadth of the country will be declaring a fatwa on me, you'll become more aware of what the inside of your mouth feels like. You'll probably decide to stick to the electric toothbrush though as they're the most fun you can have on your own in the bathroom. Ahem.

Then pick just one of those things. You don't have to go from 1 to 10; you can pick number six at random if you like. However, you must promise yourself that you will do this one thing faithfully for two weeks. Having done a fortnight of this, add another thing from your list for the next fortnight. Build it up until you're doing all 10 things. The two weeks of faithfully doing your lifestyle change is important because that is how long it takes us to form a habit. That was how long it took me to give up sugar in my hot drinks and now I can't bear to have even a few grains accidentally fall in my cup.

Pretty soon your changes will become habits. Once that happens, you should return to your list of things you'd like to change and see if there's something else you can tackle. Don't expect huge amounts of support from those around you as you are changing the familiar and that can be very disturbing for people who are afraid of change. If a person sees you as their 'ditzy' friend and suddenly you get very organised, they have to change their relationship to you from someone who takes care of you to someone who is on an equal footing and that can sometimes make them feel redundant. However, don't let the reservations of others stop you making enjoyable changes.

Defining idea...

'Change in all things is sweet.'
ARISTOTLE, GREEK PHILOSOPHER

11. Lottery life

If money were no object, where would you live? How would you live? How and with whom would you spend your days? Use this information to produce a plan for happiness.

Winning the lottery may seem like a pipe dream but leading the life you'd have if you won may not be.

The first principle in making anything come about is to know what you want. Most of us think we know what we'd do if we came into a lot of money but really we don't have a clue beyond 'pay off my mortgage' and 'go on holiday'. Fine, but then what? Think properly about what you'd do if money were no object. I once spoke to a London cabbie about this and I really agreed with what he said. 'I don't understand people who go back to their normal work place when they've won a lot of money,' he said. 'It shows a lack of imagination. I mean, if I had a lot of money, I'd be in the Med, painting on a beach.' Like many of our fantastic cabbies, the man was a philosopher and he'd thought long and hard about what would make him happy. He knew because he'd already been for a short holiday to play out his millionaire lifestyle and so he knew what his ultimate goal was. I have no doubt that when he retires, you'll find him on the Med, painting on a beach.

Wealth is not about money. Wealth is about how much you love life and lead it to the full. I noticed, during a time that I had very little money, that a free trip to the park was as exciting for my niece and nephew as the expensive outings I used to give them when I had money. It wasn't the pricey shows they were craving, it was my time and attention. So don't concentrate on the money when you think about what your perfect 'lottery life' would be like.

Most people have responsibilities that they'd take care of first like debts to be repaid and homes to buy. Then there's the helping of less fortunate members of the family and of friends. Then there are the holidays and fun times. However, what you need to figure out is what you'd do after the initial excitement had worn down. Would you return to your usual job? If so, you're very lucky as that means you do actually enjoy doing your job so much that you'd do it even if you didn't have to. Would you set up your own business? Or would you not work and live off the interest? If so, where would you live? How would you spend your day? Write out an itinerary of your perfect day, post-winning the lottery. Do you live by a beach; would you go for an early morning beach run? Who would you meet for lunch? At which restaurant?

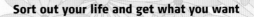

Daydreaming about a perfect life where money's no object is an enjoyable way to learn about yourself and what it is that you want out of life. You may surprise yourself. You may think you're a bit of a homebody but then you discover that you'd travel continuously if you could, in which case adventure is more important to you. Compare your choices with that of your spouse and see if you both agree. It can lead to some interesting discussions. In the case of one couple I know, it was such an exciting prospect that they sold their urban flat and moved to Cornwall to start living in the way they said they wanted to when thinking about their lottery lives. This idea can change your life, if you really put your heart and soul into it. You see, money isn't always what's holding you back, fear of taking a risk often is. Go wild and become one of life's millionaires.

> Defining idea...
>
> **A loving silence often has far more power to heal and to connect than the most well-intentioned words.**
> RACHEL NAOMI REMEN M.D., MEDICAL REFORMER, EDUCATOR AND AUTHOR

12. Tired all the time

It's normal to feel tired at the end of the day. But if you feel tired all the time, if you even wake up tired, you're in trouble.

If you suffer from this kind of chronic, day-after-day fatigue, you should check it out with your doctor. There could be good medical reasons for your fatigue – anaemia, diabetes, an under-active thyroid, to name just three – and you need proper treatment for them.

There are some pretty amazing herbs which can help boost your energy, increase your resistance, and raise your spirits, but before you start spending good money on herbal remedies, you need to check out just what's going on to cause your fatigue.

There could be a dozen different causes. You're not eating properly. You're working too hard. You're a born worrier; you can't stop even at bedtime. You're not getting enough exercise. You're bored with your job, or miserable in your love life, or stressed-out by ongoing money anxieties. All or any of these factors can bring on an aching, miserable tiredness that takes all the fun out of living, so study lifestyle factors first and work out what needs fixing.

Too much stress can leave you worn out and exhausted. Step forward the great adaptogenic herbs – so-called because they help you 'adapt' to stress by increasing your general resistance and vitality, and so help you cope better with both physical and mental stress. Siberian ginseng is the star in this field, following dozens of studies in the USSR: Russia's athletes and cosmonauts are among its biggest fans. 'An ideal all-round energy tonic,' says UK herbalist Penelope Ody, 'ideal to take whenever extra energy is needed… before a particularly busy period at work, during exams, or before long-distance air travel, for instance.' You can take it for up to six weeks at a time: then you need a fortnight's break. Don't use in an acute infection or if you're on digoxin.

Another great herbal tonic comes from Russian folk medicine. For centuries the roots of *Rhodiola rosea* or Arctic root, were chewed to stave off fatigue and exhaustion, and boost general endurance. Studies carried out by modern Russian researchers have demonstrated this useful property in – among other subjects – sleep-deprived doctors, hard-worked army cadets and students facing key exams.

Here's an idea for you…

If you're burning the midnight oil, if you need to stay sharp and focused for an exam or if you're battling a long demanding job, guarana is the herb for you. This extraordinary tonic from the Amazon rainforest (it's gathered sustainably by local people) can help keep you going cheerfully for hour after hour, with a clear mind, even on minimal sleep – though when the job is done, you'll need to crash out in earnest. Don't drink coffee when you're taking it. Faced with an implacable deadline for delivering a book, I once sailed through three days of intensive work on just four hours' sleep a night and a twice-daily dose of this wonder-working herb. Then I collapsed…

It sounds blindingly obvious, but lots of people never seem to figure out that their tiredness is caused by a serious sleep shortfall, either because they stay up too late or because they just can't get to sleep. If you're up till the small hours and then need Big Ben to rouse you for a day's work, the cure could be just some regular early nights. If sleep eludes you, even when you retire at a virtuously early hour, try my favourite cure for insomnia – passionflower. I usually take a dose of the tincture an hour or so before bedtime. Valerian, every GP's favourite tranquilliser a century ago, doesn't suit everyone, but when it does, it works brilliantly: it's often combined with sedative hops and wild lettuce. Limeflowers and chamomile – often combined in tea bags or ready-made herbal remedies – both make wonderfully calming bedtime drinks. Sip them slowly while having a bedtime bath to which you've added 10–12 drops of any of the following calming and soothing essential oils: chamomile, lavender or neroli. (Stir the oils into a little whole milk before adding them; they will disperse better.)

Defining idea...

'Fatigue makes cowards of us all.'
VINCE LOMBARDI, famous US football coach

13. Working wonders – when you're wound up like a clockwork toy

Worn out by your high-pressure life? Exhausted by the end of the day? Working till late into the night? Too tired to enjoy the weekend? Too wired to sleep?

Join the club: stress is the number one ailment of modern Western-style societies.

But don't turn to the classic pick-me-ups of caffeine or alcohol. They may help you get through a rough day but they'll do nothing for your resistance and general health in the long run. Instead, try some great stress-busting herbs, with centuries-old reputations for helping you unwind.

If the stress is ongoing with little sign of any let-up, think adaptogens. That's the name coined in Russia for a small and highly specialised class of medicinal herbs – super-tonics that boost general resistance and help you adapt both physically and mentally to ongoing stress.

The most recently-discovered is Siberian ginseng (*Eleutherococcus senticosus*) which has been researched since the 1950s in Russia. In studies involving thousands of people, it has dramatically improved resistance to extreme working conditions, disease, the stress of surgery and the toxic drugs of chemotherapy. Siberian ginseng is usually taken in courses of forty days at a time, with a two- to three-week interval. Side

Here's an idea for you...

Trying to cut down on your caffeine intake? Try rooibos or red bush tea from South Africa. It is caffeine free, great for the digestion, rich in minerals and loaded with antioxidants. It has a slightly odd aroma, but a nice round rich taste. Comfortingly, you can drink it with milk like ordinary tea. And while it works as a great pick-me-up during the day, it will help you calm down and sleep well at night-time. What more could you ask of a cuppa?

effects are very rare, and usually only at high doses, but can include insomnia and anxiety.

Ashwaganda is a key herb in Ayurveda, the thousands-year-old traditional medicine of India, and since – unlike ginseng – it grows easily and happily from seed around the world, it has become increasingly popular with Western herbalists faced with deeply stressed patients. 'An exceptional nerve tonic – one of the best remedies for stress,' says UK herbalist Anne McIntyre, who has big healthy green plants of it growing in her Cotswold herb garden. 'From my observation of patients taking ashwaganda over a period of four to six weeks, it certainly helps to enhance energy and positivity, engender calmness and clarity, improve memory and concentration, and promote restful sleep.'

Rhodiola, a little plant grown in the Arctic mountains of Siberia, is a relative newcomer to Western herbalists, but it has already made a name for itself as a great tonic for people in demanding, high-pressure jobs. When you're tired, depressed and low in energy, rhodiola might be the one for you. It's been little studied in the West, but Russian researchers tested it successfully in exhausted young doctors working impossible hours and stressed students facing exams, among other subjects.

With any of these adaptogens, look for a reliable brand, and follow the manufacturer's dosage suggestions.

There are numbers of other herbs with a reputation for effective stress-busting: among them limeflowers, skullcap, hops, passionflower, lemon balm, valerian and oats. Any health-food shop will offer a range of tablets, tinctures or teas featuring these lifesavers in various combinations. Here's a rundown of what they – and others – can do to help you calm down and sort yourself out when things are really getting to you.

Herbalists prescribe oats – usually in the form of a tincture of both grains and the grassy bits – for nervous prostration, exhaustion, depression: wonderfully nourishing for the nervous system. It is often combined with passionflower which is wonderful for insomnia, easing you into restful sleep.

Skullcap is one of the most widely used nerve tonics, almost specific for severe nervous tension. Limeflowers help relax you when you feel strung up, soothing those nervous jitters. And lemon balm is another great remedy for nervous tension, especially the kind that gets to your guts.

Prisoners, like commuters, are powerless people, but in one south London jail, according to a Times report early in 2004, the staff were dishing out herbal teas instead of sedatives in the evening – to the enthusiastic approval of the inmates, particularly the women. The two chosen varieties of tea, formulated by herbalist Dr Malcolm Stuart, contained top stress-busting herbs such as limeflowers, hops, passionflower, valerian root and skullcap, together with gut-calming fennel and yarrow, and sedative hawthorn.

> Defining idea...
>
> **'You don't get ulcers from what you eat. You get ulcers from what's eating you. '**
> VICKI BAUM, American writer

14. Become a people wizard

People are so, so different. Understanding that fact helps you to become a wizard at reading them. That's important when working to have it your way.

Unless you're one of truly identical twins, everybody in the world will approach a challenging situation differently to you. To influence them you need to tap into their way of working.

An easy way to get into a mess when influencing is to assume people will see 'our logic'. Of course, you see it as logical to start saving now so you can get on the property ladder. Unfortunately, your boyfriend sees it as logical to splash out and enjoy life now.

People see things differently. It's odd that answers we think will be common to all of us – i.e. an 'obvious' or 'right' way to approach a problem or a 'logical' way to sort it out – don't really exist. You've probably noticed this when, perhaps, discussing a film with a friend: you were insistent that the hero shouldn't have done something but your buddy has disagreed. How on earth did they see it that way?

Imagine you're trying to sell your car. To influence the potential purchaser, you'll need to notice whether they look at colours and feel the seats or whether they are interested in engine size.

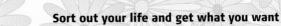

Think about the person you want to influence. Let's assume you know them well – your mum, your boss … How do they influence themselves? How does your mum decide on something? She likes to stop; mull it over for a while. What about your boss? He likes to create a table of pros and cons. And your youngest sister, Rebecca? She'll be on the internet, checking out blogs and chat-rooms to see what 'real people' (as she puts it) think.

Your four-year-old, David, likes it when you sweep him up in your arms and influence with bounce and energy – the last thing he wants is a logical lecture. Funnily enough, though, that's just the way your six-year-old nephew likes to be handled – a nice 'adult' conversation.

All very well, you say, although it is true you hadn't quite thought about it like that before. But what about people you don't know? The used-car salesperson from whom you want two hundred off the price of that second-hand people-carrier. The jobsworth at the swimming pool who refuses to give your son a student-priced ticket. Well, idea 1: ask someone who knows them. Idea 2: try one way to communicate, then try another – write, then talk on the phone, then a face-to-face visit.

> *Here's an idea for you…*
>
> **Take a sheet of paper and jot down the names of some people you find it very hard to influence: your dad or that builder who is brilliant at his job but will never budge on prices. Against each name, write down what annoys you so much about them – e.g. their stubbornness, procrastination …. Take a long, hard look at the list. Notice anything? Yep, it's normally a summary of our own weak points! Recognise these and you'll suddenly open the flood-gates to easier discussions. Something to think about and something to act on.**

You can do this more formally if you like. Draw – yes, draw! – the faces of two people you want to influence: say, your mum over some of your career ideas and, say, the car salesperson about a price. Around each face write every way you know of that they are influenced. For instance, with your mum: mull it over, quiet cup of tea, what your dad says. With the used-car salesperson, the garage receptionist hinted that he might be more amenable if you could give him some leads to other business. Finally, turn those thoughts and comments into what you need to do:

Mum. Introduce the idea over a friendly chat and cup of tea. Mention a relevant article from *Hello!* magazine and Dad's views. Leave it with her a few days.

Used-car salesperson. Tell him you could put his card up at the community centre with a flattering comment about how helpful he was in exchange for the extra discount.

Defining idea…

'I did it my way.'
FRANK SINATRA – a powerful idea
for all of us to try living up to

15. What must you get?
And what would be nice?

Of course you want the other person to change. Of course you want other things too. But, what changes do you insist on and what things would just be 'nice'?

Surprisingly, a good way to have it your way is to be more flexible and consider the options a little more. More options: more flexibility. More flexibility: better chance of having it your way.

When we are influencing somebody – perhaps to encourage them to let us borrow their amazing SLR digital camera for our trip to South America or to get them to stop playing loud music on a Sunday morning – we of course know what we want: the camera; the silence; the camera in our bag; the music off. But what happens if that's not possible? We can't have it all, can we? Our friend says the camera is simply in too much use to lend out; the music is being played by a shift worker and that's the only time she can listen to her CDs.

Will we be unable to get what we want? Have we lost? Of course not – we're not giving up that easily – because we have already given some thought to what we *must* have and what is *just nice*. What we must have is a decent digital camera for our trip; it doesn't *have* to be that specific camera. What we *must* get is some catch-up sleep at the weekend; it doesn't *have* to mean that our neighbour turns off her music. We're keeping an eye on the bigger picture.

On a practical note, take a moment to think before you act. There's some influencing you need to do. What's *really* important about this discussion you're going to have? And what's *quite* important? You want your mate's digital camera for your Andean trip because it's the best. That's what you really want. But, think again. What you actually need, of course, is just any decent camera. So, maybe if he won't lend you his, he will know someone else you could ask. Or maybe, as he's a bit of a camera buff, he's got another one you can borrow.

What about this early morning music on Sundays? You want her to shut up. But she's a nurse, working gruelling shift patterns, and listening to music is her way to relax. You don't really begrudge her that, do you? So, maybe what we want here is to get a friendship going, so that then we can talk to her about your need for sleep. Of course, it is going to take a little longer but it is likely to work and any arrangement you make will stick. It's certainly better than falling out with a neighbour.

Makes sense, doesn't it? What we're doing is asking, what would be nice, but what must we get? This doesn't mean we are losing out on what we originally wanted – we're simply being flexible; we're considering the bigger picture, the longer term and above all the relationship. And all of these are, of course, equally valuable.

It is rarely a one-off battle to *have it your way*. You'll need to be discussing further issues with your boss, the council or with your mum. Hence, all of us need to take a regular reality check on what we are seeking.

Defining idea...

'Negotiation in the classic sense assumes parties more anxious to agree rather than to disagree.'
DEAN ACHESON, US lawyer and statesman

16. No, not now! Get your timing right

Here's an idea that's very easy, very potent and yet often forgotten: choose the right time. There's a right time for everything, isn't there? So too if you want to have it your way.

It won't help your influencing if those you wish to influence are tired, stressed, getting ready to go out or watching the latest episode of *The Simpsons*.

You need to pick the right time for the targets of your influencing, not just a time that suits you. That's it. It's as simple as that. Admit it, though: you'd not really given it much thought, had you?

As you know, emotions are powerful things, so when that old lady allows her dog to go digging in your garden, you want to shout at her *now*. When your son gets home with critical red ink all over the essay you gave ten out of ten last night, you want to give his head teacher an ear-bashing *now*. And when the builder leaves old timber in the driveway and it punctures a tyre on your car as you return home, you want to sack him – *now*.

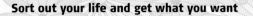
But – and it's a big BUT – 'now' is probably not the best time: you are not going to get the result you wanted. You are going to get a very upset old lady and look like a horrible bully. If you shout at the head teacher, it will only backfire on your son. As for sacking the builder, that'd be crazy. At least he turns up, works to budget and is polite; you want a clear drive, too?

Remember too that if it's not the best time for that somebody else then they will probably not be listening to you. And if they aren't listening, you are not going to influence. And if you can't influence, you can't get what you want. Here are some classic bad times to avoid:

Too soon: 'Hang on, I haven't even got my coat off yet!'

Too late: 'Look, can we talk about this tomorrow? I really need to get off home – now.'

When they are too distracted: 'Okay, but I've got a lot on at the moment. Couldn't we do this another time, maybe?'

When they are on the way to a meeting: 'I can give you one minute!'

When neither of you has had time to reflect: 'I can't believe you just said that!'

> **Here's an idea for you...**
>
> Relax with a cup of your favourite tea or coffee. Now, this person you need to influence. When is he or she at their best? Are they a morning or an evening kind of person? Do they like to 'clear their desk' before they talk to you? Or is lunchtime good for them? Or when the kids have gone to bed – or is that the worst time because they see that as their 'own' time? Possibly the weekend? Whenever it is, that's when you are going to have the conversation.

At the end of a busy day: 'Look, I've had a tough day with an evil boss and idiot clients, and my laptop's stopped working. I am really not going to listen to you table-thumping about how we should be recycling more.'

When you are too emotional: 'Where the bl**dy hell have you been?'

When they do not have enough time to respond: 'Hang on. I've got a presentation to give in 45 minutes.'

When it simply isn't fair: 'Look, I've just been made redundant myself. Can't we talk about this tomorrow?'

Defining idea...

'Who has time? Who has time? But then if we never take time, how can we have time?'
THE MEROVINGIAN, Matrix Reloaded

The aim should always be to find a time when the other person will be receptive and have a bit of time to reflect and discuss. Given the pace of life today, that's going to be difficult but, if you can't find the right time, the danger is that your whole argument will probably be ignored.

17. Thank people

A really genuine 'thank you' costs you nothing and makes the other person feel good even though you might have wrung a tough concession out of them.

And even if you don't get what you want, thank them for listening to you and giving their time. It could make it much easier when you get a second chance.

Saying 'thank you' is seriously important because all influencing is an emotional experience as well as an exchange of data and information: if we treat someone well, they cannot help but be more likely to be swayed by our thoughts. This idea is sometimes known as 'managing the emotional bank account'. Like with our financial bank accounts, it helps if we make regular deposits and keep withdrawals down to the bare essentials.

Deposits into the emotional bank account are: politeness ('thank you'), courtesy ('just to let you know, I'll be 10 minutes late'), engagement (know the other person's name, switch off your mobile phone), following up (sending a summary e-mail after the meeting), good time-keeping (be there when you said you would), and connecting (shaking hands, making eye contact, open body language, a smile). As well as 'none of the above', withdrawals from the emotional bank account are not being loyal (going behind people's backs) and lying ('I was promised this would happen' ... when you weren't!).

Here's an idea for you...

Have a 'thank you' day. Whatever happens, try very hard to thank people. Look for something you can thank them for and look them in the eyes as you do it. At the garage, as you retrieve your credit card, look them in the eyes and thank them. With your boss, after all the negative feedback he's given you, look him in the eyes and say 'thank you, that was helpful'. You'll be rewarded with a look that tells you you've done something special.

So 'thank you' is wider than the words. It's respecting someone's time and their thoughts. It's listening carefully to someone. It's being loyal. A 'thank you' approach helps that other person feel good, and if they feel good they are more likely to want to work with you and be receptive to your influencing.

Make a deliberate effort to connect with people you wish to influence. 'Old-school' recommendations are often about staying 'detached' and 'cold' when trying to influence. That's a very old-fashioned and confrontational style, especially in business today. Connect! This connection in business can be formalised into your influencing network.

This influencing network contains not only people you sometimes need to influence, but also people who will help you influence. Imagine how great it would be to have the ability to say, 'I'd like you to speak to Sally; she's someone I've known and worked with for several years; she knows a lot about this sector of the market and I think she will reassure you that we would make an excellent partner for you.'

And as your influencing network grows, this builds your 'brand': who you are and what you stand for. Just as a commercial brand will influence you or not, your personal brand will support your influencing or not. Imagine how pleasant it would be if you got this phone message: 'You don't know me, but I'm heading a new division of the business and before we start looking externally I wanted to talk to you. I have a head-count and I have a generous package and I am looking for the absolute best people. Your name keeps coming up. I wondered if you would like an off-the-record conversation later. Or we could meet any time tomorrow if that's convenient.'

Defining idea...

'**The grateful mind is constantly fixed upon the best. Therefore it tends to become the best. It takes the form or character of the best, and will receive the best.'**
WALLACE D. WATTLES,
motivational guru

Remarkable as it may seem, the building of your brand starts with simple 'thank yous'! If you want a reminder of the impact of thanking, learn 'thank you' in other languages for when you are travelling. They may be the only words you know, but you'll feel the benefit of being able to say *muchas gracias* – or whatever – in the taxi, at the hotel and after the meeting. That's all it takes to show you are trying and that will win people over quicker.

18. Don't slip off the learning curve

Learning is for life, not just your school years.

Why should learning stop just because you're an adult?

Many of us subconsciously assume that learning ends the day that we walk out of school or university for the last time. Yet as the pace of life increases, it becomes more valuable than ever to keep learning. For example, it can be important to your career to keep up with new technological advances, whether it's new software packages to master, new working practices to implement or new trends to adapt to. Also, many people are retiring at a later age than ever. A longer working life means that post-school learning becomes essential in order to keep up.

Another reason why lifelong learning is now so important is the demise of the 'job for life'. Very few people now enjoy permanent job security and business experts advise everyone, even employees of big organisations, to view themselves as though they were self-employed. This means taking responsibility for keeping your skills up to date. For many of us, the routine of our work can give a false sense of comfort which leads us to view our jobs as more secure than they actually are. Ask yourself: if you had to apply for a new job tomorrow, what would you apply for, and would your skills, as listed on your CV, make you stand out against other candidates? If not, then it's time to update them.

Knowledge is constantly growing. The amount of published material (both printed and online) is growing exponentially, as are new findings in science, as are new technologies. This not only means that a full education in many science and technology fields can now take longer than ever, but that if you are in one of those fields, you'll need to learn constantly in order to stay on track. Equally, the development of the Internet, and digital media like DVDs, MP3s and CDs, means that it's easier than ever to learn things at your own pace, in your own time.

It is true that it can be easier to learn new things at a younger age. For example, it may be easier for most people to learn a second language when they are a child than as an adult. This doesn't mean that it's impossible, just that a younger child will absorb the language with less effort. However, your brain is not hard wired during your youth. New findings in neuroscience have revealed how 'plastic' the brain is: it can remould itself. For example, when one region of the brain is damaged, it's possible for other regions to take over. Different tasks are not necessarily fixed to certain positions within the cortex. Equally, it's no longer possible to predict exactly what skills someone will need when they are a child. During the early industrial era, it was possible to plan universal education programmes on the basis that a certain set of skills would see each person through to their retirement, which meant that the only education most people needed was during their childhood. This is quite clearly no longer the case, yet we still hold to the notion that education is something for the young.

> **Here's an idea for you...**
>
> Consider signing up for a part-time class at a local college. Don't let any bad memories of school classrooms put you off; most adult evening classes are far more informal and fun. Plus you get to choose what you want to study. Who knows, not only will it stimulate your mind, but it could give your career a boost. Think about what subjects you always wanted to study, but perhaps felt were too frivolous or complicated.

Constant learning is a great way to keep your memory strong in old age. Research has shown that the more memories a person builds, the more resilience they will have to any mental decline in their later years. Being a lifelong learner can also mean being open to novelty, to be willing to 'unlearn' previous memories. If we have invested years of our lives in doing things one way, it's difficult to overturn those habits and adopt a new way. But if you can overcome any resistance to this when it's wise to, then you will have developed a mental flexibility which will serve you well in all areas of life.

Remember, when learning new physical skills, be they touch-typing or skiing, research shows that a good night's sleep will help your brain encode these new memories. This may be particularly important for older adults, who tend to get fewer hours of sleep than younger people. Equally, even if you are not that old, you may still be cutting back on sleep due to a busy work schedule. Make time to get enough sleep. It's an important factor if your brain is to operate at peak efficiency.

Defining idea...

Never grow up, but never stop growing.

ARTHUR C CLARKE,
science fiction author

19. How to find lost items

**It's one of the most annoying lapses of memory:
where did I leave my...?**

Losing things is when most of us have the biggest problem
with our memories.

These lapses can range from the merely annoying (where did I leave the TV remote
control?) to the panic-inducing ones (losing your passport on the night before your
holiday).

If you regularly lose things, don't necessarily assume you have a bad memory. It's
probably more likely that you are disorganised. If your home or work environment
is cluttered, messy and chaotic, it's going to make it harder for you to recall the
position of things. Keeping things tidy and in order and avoiding clutter can be a
good prevention against losing items. Alternatively, you're more likely to lose things
when you have a lot on your mind, and your attention is consumed with other
matters: the 'absent-minded professor syndrome'. If you are prone to forgetting
where you left things due to thinking about other things, it's probably no use to
simply tell you to 'pay more attention'; you already know you should! Just get
yourself into the habit of keeping important items in sight, or in a regular place.

However, if you do lose something, I recommend that you implement this four-
stage emergency plan.

Stage one: don't panic!

Losing something can put anyone into a panicked state of mind. This is often counter-productive and can impede you finding the item. In order to visually scan your environment for the item, you are going to need a clear head to pay attention; panic is going to work against you. So, first take a moment to calm yourself. Take some slow, deep breaths and sit down. Do not start your search until you are perfectly calm. If you can afford to, try taking your mind off the problem for a while. Sometimes, simply by relaxing, you may realise where you left the item.

Stage two: work out the last known location

Where did you last use or see the item? Or, if it wasn't you, who was the last person to use or see it? Spend a couple of minutes to think carefully about this as it's the single biggest clue you have to its location. Most objects end up being within inches of where you last saw them or where they 'should' be. Is it very near to where it should be, but fallen into, behind or underneath something? Could someone have borrowed or moved the item?

Stage three: plan your search — narrow down the possible locations

If you have answered the last question, then you should have already narrowed down the range of possible locations to search. Simply searching everywhere – for example, in every room of your house – is inefficient. You need to first work out a shortlist of which rooms this item could possibly be in and then, out of those, which it is most likely to be in. Then you need to work out which areas within those rooms it is most likely to be in. Think about where you might have been using the item. Also think about the shape and size of the item, as this will determine where it could be. Something flat, like a credit card, piece of paper or book, could be easily hidden within a pile of papers, whereas a larger item couldn't. What 'hiding places' – drawers, bags, pockets – are the right size to accommodate your item?

Stage four: search carefully and systematically

People waste a lot of time looking for objects by going over and over the same areas. It's quite common, when in a panic, to actually look straight at the object and not register that you've found it, and just continue looking, because the panic is stopping you from paying clear attention. Resolve to only look in each area once. This means you will need to take a slower, thorough and more methodical approach, but ultimately it will save you time.

> ### Defining idea...
> **Praising what is lost makes the remembrance dear.**
> WILLIAM SHAKESPEARE

Look gorgeous

Enough already with 'beauty is only skin deep' — that's as deep as it needs to be. Our looks may be superficial but looking our best makes life flow one helluva lot more smoothly. We can't all be great beauties but we can all look pretty hot. The secret is getting on top of the basics — and that's what this section is all about, making sure that the essentials are in place.

Do you feel gorgeous? If not, why not?

**There are shortcuts, and then there's sloppy.
Where do you fall?**

1. Which of these scenarios is more likely for you:
- ☐ a. You're wearing old sweatpants but terrific underwear underneath?
- ☐ b. Your outfit looks great but you don't know how many years you've had your bra and knickers?

2. Your legs:
- ☐ a. Are always smooth.
- ☐ b. Are always a bit embarrassing.

3. You wear SPF15 on your face:
- ☐ a. Every day from April through to October.
- ☐ b. On a sunny day.

4. You make a hair appointment when:
- ☐ a. You pay your stylist.
- ☐ b. You find yourself avoiding mirrors.

5. You treat yourself to a beauty treatment – salon or diy – such as a massage or facial:
- ☐ a. Every couple of months.
- ☐ b. Every couple of years.

6. You'd look really fabulous if:
- ☐ a. You had more time.
- ☐ b. You had more money.

Score 1 for every 'a' and 0 for every 'b'.

Score 4 or more

You understand the important thing about looking great – you need to have a plan and stick to it. You understand that the basics can be overlooked before 30 but after that age you need to make a bit of effort and give some time to following the ground rules. Check out idea 28 for some finetuning on your near perfection.

Score 3 or less

You may look great but you take short cuts and eventually you risk going the way of Brigitte Bardot and other great beauties who just couldn't be bothered when effort is needed. Which is fine if you're happy with it, but if not, start at idea 20 and work your way through to make sure you're ticking all the beauty basics boxes.

20. Deep-cleansing

If you've ever gone to bed without removing your make-up (don't we all?), you may need a jolly good deep-cleanse to rediscover your radiant bloom.

Soft, smooth, even-textured skin is a great blank canvas, but unfortunately this kind of an all-over body blitz on a day-to-day basis is generally impossible unless we've either an obliging neighbour or deep pockets.

There's no excuse not to exfoliate and body brush regularly though as this will keep skin looking and feeling ultra-soft. And don't forget to smother your skin with a moisturiser or almond oil afterwards.

Beauty experts recommend daily body brushing before having a bath or shower, as this removes dead skin cells and helps your body to absorb beauty products. It's also said to boost circulation and stimulate your lymph glands, which are responsible for eliminating toxins from your body. So, how do you do it? You take your body brush and, making sure your skin is dry, brush in long strokes towards your heart for about five minutes.

Here's an idea for you...

If you've got sensitive skin and you find facial exfoliators too abrasive, invest in a muslin cloth to cleanse skin and gently exfoliate at the same time.

You can also rev up your circulation and smooth rough skin with an invigorating scrub. A good loofah or some rough sea salt will do the trick. Buff away in circles, paying particular attention to feet, elbows and knees. Rinse off thoroughly and blast your skin with some cold water.

Now it's time to focus on your face. First, use a gentle lotion to remove your eye make-up (heavy creams can leave your eyes puffy). Be sure to use light inward movements to avoid dragging your skin. Then remove the rest of your make-up with a good cleanser – start at the base of your neck and move upwards and outwards in light, stroking movements. Next, exfoliate your skin to remove dead skin cells, which can make your complexion dull. A handful of oats mixed with double cream is a great kitchen exfoliator. Just rub in gently and rinse off.

Next, fill a bowl with warm (not boiling) water and add a few drops of essential oil, such as lavender or eucalyptus. Wrap your hair in a towel and inhale for five minutes (avoid this if you tend to get broken capillaries on your nose or cheeks). Now's a great time to tidy your eyebrows, as it's less tortuous to extract hairs when your pores are open.

Then slap on a face mask. Home-made methods include mashing up an avocado and massaging it into your face using the stone (avocado is naturally moisturising). Alternatively, a great way to tighten up oily skin is to whisk up an egg and rub it onto your face. Remove the mask with warm water and then pat your skin dry. Give your skin a five-minute massage using an aromatherapy oil (or natural almond oil) then remove any excess oil with a toner. Apply some eye gel, patting it gently inwards towards your nose, and finally finish up with your usual moisturiser.

> Defining idea...
>
> **'I'm tired of all this nonsense about beauty being only skin-deep. That's deep enough. What do you want – an adorable pancreas?'**
> JEAN KERR, writer

21. Look great in photos

Stars and photographers alike know all the tricks. Adopt these clever postures and easy make-up techniques and the camera *will* lie when you want it to.

Sticking your tongue into the roof of your mouth will make your lower facial muscles contract and tighten that wobbly double-chin patch. Try it in front of a mirror. Ingenious, isn't it?

Camera-shy or woefully unphotogenic people should commit this kind of tip to memory. Knowing how to show off your most beautiful features will also equip you for those horrifying times when someone feels compelled to 'capture the moment'.

If you watch models and celebrities carefully at red-carpet events, you'll notice that they'll strike a carefully calculated pose as the paparazzi gather. The result? A smaller waist, longer legs, more sculptured cheekbones.

So, next time you have to face your public, try some of the following tricks picked up from the stars and the photographers.

✿ To look your slimmest try standing with one foot slightly in front of the other and gently pivot on your feet so that your body, including your shoulders, is at a slight angle. Putting your hands on your hips can make your waist look instantly smaller.

- If you're sitting down, lean forward and rest your elbows on your knees. That way you'll disguise wobbly thighs.
- Look lively. Greta Garbo *froideur* isn't always the most flattering attitude to adopt in snaps. In fact, some professional portrait photographers insist the best pictures are always taken when the subject is looking animated and chipper. That way the subject's personality is captured. You can still engineer your 'best side' in front of the camera.
- Practise in front of the mirror. Perfect a pose you're happy with so you can strike it the moment the camera comes out.
- Brighten up. Dark colours can often be slimming to wear but black can drain the colour from the face, so choose brighter colours for your top half to bring out the best in your skin tone.
- Beware of brightly patterned clothes, as they can swamp you and detract from your face.
- Dark circles or bags under your eyes? Try lifting your chin to avoid shadows falling on your face.
- Smile. Forget looking moody, as everyone looks more attractive when they're looking happy. Plus a lovely smile really does take the focus away from the bits you're less happy with.
- Poker straight hair can pull your face down. Putting your hair up can soften your features and draw attention to your smile.
- Get the photographer to take more than one photo! The more you have taken, the more likely it is you'll be captured from a flattering angle.

Here's an idea for you...

Maximise your lips. To pout beautifully, turn to the camera and say 'Wogan'. Bizarre, I know, but glamour models swear by it.

Make-up tricks

You'd be forgiven for thinking that slapping on gallons of foundation and concealer over spots and blemishes will create alabaster skin and hence wonderful photographs you'd be proud to display. Forget it. Overdo the slap and you'll look like a waxwork or, worse, a cross-dresser. Be subtle instead.

✿ Apply a light foundation only where necessary, such as to the sides of your nose or over spots.
✿ To avoid a shiny face, stick to matt-formula make-up for your blemishes and only use creamy, reflective concealers for your eyes.
✿ Flatter your best features. Apply blush over the apple part of your cheeks, sneak a couple of extra false lashes on your eyelids and slick on some glossy lipstick. Don't forget the golden rule of make-up though: never overplay the eyes and the lips. Choose between them before you open that make-up bag.
✿ Ask for a minute or two before the camera clicks so you can touch up and dab a bit of powder over any shiny bits. Who cares if you seem vain? There are few things as insidious as unflattering photos of yourself in someone else's hands.

> *Defining idea…*
>
> **'With charm you've got to get up close to see it; style slaps you in the face.'**
> JOHN COOPER CLARKE, poet and comedian

22. Hands-on treatments

Your hands speak volumes about your toilette. If you can't stretch to salon manicures, there are easy ways to titivate your nails on the cheap.

Think of your nails as the icing on a cake – the finishing touch to your outfit, shoes, hair and make-up. A neatly manicured set says you're well groomed and glamorous.

The first steps to gorgeous hands are to wash and dry them regularly and to always use hand cream. Keep a jar by every sink in your house plus one in your handbag. Okay, most women are meticulous about hygiene and we don't need reminding to wash our hands after using the loo. However, the more you do it the better. Interestingly, one US study found that if you wash your hands five times a day you could dramatically slash your risk of catching germs and getting ill. It was based on a two-and-a-half year hand-washing programme conducted by the navy. Another reason why everyone loves a sailor!

Don't underestimate the protective powers of a pair of Marigolds. Always use rubber gloves when washing up. Also, use them when cleaning as household-cleaning products can make your skin dry and your nails dry and brittle.

Here's an idea for you...

To calm yourself in moments of stress and to relieve headaches and any tension in your neck and shoulders, apply pressure to the acupoint between your thumb and first finger (to find it, feel for the muscle that you feel when you press your thumb and index finger together). Press for one second, then 'pump' for a minute.

A nightly trick to soften hands is to smother Vaseline, or petroleum jelly, into your nails, which will have a dramatic effect on taming your cuticles. For best results wear cotton gloves to bed afterwards and you'll wake with beautifully soft hands.

You can eat your way to better nails, too, say the experts. The best foods for nails include plenty of protein (fish, meat, soya, tofu, eggs) to help them grow and prevent those white lines from appearing across them. And B vitamins, found in eggs, seafood and root vegetables, are a good way to keep nasty ridges at bay. Eat plenty of fish, fish oils and seeds, which are all rich in essential fatty acids that help nourish nails. Foods rich in zinc, such as seafood, lean meat and wholegrains, help prevent white spots. Brittle nails? You'll need to eat lots of calcium and vitamin-A foods such as carrots, peaches, leafy vegetables and tinned fish, which are great for strengthening dry nails.

Treat yourself to a home manicure every week or two and save the real thing for special occasions. Remove old polish and then shape each nail with an emery board (nail files are too severe). Don't saw away at your nails or you'll break them. Instead, use light strokes from the edges towards the centre. Massage your cuticles with cuticle cream or add a few drops of cuticle massage oil to a bowl of warm water. Soak your cuticles for five minutes, then push them back using a cuticle stick. Wash your hands, then apply a protective base coat of clear varnish to your nails, followed by a coat or two of colour. Leave your hands for twenty minutes or so to avoid smudging them, then add a sealing topcoat.

Don't forget to apply sunscreen on your hands. We rarely think about protecting our hands from the sun because we rarely burn there, but hands will give away your age better than any other part of your body and can even add a few cruel years too, so look after them. I once worked with a PR for a beauty company. She was based in LA and wore taupe leather gloves everywhere she went to protect her skin. She may have had a touch of the Howard Hughes about her, but it worked and she had the hands of a twelve year old.

Defining idea...

'Without grace, beauty is an unbaited hook.'
FRENCH PROVERB

23. Keep an eye on your eyebrows

Eyebrows can take years off you if you shape them right. Here's how to do it without looking constantly surprised.

An untamed monobrow is great if you're going for the Frida Kahlo look, but if you want to look groomed, elegant and more alert and wide-eyed, it's time to pay your brows some attention.

Think of eyebrow-shaping as treating yourself to an upper facelift on the cheap. Trim, neat, naturally ascending arched brows can make your eyes appear bigger and give you a more youthful appearance. If your brows are wild, tousled, virgin territory, you're missing a key beauty trick.

So, where do you start? There are various different brow-defining options, depending on what you want to achieve. If you've recently gone lighter or darker and don't want your eyebrows to give you away, you can try tinting, which really ought to be done by a beautician. Then there's the choice between plucking, waxing or even threading. Threading is a wonderful Middle Eastern technique that involves tiny intertwined threads being rubbed gently over the eyebrow hairs. This stings slightly, but threading doesn't leave a red mark and some find it's the least painful option. Most salon eyebrow shaping involves a bit of waxing, then tidying up with a pair of tweezers.

If you're going to splurge on a visit to the beautician, some would say that eyebrow shaping is the treatment to have done. It doesn't cost the earth, but it's a fabulous investment. If you have your brows shaped just two or three times yearly, you'll have a template to follow at home. All you need to do is simply 'tidy' them once or twice a week with a pair of tweezers.

Home plucking: the rules

If you choose to go it alone, tread carefully. You can make some pretty awful mistakes with eyebrows and end up looking permanently surprised, shifty or botoxed to within an inch of your life. Always pluck in a good light and invest in a magnifying mirror.

Here's an idea for you...

Give yourself a facial workout to help tone your facial muscles and delay the ageing process. Stand in front of the mirror daily and raise your eyebrows as high as possible and simultaneously open your eyes as wide as you can. Slowly lower your eyebrows and relax. Repeat this five times.

- ❀ Start by brushing your eyebrows, using an eyebrow brush or small, soft toothbrush. Then trim any long hairs with nail scissors.
- ❀ Aim for a natural, gently curving arch, thicker in the inner corner of the eye and tapering out over your brow bone. Focus on accentuating this natural curve by tidying up around it, above (forget that old myth, you *can* pluck above the brow) and below.
- ❀ Each eyebrow should start directly above the corner of the eye and should be the same width as your eye. Hold a pencil vertically along the side of your nose and remove any wild or stray hairs on the bridge of your nose beyond the pencil with a pair of tweezers.

✿ Then, to see where your eyebrow should end, hold the pencil diagonally from your nostril to the end of your eye and pluck anything below the pencil to open up your eyes and to avoid looking drowsy.

✿ Then work on the natural arch. To find the highest part of the arch, imagine drawing a line from the outer edge of your iris right up to your browline. That should be the highest point of your eyebrow arch. Tweeze any hairs underneath that arch. Don't go mad though. Natural is always better.

Defining idea...

'Elegance is innate…. It has nothing to do with being well-dressed.'
DIANA VREELAND

✿ If you want a fuller look, try brushing your brows sideways with your little toothbrush or eyebrow brush. Or slick them down using Vaseline or a bit of moisturiser. You can buy eyebrow gel, but it's not vital unless you have very unruly eyebrows. Slicked eyebrows do make you look instantly groomed, though, so it's worth experimenting with gels.

24. The sun rules

Forget about suncare and the consequences can be difficult to ignore. So, either catch the sun safely or fake a tan beautifully.

We're perfectly aware that the sun can accelerate ageing. It's a cruel fact of life – because brown legs look longer and thinner. That's why we still can't help ourselves when the sun comes out.

Here are the scary facts. Between 80% and 90% of skin ageing is caused by environmental factors, the biggest being ultraviolet sunrays. In fact, the sun can age you by as much as twenty years. Recent research indicates that people with malignant melanoma are twice as likely to have been badly sunburnt at least once.

So, if you can't keep out of the sun, at the very least avoid burning at all costs. Here are a few safe sun rules to commit to memory:

Start with fake tan

You'll be less likely to sit and fry in order to catch up with the other sun worshippers if you don't look white and pasty on day one of your holiday. Remember, though, that a fake tan won't protect your skin from the sun so you'll still need sunscreen.

Here's an idea for you...

Certain foods have been found to help minimise the damage caused by the sun. So, eat cantaloupe melons and lots of red, yellow and green fruit and vegetables, which are packed full of antioxidants. And dine like the Italians; a Mediterranean diet rich in vegetables, beans and olive oils can protect against the wrinkles and ageing caused by the sun. (You'll still need your sunscreen though, however many melons you put away.)

Never binge sunbathe

If you tan gradually, you're less likely to damage skin cells, which makes skin cancer less likely too. Start with, say, one hour in the sun the first day, then two the second and build up gradually so your body can adjust. According to the experts, four hours is the maximum amount of time we should expose ourselves to the sun per day. Building up gradually also means your tan will last longer.

Understand your sunscreen

Current research says SPF 15 should be the minimum protection we use. So, start your holiday by using a higher factor and switch down to a factor SPF 15. If you'd normally burn in, say, ten minutes without sunscreen, SPF 15 would provide you with 150 minutes of protection after which you'll burn, so then either reapply the sunscreen, go indoors or cover up totally. And remember you need both UVA and UVB protection to stay protected (look for the four-star rating).

Choose between chemical sunscreens, which work by absorbing the dangerous UV rays, and physical sunscreens, such as zinc oxide or titanium dioxide, which protect your skin by reflecting the UV rays away. If your skin is sensitive, you may prefer the physical sunscreens, as they're less likely to cause irritation. Many sun products contain antioxidants too, which is great because these undo some of the damage caused by sunburn and wind.

Cover up

Stay out of the sun between 11 a.m. and 3 p.m. when the sun is strongest. Don a stylish hat and kaftan, go for a siesta or head for the cool shade of the beach bar. (Drink enough and you may not be able to come out again anyway.)

Extras

If you're swimming or playing beach volleyball, buy sun products accordingly. Apparently, 85% of the sun's rays can penetrate water. Just so you know, 'waterproof' means that the product maintains its degree of sunburn protection after eighty minutes of water exposure, whereas 'water-resistant' means it maintains its degree of sunburn protection after about forty minutes of water exposure. Reapply after coming out of the water.

Apply sunscreen thirty minutes before you go out in the sun. It takes about thirty minutes for the product to bond to the skin, so it's less likely to be rubbed off. If you apply sunscreen before you go out in the morning and then re-apply once you reach the beach, you improve your protection by 60–85%.

Make sure you're using enough sunscreen. You need to dollop about two heaped teaspoons for each body part, like a leg, arm or shoulder. A 400 ml bottle will last the average person about ten days.

Defining idea...

'Your aim should be to avoid burning at all costs. Obviously it's safer to avoid sun exposure altogether, but most of us still want to spend time in the sun – so we have to make people realise that burning is not a necessary part of the suntan process.'
DR PATRICIA AGIN, photobiologist and research director at the Coppertone Solar Research Center in the US

25. Feet first

Feet generally don't get a second thought till summer, by which time you really have your work cut out for you. Instead, attend to them daily.

Paying attention to your feet can actually boost your health and well-being, as well as stopping people wincing at the sight of them.

Feet get a real beating as apparently we average between about 4,000 and 5,000 steps a day. Most of us spend a lot of our life rushing around in ill-fitting shoes, too, which can cause problems from blisters to corns, as well as exacerbate bunions, back pain and posture problems.

There's a Sarah Jessica Parker in all of us; the only thing separating most women and a serious Manolo habit is cashflow. Women seem genetically programmed to gravitate towards absurdly impractical shoes, but choosing the right shoe for the job can help minimise damage to the foot. When shopping for shoes, try to think first about heavy-duty wear. What will you be doing in those shoes? Walking to work? Rushing around shopping?

Specialists recommend we choose a low-heeled shoe (no higher than 4 cm) for everyday wear, with a rounded toe. We're also advised not to wear shoes for consecutive days because it takes them about 24 hours to dry out thoroughly; and sweaty shoes cause smelly feet and fungal infections.

Wear high heels for a special occasion, by all means, but live in them and you'll damage your feet and cause postural problems. Moreover, they can shorten your calf muscles and make them look stocky.

Wearing tight shoes can also cause bunions, curvatures in the toes and swollen, tender joints. It's worth giving your shoe wardrobe a serious rethink, because wearing tight shoes can make the problem worse. A chiropodist can help you limit further damage by recommending shoes with a straight inside edge, which should prevent excessive pressure on the joint. Also, protective pads can be worn to ease pressure on the joints and shoe alterations or orthotics (special insoles) can help the feet function more effectively. In severe cases, surgery may be necessary.

Regular foot maintenance makes sense and few treatments will make you feel more enlivened than a pedicure or a session with a chiropodist, so budget for a treatment once every three months. The rest of the time:

Here's an idea for you...

Stimulate acupressure points on your feet. Stiff neck? Gently walk your thumb and fingers across the ball of your foot below your toes then around the base of your big toe. Aching back? Slowly walk your thumb down the inner edge of your foot following the bones along the arch.

✿ Regularly remove hard skin with a pumice stone.

✿ Trim your toenails with proper nail clippers, cutting straight across and not down at the corners, which can cause ingrown nails.

✿ Get into the habit of washing your feet each night with warm soapy water, but don't soak them for too long or too often in water that's too hot or you'll destroy the natural oils.

✿ Stretch your feet and exercise your muscles by making big circles with your feet – clockwise and anticlockwise – and repeat four or five times each.

✿ Make sure you dry your feet thoroughly, especially between the toes. Smother moisturising cream all over your foot, avoiding the area between the toes, and then apply some foot powder.

✿ Treat your feet to a regular, soothing foot massage. You can either buy specialist foot products for this, use your favourite body cream or try essential aromatherapy oils diluted in carrier oil.

Defining idea...

'If high heels were so wonderful, men would be wearing them.'
SUE GRAFTON, writer

26. Boost your bust

Sadly, half of women hate their breasts. Whether they're too small, too big or entering a downward spiral, there are plenty of ways to enhance those statistics.

Although men tend to view breasts as an amazing wonder to behold, they're basically just globes of fatty tissue, mammary glands and muscle. The Coopers ligaments that hold them in place aren't actually very strong, which is why women live in fear of drooping. They can be stretched permanently if you don't support your breasts with a well-fitting bra, and 85% of us wear the wrong size. Pregnancy, breastfeeding, age, gravity and doing lots of sport in a flimsy or wrong-sized bra can also take their toll and cause dreaded 'tennis ball in a sock' droopiness.

The bottom line is, nothing short of surgery will change the shape of breasts. However, good posture and strength-building exercises can help improve the back and chest muscles and perk the whole area up considerably. If you love swimming then backstroke can help boost your bust. In addition try these excercises three times a week:

Press-ups
These are considered the best move for a firmer chest.

Get down on your hands and knees and put your hands a little more than hip distance apart, keeping your hands in line with your shoulders. Keeping the part of your thigh just above your knees on the ground, lower your chest so that your

Here's an idea for you...

Get to know your breasts. Take a moment in the shower to check up and down your breast and armpit area. Check for lumps or hard areas by either moving your fingers up and down or by gently pressing in a circular motion.

elbows come out slightly to the side and then slowly push up again without locking them. Keep your stomach pulled in tight and don't allow your back to sag. The wider apart your hands are the more you work your chest. Aim for three sets of ten to fifteen press-ups.

Pullover

Lie on your back, holding a 2.25–4.5 kg (5–10 lb) weight in both hands above your head. Keeping your elbows bent and your arms about shoulder width apart (either side of your head) slowly lift the weight up over your head towards your belly and back. Build up to three sets of twelve to sixteen repetitions.

The back extension

The back extension can help support your breasts and improve your posture. After each set of press-ups, lie face down on the floor, lift one arm and the opposing leg a few inches straight in the air simultaneously and hold for a count of ten. Do this move twice on each side. Back extensions will strengthen your upper and lower back muscles, which will help improve your posture.

Bust beautifiers

Décolletage is a prime spot for sun damage. A crêpe-like bust is incredibly ageing, so look after it.

✿ Wash the area with face wash, which is gentler than many body washes and won't strip it of the oils that keep it young.

❀ Always make sure you wear at least SPF 15 if exposing your cleavage to the sun.

❀ Spots often occur on this area because it gets hot and sweaty beneath your clothes. Anything containing salicylic acid should help treat spots, or dab some tea tree oil on them to help dry them up more quickly.

❀ If you want to cover spots up, chances are your face concealer will be too light, so experiment with a darker one.

❀ The skin on your bust is often neglected, but moisturising will help hydrate the area and make skin look softer, smoother and firmer.

Bust-firming creams will do the same trick as moisturisers and they usually contain ingredients to temporarily tighten the area

You can boost a small bust with: high necklines ❀ roll-neck sweaters and big chunky knits ❀ sleeveless tops, halternecks and high necks with cutaway sleeves ❀ jewellery that draws attention to the chest (chokers take attention away from a flat chest) ❀ pretty tops, strappy dresses and camisole tops.

To minimise your bust try: V-necks (they divide and lengthen the torso) ❀ sweetheart necklines and wraparound cardigans ❀ dark colours in matt fabrics on the top half ❀ tailored shirts ❀ curvy jackets nipped in at the waist ❀ coat dresses.

Make sure your bra fits you: if the band at the back rides up, you need one with a smaller back size; if the underwire is digging in under your armpit, your cups are too small; if you have indents where the straps have dug in then look for one smaller in the back and bigger in the cup; and if your breasts are falling through the bottom of the underwire, you need a bigger cup size.

> *Defining idea...*
>
> **'A woman without breasts is like a bed without pillows.'**
> ANATOLE FRANCE, writer

27. Points on posture

How you hold yourself can make you look and feel longer, leaner and more confident. Shoulders back now, ladies.

To improve your posture in days gone by you simply balanced a few books on your head and walked elegantly around a room. These days improving posture is an altogether more athletic pursuit.

The key to great posture is to stabilise your core, i.e. the muscles that run around your body – your natural corset if you like. Pilates is the ultimate tummy-flattening, posture-boosting discipline as it's based on firming precisely these muscles. Pilates can also be a great libido booster as strengthening your abs, back and pelvic floor can enhance sexual function and response.

Try the Pilates 'zip and hollow' method, an easy but effective posture booster. Whenever you zip or button up your trousers, pull in your pelvic floor muscles while you hollow your lower abdominals back towards your spine. That way you're working the deepest layer of abdominal muscles. You can do this exercise anywhere, in fact, and it's even more effective than sit-ups in terms of firming your tummy.

Stand tall

* Imagine there's a string pulling you up from the centre of your head. Whether you're walking, sitting or standing, think tall and 'feel' that string gently pulling you up. Your stomach should be pressed flat.
* Relax your shoulders down into your back. When they feel tight, raise them up to your ears, squeezing them up and together as hard as you can, as if you're doing an exaggerated shrug, then just drop them and feel the tension ease. Try squeezing your shoulder blades together behind you; it's a great way to keep your shoulders back.
* Position your pelvis as neutral as possible and keep your waist long. Don't let your ribcage 'fall' into your hips.
* When you stand, make sure you soften your knees. If you lock your legs, you'll end up arching your back and throwing the rest of your body out of line. Also, make sure you put equal weight on each foot. If you're standing with more weight on one foot or with one foot turned out you'll look crooked.
* Keep your chin parallel to the floor.

Here's an idea for you...

Been sitting down for too long? Counter bad posture with this exercise. Begin on all fours with your weight evenly distributed and your hands and knees shoulder-width apart. Pull your left knee towards your chest with your right hand, simultaneously curling your head towards your chest. Uncurl slowly, extending your left leg and right hand until they're horizontal to the floor; your back should be in a straight line. Repeat on the opposite side after placing your left knee and hand slightly forward of the starting position. Do five sequences; you should find you're moving across the floor.

Sit up straight

✿ Sit at the end of your chair and slouch completely. Draw yourself up and accentuate the curve of your back as far as possible. Hold for a few seconds and then release the position slightly (about ten degrees). This is a good sitting posture.

✿ Make sure your back is straight and your shoulders back. Your buttocks should touch the back of your chair. A small, rolled-up towel or a lumbar roll can be used to help you maintain the normal curves in your back.

✿ Distribute your body weight evenly on both hips.

✿ Bend your knees at a right angle, keeping them slightly higher than your hips. Keep your feet flat on the floor. If necessary, use a footrest or stool.

✿ Never cross your legs.

✿ Try to avoid sitting in the same position for more than thirty minutes.

✿ At work, adjust your chair height and workstation so you can sit up close to your computer screen and tilt it up at you. Rest your elbows and arms on your chair or desk, making sure you keep your shoulders relaxed.

Strengthen those abs

Start on your hands and knees. Whilst exhaling raise your right arm and left leg until they're level with your torso. Keep your hips even and look down so that your neck is aligned. Contract your abs, but don't tuck your pelvis under or arch your back. Pull in your pelvic floor muscles and pull your tummy button in towards your backbone. Slowly return to the start and then repeat on the other side. Do two sets of eight repetitions on each side.

28. First impressions

How to achieve the wow factor and have everyone eating out of your hand the moment you walk into a room.

We all know someone who exudes charisma, a certain something that gets her noticed wherever she goes. She's one of the lucky ones. Her charisma is innate. But I strongly believe that you can approach it methodically.

Let's look at what the experts say about first impressions. Well, apparently 55% of the impact we make depends on how we look and behave, 38% on how we speak and only 7% on what we actually say. That's great news for the Eliza Doolittles among us, but it gives all of us something to work on.

Dress the part

Think of that foxy, pink dress in which you never fail to 'pull'. A great party cracker, but it'll do you no favours at that board meeting. So, the first rule of thumb is to keep the occasion uppermost in your mind and dress accordingly. That goes for make-up, jewellery, fragrance and shoes, too.

I once heard a chilling tale of a young woman who strayed from the acceptable uniform (navy below-the-knee skirt-suits) for women who wanted to be taken seriously in the City investment bank where she worked. Always wanting to steal the limelight and turn heads, she apparently sashayed into her prim, stuffy office one morning in a pair of bottom-caressing, silky, flared trousers. Big mistake. Rather

Here's an idea for you...

Try an aromatherapy upper. Bergamot is said to increase self-esteem and grapefruit can be refreshing and revitalising. Try wallowing in an aromatherapy-infused bath before you head out or pop a few drops on a tissue and inhale deeply two or three times *en route* to the event.

than having the desired effect, to elicit desire, her boss gave her a public dressing-down for 'coming to work in pyjamas and looking ridiculous'.

While you may condemn this anachronistic attitude, learn from it too and always wear what's appropriate for the occasion. Your overall appearance is the first thing that will be noticed and you'll feel far more confident if you know you're looking suitably businesslike/smart-casual/glamorous.

Comfort counts

Hot date? Swanky black tie party? Whilst shopping for a new outfit for an exciting 'do' is part of the pleasure, you'll be more confident if you're comfortable. So, break in new shoes, play around with underwear and road-test jewellery if you're allergic to certain metals.

Be prepared

Spend as long as you can afford preparing. Promising new date? Splurge on a blow-dry. Big party? Get a manicure or facial. Pampering yourself will instantly make you feel more attractive and more confident, which will show.

Expect to be liked

A good way to offset nerves, anxiety or a feeling of dread is to imagine yourself making that great first impression. Repeat to yourself, 'I will shine. I always live up to expectations. I'm friendly. People like me. I look fantastic.'

The first hello

Perfect a firm, confident handshake, remembering that eye contact is vital. Smile and look happy. The impact will be immediate and you'll generate warmth and friendliness. People like people who like them, and a smile is an instant signal that you do.

Slow down

Nerves can turn even the most mellifluous voice into a gabbling Minnie Mouse on helium. Relax. Make a point of trying to talk slowly. Also, breathe deeply, walk slowly and carefully and maintain that eye contact, however nervous you're feeling.

Rehearse your chat

Never know what to talk about? Do your homework and perfect a few conversational icebreakers. If it's a scary meeting then research topics that are pertinent to the people you know you'll be meeting, such as the region they're from, or what's going on in the news. An instant way to get the conversation flowing is to ask the other person about themselves. So ask them how they got to the event or how they know the host. Show an interest in them and look for common ground like favourite holiday destinations or mutual friends. A good easy-to-remember trigger in terms of conversational topics is FORE: Family, Occupation, Relaxation and Education.

Defining idea...

'[Charm.] It's a sort of bloom on a woman. If you have it, you don't need to have anything else; and if you don't have it, it doesn't much matter what else you have.'
J.M. BARRIE

---

29. Back beauty

If you've never given your back a second thought, now's the time to make up for the neglect.

Try the following and give your back the attention it deserves.

Tone it

Disciplines such as swimming (backstroke), Pilates and yoga are fantastic routes to a long, slender back and shoulders. Also, try the Alexander Technique, a postural alignment method of adding inches to your height. Rowing is another excellent back firmer. Try this rowing-based exercise:

1. Hook a resistance band up to a heavy object such as a table leg; attach it three quarters of the way down the leg towards the floor.
2. Do a few stretches to warm up.
3. Stand with your feet hip-width apart, a few feet away from the table. Bend your knees into a half squat with your hips behind you and lean forwards, keeping your back straight and your head in line with your spine.
4. Take hold of the resistance band with both hands (palms facing). You should feel a stretch along the side of your body.
5. Keeping your back, legs and hips in the same position, exhale and bend your arms to pull the band towards your ribcage, making sure your elbows stay close to your body. Then, gently return to the starting position, making sure you maintain the tension in the band.

6. Repeat the move fifteen times, building up to two sets of repetitions.
7. Stretch afterwards. Standing a few feet away from a table or chair, bend your knees into a semi-squat and lean forwards, placing your hands shoulder-width apart on the table or back of the chair. Step backwards and lean forwards so that your back and head are in line with your shoulders and arms. Hold for twenty seconds; make sure your knees are bent and your back isn't arched.

Here's an idea for you...

Tense shoulders? Sore back? Try an aromatherapy bath. Add a few drops of Scotch pine, which is warming and good for sore muscles, or clary sage, which has anti-inflammatory properties.

Firm up those shoulders

Try this move, which targets your deltoids, the muscles that run from your collarbone at the front and each shoulder blade at the back, covering your shoulder and attaching at the back of your upper arms. All you need is a light chair that you can pick up without straining. Aim for a set of six repetitions, three times a week.

1. Stand with your feet hip-width apart and close to the chair. Viewed from the side, there should be a straight line from your ear to your shoulders, hips, knees and ankles.
2. Breathing in, bend your knees and push your hips out behind you as if you're about to sit down. Keeping your arms shoulder-width apart, gently take hold of the sides of the chair. Focus your attention on the chair.
3. As you breathe out, lift the chair to shoulder height, keeping your arms shoulder-width apart. Keep your shoulders down, your chin tucked in, your spine nice and long and your abs tight. Tuck your pelvis slightly under and hold this position for three to five seconds without holding your breath.
4. Gently lower the chair and return to the starting position.

Clear up a spotty back

Spots can ruin the effect of any strappy number. Keep the spotty area thoroughly clean, change your towels and bedlinen at least twice a week and cleanse your back at least once a day.

When you're cleansing your back, the key is to slough off the dead skin cells that cause blocked pores and spots. Apply a good-quality – ideally medicated – cleanser using your fingertips, then remove it with a muslin cloth. Try tea tree oil too; it has good antibacterial action, so either dab some on the spots themselves or add six to ten drops to a warm bath and lie back in the water for up to ten minutes. Don't use it with soap – which may interfere with its healing properties.

The back's a difficult area to reach yourself so you may want to invest in a salon treatment; the Guinot back cathiodermie treatment uses a combination of mild electrical current and Guinot gels and creams to revitalise the skin. Also, consider a visit to your doctor, as spots on your back may be the result of a hormonal imbalance.

30. Hair care

Considering you have between 80,000 and 120,000 hairs on your head, it's little wonder you sometimes experience discipline problems. Here's how to stay in control.

Hair is a mischievous minx. You shower it with love and affection, exotic lotions and regular outings to the best salon you can afford, and still it laughs in your face.

Hair is composed of three layers. The outside is called the cuticle, and is made up of lots of cells like tiles on a roof. When the tiles lie flat, your hair will be smooth, healthy and look glossy because the light will bounce off the surface. However, when you've subjected it to too much brushing, combing, processing, heat and extremes of weather, some of the cells will be damaged. Think of the cumulative effect of these forces like a whirlwind hitting your roof. The surface ends up rough, pitted and drab and may split into layers. And that's when you need to do some excellent repair work, or get a decent trim and start again. Try the following solutions.

Assess the damage

How healthy is your hair? Hold a strand between two pairs of tweezers about 7.5 cm (3 inches) apart and pull. If it's healthy is should stretch another 30% more (about 2.5 cm or 1 inch) before it breaks. If it breaks before that, it may have lost some of its elasticity due to chemicals, styling or sun damage.

Here's an idea for you...

If your hair's looking dull, take a close look at your diet. Be sure to eat plenty of protein-rich foods, such as lean meat, fish, tofu and dairy products, to encourage healthy hair growth. Also eat plenty of red meat, green leafy vegetables, eggs and fortified breakfast cereals, as hair loss is linked to a deficiency in iron.

Next, run your fingers through your hair and feel your scalp. It there's little movement of the skin and it feels tight, your circulation may be poor. If it feels spongy, your scalp may be inflamed or suffering from a build up of toxins. A scalp massage may help.

How does your hair feel after shampooing, but before you add your conditioner? If it feels rough, your shampoo may be too harsh and you may need one for combination hair or with rich conditioning oils.

Massage your scalp

Next time you shampoo, focus on cleansing your scalp rather than just your hair and use a conditioning shampoo (one that contains jojoba or sweet conditioning oil will do). Don't be put off if you have greasy hair, as these oils could actually help regulate further production of oil because they trick your hair into believing it's producing the oils itself. As you shampoo, massage your scalp with your palms and fingertips to help soothe the skin, encourage blood circulation and boost skin renewal.

Try a salon-style treatment or an overnight fix

Take one teaspoon of hair-treatment oil (or almond or olive oil). Starting at the front of your hair and working backwards towards the nape of your neck, massage it deeply into your scalp using the pads of your fingers, kneading as you go. Leave the oil to soak in for about ten minutes, then shampoo out with a mild shampoo. Next, apply a conditioning treatment. Wrap a towel or cling film round your head to generate heat, which will help the treatment to penetrate more deeply into each hair shaft. Leave for about an hour, then rinse well.

Alternatively, mix together three tablespoons of avocado, two tablespoons of carrot juice, three tablespoons of olive oil and a drop of essential oil such as ylang ylang or jasmine. Work the mixture into wet hair and cover with a scarf or cling film. Rinse hair (don't shampoo it out) the next day.

Dos

✿ Shampoo gently, one section at a time, working down the shafts of the hair in line with the cuticles.

✿ If you can bear it, rinse with cold water from a jug or a blast of cold water from the shower to tighten the cuticles. Alternatively, rinse with the juice of lemon or a capful of vinegar diluted in a litre (two pints) of cold water; the acid will tighten the cuticles, which will help your hair shine. Then condition and rinse again.

✿ Dry your hair on the coldest setting of the hairdryer and use a warmer setting only for styling. Point the dryer down the hair shaft and follow your brush with the nozzle. Finish each section with a blast of cool air to close the cuticles.

Don'ts

✿ Don't rinse your hair in bath water as this contains alkaline soap residue that leaves dulling deposits on the hair.

✿ Don't towel dry, as it can tangle and roughen the cuticle.

Defining idea...

'The hair is the richest ornament of women.'
MARTIN LUTHER

31. Creating curves

A dainty waist means big sex appeal. Here's how to hone, firm and whittle yours in weeks.

Studies show that the waist to hip ratio – going in and out in all the right places – is a better gauge of a woman's attractiveness than the size of her breasts.

The trouble is, these days we're so hung up on boobs. We know our bust size, our friends' bust size, our colleagues' bust size and the bust size of virtually every Hollywood actress and soap star on the box.

In our mother's day, waist size was the only statistic worth comparing. My mother always bangs on about the fact she got married with a 23-inch waist. Me, I'd have been pleased with a 23-inch thigh. But back then, waists were the measure of attractiveness; along with a squeaky clean reputation and a fetching ankle. By contrast, how many of us now even know the size of our waist?

We ought to because men of all cultures fancy women with small waists. Or to be precise, women with a 0.7 hip:-to-waist ratio, i.e. waists that are 70% the size of their hips. And that doesn't necessarily involve being thin! Think Sophia Loren and Marilyn Monroe. And although one recent study on *Playboy* centrefolds showed that women's waists are getting slightly wider, curves still reign supreme.

The reason for this is biological. A small waist that curves into a generous hip equals fertility and youth – it's a sign that a woman has high levels of oestrogen and low levels of testosterone. In fact, in studies of IVF patients, women with a hip to waist ratio of more than 0.8 were less likely to conceive. (Apparently having an index finger a couple of centimetres longer than your ring finger is another sign of high fertility.)

> Here's an idea for you...
>
> **Invest in a gorgeous corset. Anything that boosts your bust and cinches your waist will do wonders for your rating in the bedroom.**

What's tricky about waists is that their size is largely inherited; you're either an apple shape, an hourglass or a pear. However, the good news is that you can trim an inch or so from your waist by losing weight and doing some waist-whittling exercises.

Love handles won't simply disappear. You have to shed the fat first. Experts say that if your waist measures between 81 and 89 cm (32 –35 inches), you're overweight. If that's the case you'll need to follow a low-fat, low-cal diet and do three to five sessions a week of cardio exercise such as running, dancing, cycling or power walking.

Waist-whittling exercises

Twist crunches

Lie on your back with your knees bent, your feet flat on the floor and your fingers touching your ears. Contract your abdominal muscles and slowly lift your torso off the floor. When you can't lift any further, contract your side muscles and turn to the left. Then return your torso to the floor and repeat on the other side. Build up to three sets of ten on each side.

The bridge

Adopt the press-up position, resting on your elbows. Pull your stomach muscles in tight towards your backbone, keeping your bottom down and your spine straight. Hold this position for as long as you can, being careful not to arch your back. To make it easier, drop to your knees. Keep looking down to the floor at all times. Build up to thirty seconds and repeat three to five times.

Defining idea...

'The curve is more powerful than the sword.'
MAE WEST

Horizontal side support

Start by lying on your left side, resting on your left arm and with your legs extended outwards and your right foot on top of the left. Slowly lift your pelvis off the floor while supporting your weight on your left forearm and feet. Hold, keeping your other arm by your side, for ten to fifteen seconds without letting your pelvis drop down. Repeat five times on each side.

32. Go for the glow

Short cuts to re-energising your skin.

Anything that gives you a healthy boost in energy should also do miracles for your looks. But if your skin isn't glowing as much as you'd like, then try this.

The basics of building more energy are also those necessary for looking your best; adequate sleep, plenty of good quality food especially fruit and vegetables, and some regular exercise to boost your circulation (increased blood flow to your cheeks helps enormously). Once they're in place, what else can you do?

Luminous skin depends on how much light your skin absorbs in relation to how much it reflects. For it to reflect well, there has to be a good scaffolding of collagen fibres that allows your skin to 'mirror' light back. Unfortunately, collagen begins to break down after the age of about 35 to 40. It breaks down even faster in those that smoke and those that overdo UV sun exposure and these should be the first bad habits you eliminate if you are serious about supercharging your skin's appearance.

This three step plan should help improve your skin in a matter of days.

Polish your skin

Dead skin cells make your skin dull because they don't reflect light. Smooth them away with a religiously-adhered to cleansing programme – known as exfoliation. Scrubs can be too harsh especially for older skins and the best way is to remove

103

Here's an idea for you...

Eyedrops that get rid of blood shot eyes are your quickest route to a re-energised look. Navy eyeliner is the second quickest. It neutralises 'red eye syndrome' better than black or brown and makes the whites of the eyes zing. On the whole keep makeup to the upper lids and lashes. The eyes of people looking at you will be dragged upwards, away from sagging.

them gently every night with your normal cleanser. Try cleansers that contain alpha- or beta-hydroxy acids that lift away dead skin cells. An alternative is a thick cleanser which you massage in and then remove with a flannel, exfoliating as you go. The extremely expensive Eve Lom cleanser is the original and my favourite. I am too ashamed to tell people how much it costs and I use supermarket moisturizers and make-up so that I can justify its expense (but a pot does last me six months). There are cheaper versions available – try any where a flannel is part of the package. Liz Earle's (available on the internet) is also good.

Even out skin tone

One of the reasons skin doesn't reflect light is the increase in pigmentation (melanin) as you get older due to cumulative sun damage. The most obvious suggestion is to wear a moisturizer with sun protection all year round, and on bright days, sun lotion on your face every time you go out in the sun. A hat is even better.

Glucosamine (the same supplement that is used for arthritis) is being touted as a new treatment for dull skin, delivering results in around eight weeks. You can find it in lotions now (Olay do one). Another nutrient known to minimise ageing pigmentation is niacinamide (Vitamin B3).

Rebuild your scaffolding

Collagen damage can be repaired with retinoids – a form of vitamin A. There are many lotions available that contain retinoids, generally the more expensive they are the more active ingredients they contain. Retinoids don't go well with sunlight so it's best to use them at night. Which is a good idea anyway because skin cell regeneration is slightly higher at night: that makes it the perfect time to apply treatment creams.

That's the basic skin care routine but it's not just dull skin that makes us look tired. Sagging, lifeless skin is for many of us more ageing than wrinkles. One solution? Ditch your pillow. Squashing your face at night eventually leads to permanent lines. A small study of Japanese women discovered that we have more wrinkles in the afternoon than the morning, and the scientists therefore assumed that gravity plays a powerful role in causing wrinkles. Ergo: lying flat on your back, preferably without a pillow, will combat the effects of gravity that were at work during the day. I have tried this because I suffer from droopy eyes – and it worked. Another idea is to keep eye cream in the fridge and one of those gel-packs to wear over the eyes in the bath. Coldness combats under-eye puffiness.

Defining idea...

'Beauty is in the eye of the beholder and it may be necessary from time to time to give a stupid or misinformed beholder a black eye.'
MISS PIGGY

How fast is your metabolic rate?

Your metabolic rate is how fast you burn calories. The faster it is the easier it will be to stay at a healthy weight.

❏ I am male (are you sure you're reading the right book?).
❏ I am under 50.
❏ I get on people's nerves by fidgeting.
❏ I never forget to eat.
❏ I think eating breakfast is important and I always do it.
❏ I don't feel the cold.
❏ I exercise until my heart beats fast three to four days a week.
❏ I do weight bearing exercise at least three times a week.
❏ I prefer active holidays to lying on the beach all day.
❏ I drink at least 1.5 litres of water a day.
❏ I have good muscle definition.

Score 1 for every box you ticked.

5 or under

Your metabolic rate is probably fairly slow. You're likely to put on weight easily and lose it with difficulty. The clues to how to speed up your metabolic rate are in the questions – although adopting all of them might be challenging. However read idea 37 for more inspiration.

6 or over

Your metabolic rate may be higher but if weight is still an issue for you, look again at the questions where you said 'no' to see if they give some clues. You could also read idea 39 for some more ideas.

33. A weighty issue
(or, a weighty question)

Have your waistbands been feeling a little tighter recently? Or are kaftans the only clothes you really feel comfortable in now? Here's how to work out roughly the right weight for you, plus some news you can use about body shape.

Judging by the newspaper headlines screaming about some new statistic or research about obesity, you'd think there was a moral obligation to be thin.

Often the subtext is that fat people get sick and are a burden on our medical resources. And then there are the images of super-slim models and celebrities that confront us in magazines and on our TV and movie screens. The underlying message here is that this is the way you're supposed to look, especially if you want to be happy and successful, not to mention being sexually attractive. Yet half the world is starving. It's enough to make you choke on your chocolate bar, isn't it?

Obesity is undeniably a growing problem in the Western world, due mainly to the over-consumption of the wrong kinds of foods and decreased activity levels. Experts warn of the host of health dangers to which carrying too much weight exposes you, including heart disease, diabetes, high blood pressure and, for women in particular (though not exclusively), fertility problems. It's not guaranteed that you'll develop these kinds of health problems – obesity just heightens your risk, which is of course why most of us just carry on regardless – until something goes wrong. The chances are that if you're already suffering any of the conditions mentioned, your doctor has grilled you on your diet and suggested losing weight.

For the majority of us, slimming down is more of a preventative health measure or something we want to do for cosmetic reasons: i.e. we just don't like the way we look. This is fine, as long as it isn't interfering with daily life and manifesting itself as disordered eating (anorexia, bulimia, faddy eating and so on). If that is the case for you, please seek help through a doctor or therapist. Life is too short and too precious not to enjoy it to the full.

Working out if you're really overweight is easily done using the Body Mass Index calculation. I have to point out that this method is not without its critics (partly because if you're quite well-muscled, you'll be heavy, not fat, because muscle weighs more than fat) but my feeling is you have to start somewhere! All you have to do is weigh yourself and record the result in kilograms. Then measure your height in metres. Then do the following sum:

Here's an idea for you...

Measure your waist and hips. Many experts are now saying that abdominal fat is the killer, with apple-shaped people who have relatively slim hips and a larger waist being more at risk from developing heart disease than the pear-shaped – those who carry their fat on their hips and thighs. The ideal waist measurement for men is less than 95 cm (37 inches) and less than 80 cm (32 inches) for women. Over 100 cm (40 inches) for a man and over 90 cm (35 inches) for a woman indicates the greatest risk to health.

Weight in kilograms divided by (height in metres × height in metres) = BMI

Example:
You weigh 70 kg and you are 1.6 metres tall

$$70 \div (1.6 \times 1.6) =$$
$$70 \div 2.56 = 27.34$$
$$\text{BMI} = 27.34$$

Check your own result against the ranges below

BMI for men	BMI for women	
Under 20	under 19	underweight
20–24.9	19–24.9	normal
25–29.9	25–29.9	overweight
30 plus	30 plus	obese

Defining idea...

'I'm not overweight. I'm just nine inches too short.'
SHELLEY WINTERS

I fall into the upper level of normal weight, which is fine from a fatness perspective, but I know that I've crept up two dress sizes in the past decade and so estimate that losing three kilos (and keeping it off!) would take me where I want to be. That's my weight-loss mission; now work out yours.

34. Food accountancy made simple

You can eat them, count them or ignore them, but here's why knowing your calories from your onions is the key to losing weight.

Many books make calories unnecessarily hard to understand, but the concept is really quite simple. Once you have grasped what calories mean, you have a powerful tool to help you control your weight.

Put simply, calories are just the basic units by which both the energy values of food and the energy needs of the body are measured.

You may be familiar with diets that advocate counting your daily calorie intake. It's now seen as a rather old-fashioned way to slim, not least because you have to weigh things obsessively and eating anywhere but at home becomes a nightmare. It can also make you very boring to be around as you proceed to tot up the number of calories on everyone's plate. You may find that friends stop returning your calls! However, it is really important to have some general knowledge about the calorific value of foods so you can make the best choices about what you're going to eat.

Most foods are a combination of protein, fat and carbohydrate in different ratios depending on the food. Gram for gram, fat contains 9 calories, protein and carbohydrates 4 calories and alcohol, if you're interested, 7 calories. Basically if you eat anything in excess, there's the potential that it will be more than your body

Here's an idea for you...

Include soya products in your diet. A particular isoflavone in soya may hold the key to improving the rate at which your cells burn up fat. It also boosts your metabolism slightly and reduces your appetite. From a looks perspective, I have it on good authority that soya helps to make your nails grow too!

needs in terms of energy or calories and will end up stored as fat. Of course it's easier to reach your maximum calorie needs quickly if you cram in lots of high-fat foods, as they have the most calories. Also, the most nutritious choices may not always be available, especially when you are away from home.

How many calories do you need?

I'm going to give you a basic formula to work this out (calculators at the ready!) but it will only be an approximate calculation. It should still be enlightening, though. The reason it is only an approximation is because if we were going to be really scientific, we would have to factor in other information. Your gym or local health centre can probably help you with these calculations if you want to be more precise.

One of the factors that makes a difference is your age, because your calorie needs diminish as you get older. By the way, this is for adults only, so please don't try this on your kids. Your sex is important too. As men have more muscle than women and muscle burns up more calories than fat, men need more calories just to exist.

Now let's play with some numbers:

First work out your *basal metabolic rate* (BMR) which tells you the energy you need to stay alive. Multiply your weight in pounds by 10 if you're a woman, or 11 if you're a man. (If you're a metric sort of person, first multiply your weight in kilos by 2.2 to get the poundage.) Next, factor in how active you are by multiplying the sum above by 0.2 if you only do very light activities, by 0.3 if you do a little more formal exercise such as walking as well as housework, by 0.4 if you are moderately active and you rarely sit still or by 0.5 if your job involves manual labour or you play lots of sports. The result is the number of calories you need on top of your BMR.

Eating and digesting food uses up around 10% of your calorie needs, so, after adding your BMR and the extra calories you worked out for your activity levels together, work out what 10% is. Now add all three of those figures together and you'll have the number of your total calorie needs per day.

To lose half a kilo (a pound) a week, you need to cut your daily calories by 500 (or cut fewer than that and make up the difference with exercise), which is a safe amount to aim for. Although this might not sound a lot, it's easier to achieve in the long term and easier to sustain. If you lose lots of weight very quickly, you're more likely to put it back on and get into that yo-yo dieting spiral.

OK, end of accountancy lesson. Who'd have thought that playing with numbers could be such fun!

Defining idea...

'**If you are going to lose weight and avoid gaining it, eating less is more effective than exercise alone... Doing both is the most effective combination.**'
Sir JOHN KREBS, Chair of the Food Standards Agency

35. Why size matters

It's not just what you eat that counts on the road to losing weight, it's about how much you eat too. How does your sense of portion control measure up?

What do you think a portion size of say, breakfast cereal or meat should be? I hope you're sitting down because it will probably be a shock. I know it is to me every time I see this particular truth in black and white!

According to healthy eating guidelines, a serving of breakfast cereal should be one ounce and a serving of meat should be two to three ounces. Cereal belongs to the food group of which we can have 6–11 servings a day, but it could be very easy to eat all of it at breakfast alone. The meat group, which also includes fish, dry beans, eggs and nuts, should be contributing 2–3 servings a day to our diet. Again, it's astonishing how quickly that can add up.

The simple fact is that most us eat too much and have lost all idea of what a portion size should be. This is due to a variety of reasons but the most significant is that food is so readily available in our affluent society. We don't have to go and hunt for it – we can just gather it at the supermarket. When eating out or buying takeaways we demand value for money. What better way to appear to offer good value than with enormous portion sizes? At home we'll cook a meal which could serve four or six people, but it's often eaten by just two or four. Portion control is essential to weight loss. You could be eating all the right things and still gain weight because you're overeating.

Here's a checklist of the sorts of foods we should be eating for a healthy balance of nutrients. It gives a range for the number of daily serving (e.g. 6–11 servings). The upper end of range really intended only for a very active man; most of us, especially sedentary women, should look to the lower end. There are also a few handy little visual ideas of what that amount looks like. It helps to get good at estimating these by eye because you can't carry around a set of scales everywhere you go. Well, you could, but it would look a little obsessive.

Bread, cereal, rice and pasta – 6–11 servings

A serving is:
1 slice of bread (the size of an audio cassette tape)
1 small bread roll
2 heaped tablespoons of boiled rice
3 heaped tablespoons of boiled pasta
2 crispbreads
2 egg-sized potatoes
3 tablespoons of dry porridge oats

Fruit and vegetables – 2–4 servings of the former, 3–5 servings of the latter

This is based on US recommendations. In the UK, the suggested amount of fruit and vegetables is 'at least 5' a day.

Here's an idea for you...

Squeeze a lemon. Citrus fruits are a great source of vitamin C and also a phytonutrient called limonoids, which can help to lower cholesterol. These phytonutrients are concentrated in the rind, so try to incorporate the zest of citrus fruits into your cooking. They work especially well in sauces and garnishes.

A serving is:

2–3 small pieces of fruit, such as plums
1 heaped tablespoon of dried fruit such as raisins
1 medium-sized piece of fresh fruit such as half of a grapefruit or a melon
1 side salad, the size of a cereal bowl
3 heaped tablespoons of cooked vegetables such as carrots

Meat, fish, eggs, nuts, dry beans – 2–3 servings a day

A serving is:
60–90 g (2–3 ounces) of cooked lean meat, poultry or fish. This the size of a deck of cards or the palm of your hand.

150 g (5 ounces) of white fish (or three fish fingers)
120 g (4 ounces) of soya, tofu or quorn
5 tablespoons of baked beans
2 tablespoons of nuts and nut products

Defining idea...

'A fat person lives shorter, but eats longer.'
STANISLOW LEC, Polish poet and satirist

Milk, yoghurt and cheese – 2–3 servings a day

A serving is:

200 ml milk
1 small pot of yoghurt
90 g (3 ounces) of cottage cheese
30 g (1 ounce) of cheddar or other hard cheese. This is roughly the size of a matchbox.

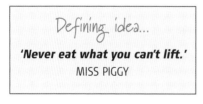

Defining idea...

'Never eat what you can't lift.'
MISS PIGGY

36. With friends like you, who needs enemies?

How do you feel about your body? Having a poor body image is a surefire way to sabotage your diet, so shape up with a little self-love.

I know a man who looks like the nerd from central casting. He's overweight, has comedy ginger hair and wears rather thick spectacles, but he truly believes he's a love god.

He really does do rather well with the ladies because he is a fabulous man. He is kind, funny and clever. The point is that he has no problems with his body image. Conversely, in my years as a journalist I have met many of the world's most beautiful women and they have all expressed negative feelings about their bodies, complaining about bellies, cellulite, feeling gawky, ugly and many other 'flaws'. It's not simply a female affliction either – just as many gorgeous men worry about their flabby bellies and 'man breasts'. No one is immune from disliking their shape and looks, but some people seem to manage to get over the problem more readily.

This is not easy in a society that prizes slimness and makes negative judgements about people who are overweight. It's a prejudice that finds its way into the workplace and relationships, eating right into your self-esteem. The issue intensifies if hating the way you look turns into a negative view of your personality and character. 'I'm fat and stupid' or 'I'm not worth anything, no one likes me' are examples of this kind of dangerous auto-suggestion.

> **Here's an idea for you...**
>
> Dieters often wear black from head to toe because it is 'slimming', but adding touches of colour can really lift your mood. Use red for energy, blue for communication, green for emotional encounters, yellow for intellectual sharpness and purple when you want to appear calm.

If you don't like yourself, it is going to be really hard to make the lifestyle changes that will help you lose weight. Often these sorts of thoughts are coupled with the habit of comparing yourself with others, especially with images in the media of celebrities and models. The truth is that these people's lives depend on how they look and they have the time and money to spend on an array of products, services and people who will keep them looking fabulous. What's more, the images you see are often 'improved' – for example, photos of models are often airbrushed to remove 'flaws'. For most of us, comparing ourselves to the thin and famous is just going to be a recipe for misery. That's rule number one: don't do it.

You need to develop a more realistic picture of how you would like to look: to look like you, but in better shape. Once you have done that, you can try some other self-esteem boosting tricks. Try writing down all the things you like about yourself, then turning them into positive statements and saying them to yourself every day like a mantra. If that seems too hard, ask your friends or family to write down what they love about you. You never know, you might finish up discovering things you had never even dreamt of that will warm the cockles of your heart.

Next, if someone pays you a compliment, accept it without putting yourself down. Avoid conversations like this:

Friend: 'You look really well.'

You: 'Yes, but I really need to lose some weight because hardly any of my clothes fit anymore.'

Instead, try something like:

'Thanks. I feel great, too. How are you?'

Exercise is good for your self image. Not only will you see physical results, but you'll feel benefits, from the satisfaction of doing something positive for yourself to a greater sense of wellbeing. Exercise has been proven to stave off depression.

Finally, rather than seeing your body as a collection of parts that you think are awful or could use improvement, focus on it as a whole and think of the wonderful things you have done or will do with it. Cuddle someone, run a marathon, give birth, climb trees, build something, help old ladies across the road.... it's your list, you finish it.

Defining idea...

'God made a very obvious choice when he made me voluptuous: why would I go against what he decided for me? My limbs work, so I'm not going to complain about the way my body is shaped.'
Drew Barrymore

37. Burn fat faster!

Eating less and moving more will result in weight loss. If you rev up the exercise part of the equation, you'll lose kilos quicker.

Taking a bath burns calories. And, given the choice, who wouldn't prefer a nice long soak to a nice long session on the rowing machine in the gym?

Most daily activities, such as watching TV, doing housework and sleeping use energy, but they are unlikely to exceed your energy intake from food. The secret to burning fat faster is to maximise the fat-burning potential of everything you do, from your daily chores and activities to proper workouts. Here are some tips for you to mix and match as you like.

Try working out for longer
If the prospect of an intense workout at the gym or a 15 km hike around your local park horrifies you, try working out less fast, but for longer. For example, walking briskly for an hour burns the same amount of calories as running for half an hour.

Have a more energetic day
You can burn up to 300 calories more simply by being more active in the way you do everyday things. Instead of ambling along to work, stride briskly. Do those dull old household chores you've been putting off for ever, such as cleaning the

windows, scrubbing the kitchen floor, tidying the garden and redecorating the bedroom. Put some good old-fashioned elbow grease into it and you've got yourself a workout. Why not start your day in an upbeat mood and dance to a few songs on the radio or on your CD player? And when you next go to the shops, walk instead of driving or taking the bus.

Build some muscle

Use weights, either on gym machines, in a workout class or as part of a home fitness routine. This will help you burn fat and not just because simply lifting weights uses energy. Pumping iron (I know, it's such a male term, but women, please take note) builds muscle tissue, which is metabolically more active that fat tissue. Muscle uses more energy than fat just to exist, so the more muscle you have, the more calories get used, even when you're resting. You really don't need to look like Arnold Schwarzenegger for this to be true.

Learn to love intervals

I don't mean going off mid-performance to have an ice-cream or a glass of wine, I mean interval training. The idea is that you can increase the amount of calories you burn during any exercise by increasing your speed, the intensity or the duration, even for brief intervals. If you are walking, swimming or cycling, you could go steady for about 15–20 minutes, then go faster for a couple of minutes, then slow

Here's an idea for you...

Following a good workout, after an hour, go for a healthy protein and carbohydrate snack, such as a tuna and salad sandwich. This will help your body through its 'after-burn', when it replaces short-term energy loss with energy from your fat stores.

121

down again and speed up in random bursts. To earn extra good marks, increase the duration and frequency of the intervals of harder work. It's tough, but really effective.

Remember, the fitter you are, the better your body becomes at using its fuel, which translates into a leaner, more toned you. The more exercise you do, the quicker you'll see results. This makes it worth learning to love exercise.

Defining idea...

'Consider joining a group or exercising with a friend. Commitments made as part of a group tend to be stronger than those made independently.'
AMERICAN COLLEGE OF SPORTS MEDICINE fitness book

Defining idea...

'My idea of exercise is a good brisk sit.'
Phyllis Diller

38. What does it say on the label?

It has a little healthy eating logo on it, so it must be good for you, right? Reduced fat means I can eat a bigger portion too, doesn't it? No and no! Learn to read labels and help yourself lose weight.

I'm something of a label freak and it's not just because I like a little bit of Gucci and Prada. If you read food labels, you can transform your body because you know much more about what you are eating.

It's not some nerdy hobby of mine. I had to start reading labels when my daughter was diagnosed as having a peanut allergy, as nuts can be hidden in all kinds of food and a reaction can be potentially fatal. Once you start reading labels, you discover interesting things – juice drinks with vegetable oils in them, for instance, or something you thought looked like a delicious fruity yoghurt that is just fruit-flavoured, not full of fruit. That 100 g (3.5 ounces) of your favourite cheddar cheese might turn out to add up to 410 calories and 34 g of fat.

As a starting point, you should know that food labels have to tell us things like the sell-by date and also state the country of origin. There has to be a list of ingredients too, with whatever the food or product contains most of named first and the rest listed in descending order. This is interesting when something looks full of meat,

Here's an idea for you...

Check the labels of various loaves of bread next time you're at the shops. Bread is a healthy food to eat, especially if it's wholemeal, but the fat content of a slice can vary quite dramatically between the brands, from around 60 calories a slice with 0.9 g of fat, to 115 calories a slice with 2.7 g of fat and even more!

for example, and then you see that meat is actually the third thing listed rather than the first! Labels also give a nutritional breakdown, usually expressed per 100 g, but sometimes as a percentage of the RDA, which is the recommended daily amount suggested by the government and calculated to prevent nutritional deficiency in at least 95% of people. You can check the RDA against calories, fat, protein and so on. All of this is useful when you compare similar-seeming foods in the supermarket. It all becomes slightly more complicated when you start seeing extra little logos and words such 'lite' or 'reduced fat'. When you're trying to lose weight you're more conscious of these extra labels, but don't just take them at face value. Here's what they really mean:

❀ **Lite/light** – Although manufacturers are encouraged to say what they mean by this, there are no real rules to say how much fat and how many calories should be in something that describes itself this way. The only way to work out whether it is as diet-friendly as it appears is to check the nutritional label yourself against a standard, i.e. non light, version. Check it against the per 100 g breakdown and you'll be able to judge for yourself what the difference is. Light in fat can still contain as many calories as a standard product because sugar has been added to compensate for example.

✿ **Low fat/fat free** – By law you can't be misled on this one, but it's still not straightforward. The UK Food Standards Agency suggests to manufacturers that 'low fat' should only be claimed when the fat content is less than 3 g per 100 g. 'Fat-free' should be for foods that only have a trace of fat – under 0.15 mg per 100 g. Claims of '90% fat-free' used to be used quite freely and implied that it was perhaps a better bet than low fat. However, it basically meant that a food was still 10% fat – so it was actually not as good as low fat. Confused? Luckily, voluntary guidelines for labelling mean that this particular description is being used far less, but if you do see it, you have been warned!

✿ **Reduced fat** – It sounds good, but the recommendation is that it can only appear on foods that have less than three quarters of the amount of fat of the standard product. Again, to really understand what you're getting, you'd have to check against the original product. Reduced fat taramasalata dip, for example, still contains 25 g fat per 100 g. So it's better than regular taramasalata, but not necessarily the best choice of dip (tomato-based salsa is an alternative).

Finally, beware 'healthy eating' style logos and labels. Quite often when fat is reduced in these types of products, fillers are used to bulk them up, and the sugar and salt contents may be high too. Maybe the calories are reduced because it's a tiny portion! As ever, do a comparative label check.

> *Defining* idea...
>
> **'It helps to know your labelling law here: a strawberry yoghurt must contain some strawberry. A strawberry-flavoured yoghurt has had a brief encounter with the fruit, while a strawberry flavour yoghurt has not even been within sight of a strawberry.'**
> Felicity Lawrence, author of
> *Not on the Label*

39. Easy ways to lose a pound a week without trying too hard

Simple food swaps, cutting back on high calorie treats and pushing yourself to be a little more active can help you achieve realistic, long-term weight loss. Mix and match these tips and you will look and feel slimmer with minimum effort.

There is always a less fattening choice of snack to be made, or a calorie-minimising way to cook. Take one of my favourite meals, the Caesar salad. It's a salad, so it must be good for you, right? Wrong!

Unfortunately, the Caesar salad has one of the most fattening dressings known to the hips, plus enough cheese and croutons to demand its own place setting at dinner. What can you do, apart from gaze at it longingly from across a crowded room? You can make a lighter version, that's what. Just replace the fried croutons with baked ones, reduce the cheese drastically and go very light on the oil. There's always a solution, you see.

One of the best solutions to losing a little bit of weight every week is to make changes that are so simple, you'll barely notice them. It's safe and possible to lose half a kilo (a pound) a week if you shave 500 calories per day from your food intake (or expend it through activity). The maths behind this is that 3,500 calories equals half a kilo (a pound) of fat. So, divide 7 days into 3,500 and you get that magic 500 number. Do some more maths and you'll see that 500 g a week is 2 kg a month and 12 kg in six months. Get started with the following clever little ideas:

Say no to crisps

This is one of the most popular snacks, but a regular 40 g bag has around 200 calories and 10 g of fat. Even lighter versions come in at slightly over half of that amount. So if you stopped having a bag each day at work, you'd save at least 500 calories a week.

Avoid large portions

A large burger, fries and fizzy drink will easily stack up to 1000 calories, if not slightly more. If you can't cut them out, at least opt for the regular or small sizes which will cut the calories in half.

Watch what you drink

On a night out, three 175 ml glasses of white wine will cost you nearly 400 calories. Three spritzers will be half that. A half pint of strong lager clocks up around 160 calories, while a half of ordinary strength is about 80 calories. Steer clear of cocktails too – a pina colada is easily 225 calories, while a vodka and slimline tonic is just 60.

On your bike

Eco-friendly, fun and jolly good exercise, an hour's cycling should take care of nearly 500 calories.

Sandwich swap

If you have a little low fat salad cream in your lunchtime sandwich instead of lashings of butter, you could save up to 500 calories during your working week.

> *Here's an idea for you...*
>
> **Chew sugar-free gum or clean your teeth after a meal or a snack. As well as cleaning your teeth and giving you sweet breath, it sends you a psychological message that you have finished eating and that it is time to do something else. Make a clean break when your meal ends so that you really know that it is over.**

Rethink your Saturday night take-away

Choose chicken chow mein and boiled rice over sweet and sour chicken and fried rice, you'll save around 500 calories.

Walk more

If you walk to work, the shops or just for fun (but at a reasonably brisk pace) you'll burn up around 250 calories an hour.

Wash the car

Save money and burn energy by valeting your car. Wash it, polish it and vacuum it inside and you'll use up a few hundred calories,

Have a skinnier coffee

You could save yourself 170 calories if you opted for a regular white coffee, made with skimmed milk, rather than a cappuccino made with full fat milk.

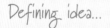 Defining idea...

'Another good reducing exercise consists of placing both hands against the table edge and pushing back.'
Robert Quillen

Party snacks

Think such small little nibbles don't count? If you had two tablespoons of tzatziki dip that would add up to around 40 calories. Two tablespoons of taramasalata, however, is 130 calories. Thick meat pate on French bread can cost you about 250 calories, whereas a small helping of smoked salmon on rye bread is a mere 130 calories. A cocktail sausage is around 70 calories. Wrap it in pastry and serve it as a sausage roll and you're looking at 200 calories.

40. Does being overweight really matter?

Perhaps you never got back into shape after having kids or maybe you've always been a little plumper than you would like. How do you know if it's really a problem?

A very attractive, curvaceous woman in her early sixties once said to me, 'Eve, darling, don't ever get too thin, it's so ageing.' And she was right!

I have friends who are in their early thirties and are incredibly proud of their skinny little size 8 or 10 frames, but look at least ten years older with their dried-up faces and flat little bottoms. I think a few curves and a couple of extra kilos are flattering and sensual – and that goes for men too.

When does a little plumpness become unacceptable? It depends on your viewpoint. If carrying a *few* extra kilos doesn't bother you, then it is not an issue. If it annoys you because you want to be in better shape, or it diminishes your confidence or stops you wearing the clothes you want to wear, then you should do something about it. If you have more than a few extra kilos, it does start to matter and when you're properly overweight it starts to matter very much indeed.

Here's an idea for you...

Get out your tape measure and calculator. Divide your waist measurement by your hip measurement (in centimetres). If the result is more than 0.95 for a man or 0.87 for a woman, you are apple-shaped. If you are apple-shaped, with more fat around your middle, your risk of heart disease is greater than if you're pear-shaped, with more fat on your bottom.

Fatness is a worldwide epidemic. In the UK alone, it is estimated that two-thirds of men and half of women are overweight, with one in five being obese, that is at least 12.5 kg (28 lb) overweight. Experts are predicting that one in four adults will be obese by 2010.

Obesity makes everyday life uncomfortable is so many ways, such as being unable to run for a bus, a lack of choice in clothes, rude stares and comments from other, thinner, people, and sleep and fertility problems. It is also the commonest cause of ill health and potentially fatal diseases. Obesity contributes to heart disease, diabetes, gallstones and some cancers. Just being overweight – and that's more than say a kilo or so – can raise your blood pressure and give you problems with cholesterol. Even dental decay is more common in overweight people.

In case you're in any doubt as to why being overweight does matter, here are some fat facts to consider:

According to the British Heart Foundation, heart and circulatory disease is the UK's biggest killer. Although the numbers are in fact slightly lower than twenty years ago, this is because of medical advances, not because we are getting healthier! There are other risk factors too, such as smoking, poor psychological health and inherited infirmities, but the truth is that 30% of deaths from coronary heart disease are directly linked to an unhealthy diet. The World Health Organisation estimates that somewhere between 1 and 24% of coronary heart disease is due to doing less than two and a half hours of moderate activity a week.

The fatter you are, the greater your risk. A weight gain of just 10 kg doubles your risk of heart disease. Reducing your weight even by 5 or 10% can have a beneficial effect on cholesterol levels.

Excess weight plays a part in high blood pressure, which can lead to blood clots, stroke and heart attacks. You can reduce these risks through diet: less salt, lower fat consumption and a huge increase in fruit and vegetable consumption.

Although the exact relationships are not fully understood, diet and cancer have an association too. A recent report suggested that as many as 40% of cancers have a dietary link. Breast cancer risk rises with a high fat diet or being overweight.

Clearly there's still a lot of research to be done, but it is certain that being overweight isn't fun and it isn't clever – and it can be about a lot more than the way you look.

Defining idea...

'Imprisoned in every fat man a thin one is wildly signalling to be let out.'
Cyril Connolly

41. Spot reduction: the facts and the fiction

How much can you change your natural shape? Is it possible to lose weight from specific areas of your body? There are many myths surrounding those questions. Here's the truth.

What did you inherit? I don't mean a cottage by the sea or your Great Uncle Stan's stamp collection – I'm talking about things like Mum's thighs and Dad's height.

As well as your gender and your nutrition in childhood, the main influence on your body shape comes from your parents. You can take after one or other of them, or be a mix of both.

Broadly speaking, human shapes can be split into three main types, ectomorphs, mesomorphs and endomorphs. Ectomorphs are tall and thin and are often quite angular or even delicate-looking. They have a low body fat percentage and not much muscle, either. Although they usually have few weight problems when young, they are likely to put on weight around the stomach area as they age. Mesomorphs tend to have quite a bit of muscle and indeed a higher muscle to fat ratio than the other two types. They appear well-built with strong arms and legs. A mesomorph stays in good shape if active. However, a sedentary mesomorph will gain body fat. The endomorph is altogether rounder and softer looking, with more fat than muscle. They put weight on easily, but with regular physical activity can achieve good muscle tone.

As well as the basic shapes, you can have an android or gynoid influence. The android is an apple shape, with most weight carried on the top half of the body (and of course, sooner or later around the abdominal area). This shape is more closely associated with ectomorphs and mesomorphs as they age and especially men, while it affects endomorphs more generally. The gynoid influence, which is a pear shape, i.e. heavier on the bottom half, is a more female shape and can occur across the three groups. While we can be a combination of the groups, most of us do tend to fall into one identifiable type. The key is to identify the closest to your shape and work with it, rather than battling against it, to be in the best possible shape you can be.

Here's an idea for you...

To get an idea of whether you really need to lose weight or indeed to track your progress, you can have your body fat measured electronically. A harmless electric current is passed through your body which estimates body water, showing the amount of muscle you have. The difference between your overall weight and lean tissue weight gives an idea of your body fat. Gyms and health centres usually offer this service (for a price) or you can also buy special scales to use at home.

Movers and shapers

You cannot spot reduce and lose weight from specific areas of the body. Research has shown that we all tend to lose weight from the top down, so, first it shows in your face, then your chest and stomach area, followed by hips, thighs and legs. Abdominal fat seems to be fairly easy to shift – good news for apple shapes, less good for pear shapes. But of course as abdominal fat is a risk factor in heart disease, pear shaped people can afford to be a little smug. But I'd rather be slim and in proportion, I hear the pear shapes say. A fat pear shaped person will slim into, well, a slimmer pear shaped person. And there's not a lot more you can do about your basic shape apart from surgery, which I don't recommend, but it's up to you. There is also exercise, which I do strongly recommend. One of the best tips for the pear-shaped person is to focus your strength training efforts on your top half to create more balance.

How much can exercise change your shape? Toning exercises certainly work to either increase your muscle bulk or streamline your muscles. However, if you've got lots of fat covering your muscles it will be harder to see muscle definition, plus you could just end up looking bigger. It's best to lose some body fat first. Contrary to popular myth it's not possible to turn fat into muscle or the other way around. Fat is fat and muscle is muscle.

Defining idea...

'I'm in shape. Round is a shape, isn't it?'

ANONYMOUS

42. Give it the brush-off

Here's a cheap and cheerful solution to your cellulite woes. Daily skin brushing can help soften and smooth out orange-peel thighs. And you'll soon see the results.

You'd be forgiven for thinking that you need a vast budget, and a coterie of beauty therapists and personal trainers to really banish cellulite. In fact one of the most inexpensive ways to tackle a dimply bottom is to give it a good firm brushing.

Most beauty experts and authorities on cellulite agree that regular body brushing can dramatically enhance the texture of your skin and help the dimples appear less noticeable. The advantages are you can do it every day in the comfort and privacy of your own home, that it takes no more than three to five minutes of your time, and that it costs nothing – well, a decent brush costs about the same as a bottle of wine. And that you can usually see results within days.

Body brushing can help minimise cellulite in two ways. Firstly, it helps remove surface dead cells, which makes the skin on your rear end look smoother and more even-textured. Think about how much smoother and more radiant your face looks after you've exfoliated; you get the same effect on your bum too!

Secondly, dry skin brushing is considered an effective way to stimulate circulation and boost lymphatic drainage – deficiencies in both of these systems are believed to be major contributing factors to cellulite.

Ever noticed how blotchy and pasty your face looks when you've been sedentary or lolling about lazily for days on end in a centrally heated or air-conditioned room? Compare this to how it looks when you've taken some exercise, washed, exfoliated and patted your skin. Boosting your circulation improves skin dramatically.

In fact many experts describe cellulite as a disorder of the lymphatic drainage system and your circulation. When these two body systems work optimally, your circulation delivers oxygen and important nutrients to your cells via blood, and the lymphatic drainage system removes the waste-products.

Here's an idea for you...

Get the circulation in your bottom and thighs going, and smooth the skin at the same time, with a home-made scrub. Mix two tablespoons of finely ground oatmeal together with one tablespoon of almond oil. Rub into the skin, then rinse off in the shower.

Think, then, of the healthy fatty tissues on your bottom and thighs. This tissue has a blood supply which provides nutrients and oxygen, and a drainage system taking waste-products away. When this flow of fluid slows down, either because you live the life of a couch potato, or have a very sedentary job, your limbs don't get much action and your skin in that region suffers.

Your skin cells that separate the fat cells in your bottom and thighs are like bits of elastic. The more sedentary you are, the less nourished they become, and gradually they become thicker and less flexible. If you're a confirmed couch potato, the continued sluggish movement of fluid round your body makes these fibres even thicker and tougher. And, because these fibres lose their elasticity, the fat that lies beneath them ends up bulging out between them, creating the dimples we know as cellulite. All of this is made even worse by the excess fluid in the bottom and thigh area – which is another result of poor lymph flow and blood circulation.

Dry skin brushing, then, can help get your blood circulation and lymph flowing again. Plus some experts also believe that skin brushing helps encourage new skin cells to regenerate and boost collagen production, which in turn helps elasticity.

Convinced? Judge for yourself. Try it every day before your shower or bath and brush your skin in long strokes towards the heart.

How to body-brush

Start at your feet and brush your soles, toes and ankles and top of each foot gently but firmly with long, sweeping movements. Brush the front and back of your lower legs, working towards your knees. Then rest your foot against the bath or a chair and brush from your knees to your upper legs and thighs, waist and buttocks using long, smooth strokes. Repeat on both legs.

Many women get cellulite on their upper arms, so don't neglect your upper body. Start at your wrist and brush your inner arm in upward strokes towards your elbow. Then brush the palm of your hand, then the outer side of your hand, and move up towards the back of your arm. Repeat on the other arm. Follow with gentle circular movements over your stomach and chest.

Then shower or jump in the bath to remove the dead surface cells.

Defining idea...

'**The buttocks are the most aesthetically pleasing part of the body because they are non-functional...as near as the human form can ever come to abstract art.'**
KENNETH TYNAN, legendary theatre critic (and confirmed bottom-man)

43. Goodbye Mr Chips

Cut back on fat and you'll reap rewards on your bum and thighs. Try some simple and painless ways to reduce fat in your diet.

If you're reading this, no doubt your priority right now is on your behind. And, given that being overweight is a major factor in cellulite, it's time to slash some of the naughty stuff from your diet. Let's start with some home truths about dietary fat:

Weight for weight, fat contains twice as many calories as sugar.
1 g of fat contains 9 calories, while 1g of sugar contains about 3–4 cals – so one of the best ways to cut back on calories is to reduce your fat intake.

Fat calories make you fatter than carbohydrate and protein calories.
That's because fat is closest to the form it needs to be for storage – to metabolise it requires just 3 calories for every 100 calories you eat. That leaves a whopping 97 to be stored in your fat cells.

Compare this with the number of calories required to metabolise carbohydrates, about 10–15 calories which leaves only 85–90 to be stored. Protein wins hands down though; it requires an amazing 20 calories to use it. So if you want to boost your metabolism, stick to protein and carbs and go easy on the fat.

Try sticking to a moderate fat restriction eating plan (where it accounts for between 30 and 35% of your total calorie intake). You're much more likely to keep the weight off this way than by restricting it to 20–25% because it's more palatable and therefore easier to stick with.

You don't have to suffer on a fat-free regime to lose weight. There are plenty of painless ways to cut back:

❀ **Ban** margarine, butter or cheese in your sandwiches (and use tuna, turkey and low fat ham as fillings). Mustard and low-fat dressings make good alternatives to spreads.

> *Here's an idea for you...*
>
> **Can't say no to afternoon tea? Try munching warmed fruit loaf with your cuppa instead of butter-laden crumpets; fruit loaf is rich in fibre and iron and is gooey and moist so you won't need oodles of butter.**

❀ **Reduce** red meat consumption by adding beans or root vegetables such as parsnips and turnips to casseroles or hotpots to bulk up your servings.

❀ **Keep away from** foods preserved in oil; check the labels and stick to brine or fresh water instead.

❀ **Stop frying food**; instead barbecue/griddle or grill your fish or meat.

❀ If you're making meat casserole, leave it to go cold, then **remove any fat** on the surface.

❀ **Never add** butter to your potatoes; try mustard or fromage frais in mashed potatoes instead.

❀ Drink clear broths or vegetable soups **instead of** creamy ones.

❀ **Never add cream** to pasta sauces or soups.

Defining idea...

'No diet will remove all the fat from your body because the brain is entirely fat. Without a brain, you might look good, but all you could do is run for public office.'
George Bernard Shaw

Try these swaps:

❀ Instead of steamed puddings and cream, opt for crumbles; they'll keep your fruit intake high. Plus if you swap heavy crumble mixture for brown-breadcrumbs and a sprinkling of brown sugar you'll keep it lower calorie still.

❀ Instead of toast smothered with butter try hummous – it's a good source of protein, plus it's high in soluble fibre which lowers cholesterol levels.

❀ Love roasts? Swap red meat for white meat – and use spray olive oils and balsamic vinegar to add taste and cut back on fat.

Good fats

But don't eliminate all fat from your diet. Firstly, studies show you'll lose more weight if you include small amounts of fat in your diet. Secondly your body needs one to two daily servings of essential fatty acids and mono-unsaturated fats each day for energy, eye function, brain-power, and healthy skin and hair. Fats are also needed to absorb fat-soluble vitamins A, D, E and K which are important for vision, strong bones, and to help fight disease.

Here's where to get your daily fat:
80 g (quarter to one-half) of an avocado
One tablespoon of olive or rapeseed oils
10 g (half an ounce) butter
2 tablespoons of low fat mayo

2 tablespoons sunflower or pumpkin seeds
4-6 walnuts
3-4 tablespoons hummous
150 g oily fish such as sardines or mackerel

44. Getting a leg up

Walk your way to firmer, sexier legs – with a little help from MBTs, or Masai Barefoot Technology trainers.

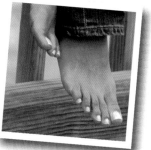

Can the type of shoes you wear really make a difference to the dimply stuff on your bottom? Here's the lowdown on the trainers nicknamed 'fatburners'.

Sounds like a fairytale, doesn't it? You put on a pair of shoes and, as if by magic, your cellulite starts to disappear…Well, let's not get too carried away – you do have to actually walk in them. And first you have to learn how to walk in them. Their thick, curved soles give them a platform, and make you walk in a different way, so that your feet are 'rolling' rather than the heel absorbing most of the impact as it does with normal footwear.

Like many aids to reducing cellulite, these trainers were designed for their health benefits, with the inch loss to orange-peel thighs a welcome bonus. They were originally developed in the 1980s by a Swiss professor, Karl Muller, to help cure back and joint problems by correcting the posture and altering the load on the spine.

Now that their many benefits have been revealed, celebrities as well as sports professionals have had themselves fitted for a pair. Jemima Khan, Madonna, Gisele Bundchen, Sadie Frost and Zoe Ball have all been seen rolling along with a pair of MBTs on their feet, and glossy magazines such as Vogue have featured them.

Here's an idea for you...

To get the maximum benefit from wearing MBTs you need to walk as much as you possibly can. So leave the car in the garage and walk to work/to the station/into town/to see friends. Carry your work shoes or evening Manolos with you and change when you get there – the longer you wear your MBTs the better the results. The extra exercise will help you lose inches and tone up your bottom even more.

How do they work?

The curved layers of the sole emulate walking on natural, uneven surfaces – which our bodies were designed to do – as opposed to the artificial hard and flat surfaces we mostly walk on today. This forces the body into a more upright posture and means you use muscle groups that are normally neglected. With better posture – think of a proud Masai warrior walking across an African plain – your back and joints are strengthened, circulation is improved and you even breathe more efficiently.

Because the body is working more efficiently and extra muscles are being used, more calories are being burned and weight loss is speeded up. MBTs improve muscle activation by 38%, so any workout is 38% more effective. Bottom and leg muscles are toned up more quickly – even while standing the muscles continue working to maintain a centre of balance.

Losing excess fat on bottom and thighs means less cellulite. With improved muscle tone over the whole of the lower body, any remaining cellulite will be less visible, and more efficient circulation will boost blood supply to the skin tissues, further improving skin texture.

What do they feel like?

MBTs take a bit of getting used to. The thick layers of curved sole feel awkward at first because they make you feel as if you're walking on an uneven surface (that's

the point). After wearing them for the first time –
usually for just half an hour's walking – you'll feel as if
your legs have had a good workout (which they have)
and may ache a bit. But once you've got used to them
it feels like floating – some wearers can't bear to be
parted from them.

Other wearers have felt a burning sensation in their
feet after walking in them. This is due to the increased blood flow to the foot muscles
and should disappear after a few weeks. However, if it doesn't, the manufacturers
advise a visit to your GP as it could indicate some kind of vascular problem. If you get
backache after wearing them it's because the back muscles are getting used to a
different posture, and should settle down after a while. In fact, some MBT wearers
have reported a big improvement in their back problems, including lower back pain.

The right fit to get fit

The big plus of MBTs is you don't have to change your daily routine at all to get any
of these benefits – you just put on a different pair of shoes. MBTs come in several
styles and colours and there's even an open-toed sandal for summer. They are not
much more expensive than high-quality 'normal' trainers, so whichever way you
look at it they are probably a worthwhile investment.

You can't buy MBTs mail order because they need to be properly fitted to make sure
you are using them correctly. They come in slightly more varied sizing than
standard footwear and need to fit snugly. The trained fitter will also give you a
lesson in how to walk properly in them. There is now an international following
and MBTs are becoming more easily available through sports shops and department
stores. For prices and where to buy visit www.mbt-info.com. Roll on!

Re-energise your relationship

Even the best relationships go through the doldrums sometimes. Trouble is it happens so gradually that we don't really notice until one or both of us is halfway out the door. This section is full of clever ideas to revitalise your relationship whether you are still at the honeymoon stage...or nearer the divorce courts.

146

Have you got what it takes to be a lover?

According to the god of human relationships, psychologist John Gottman, there are several characteristics that good couples share which set them apart from couples who are likely to split. Pick the scenario that best describes your partnership style *most* of the time.

1. How easy do you find it to apologise to your partner after a fight?
- ☐ a. Very easy. I make a real effort to see where they are coming from and if there's any area where I am at blame, I'm happy to apologise first.
- ☐ b. Difficult. I know it takes two, but the truth is that it's his fault nearly all of the time.

2. My partner is still very hurt by some things I said to him years ago:
- ☐ a. Maybe but he doesn't say.
- ☐ b. Yes, every time we fight he brings it up again.

3. When we aren't getting on:
- ☐ a. It's not too long before one of us cracks and gives the other a hug.
- ☐ b. We avoid each other completely. We can't even bear to be in the same room.

4. We're the kind of couple:
☐ a. Who talk all the time even when we're not getting on.
☐ b. Who can go days without speaking to each other. We retreat into our shells.

5. When one of us has a problem:
☐ a. We will tell the other and try to work it out together.
☐ b. We solve it alone for the most part – and even resent the other one trying to understand or help.

You'll have guessed already that the 'a's demonstrate the 'right' way, the 'b's the 'wrong' way. The characteristics of lovers are

❀ You don't blame or criticise each other;
❀ You show respect for the other's viewpoints and ideas;
❀ You maintain physical intimacy even when you're angry with each other;
❀ You are emotionally available to the other person.

If you were short on 'a's – and it only takes being short on one to push a relationship into decline – start by reading ideas 54 and 63.

45. Who do you think they are?

As soon as girls are old enough to understand the spoken word, they are told stories of handsome knights and Prince Charming, encouraging them to daydream Mister Perfect from an early age.

Yeah, a great way to while away the hours of your youth but, ladies, don't be fooled. For grown-up women, this is the enemy of a sane and fulfilling adulthood.

That's not to say a woman shouldn't have standards. Standards are what keep us from ending up with the frog instead of the prince. But if you are serious about meeting someone, you need to forget your 'perfect' man nonsense and think more laterally about who you *both* are.

A great technique for understanding what you want is called visualisation. This means that you imagine yourself in a situation with your said partner and then note what is happening; it's a way of getting closer to your real desires. For example, in your fantasy, what are you doing? If you are laughing together, lying on a beach, that may tell you that you want someone you can relax with, maybe travel with, be easy in their company. If it's a passionate clinch, it may be that sex and attraction takes precedence for you. Next, take a list and write down a 'wish list' of your ideal partner's qualities, aiming for around ten. You will probably find that you write bland things first, like 'a sense of humour', but try and be as specific as you can.

Here's an idea for you...

Tell everybody that you are looking to meet someone. This is also an important visualisation technique. Rather than saying you are desperate to hook up with the love of your life, explain that you are ready to meet someone lovely and have a nice time. It will make it more of a reality in your own mind and move it to the forefront of your life: it might also mean that your cousin suddenly considers the guy she knows at work as a possible date, which may never have occurred to her before. The more you put out there, the more you've got a chance of things coming back...

Then reread it. If you have written 'rich' but also 'loves walks in the country' are you being realistic? (Not that the two are mutually exclusive. After all, you could be talking walks around his *estate* in the country...) If you are looking for a dynamic businessman, then is it really sensible to imagine him devoting his time to hillwalking with you every weekend? It may be that he has to work long hours to be so successful, and you need to be prepared for that compromise. Otherwise, you are storing up a whole lot of misery for you both before you even meet...

What is most important to you? Would you prefer to accept security and appreciate the time you can spend together, or would you prefer lots of attention and fewer flash dinners? You could strike lucky and get both, but a little thought now could save you from ignoring your perfect guy because he doesn't seem to fit some very narrow criteria. By the same token, a little soul-searching may be needed. If you want someone free-spirited, are you willing to accept that you may have to share or even carry the more grown-up responsibilities of the relationship? If you'd love a playful 'lad', will you be prepared for the fact he may want to keep his Saturdays free for football matches with his mates? This isn't about making someone change but rather the opposite: being compatible after the first flush of lust is the key to staying happy, so rather than trying to force someone into an uncomfortable role later, be upfront early on. It will save a lot of heartache all round.

There is also an important thing to consider here: what the other person wants. If you meet someone that you like who hasn't shaken off their fairy-tale fantasies, unless you really do spend a lot of time in a pink ball gown and glass slippers, then consider walking away. How do you know? If he says he loves your high-powered consultancy job then complains that you don't iron his shirts (which makes him feel special), think carefully. If he leaps at the suggestion that you get a cleaner who can take the (washing) load off you both, then great. If he looks disappointed and questions your commitment – forget it. You may find that this request is just the beginning of a very long list entitled 'Hoops to jump through'.

> *Defining idea...*
>
> **'We come to love not by finding a perfect person, but by learning to see an imperfect person perfectly.'**
> ANONYMOUS

46. After the confetti...

So you got married and it was a wonderful day; you've even got the pictures to prove it. But what happens after you've found the last of the confetti and everyone has seen the video? Your life together begins in earnest, and it can be tough at first.

Lots of people find that they feel a bit flat after the wedding. It's a completely natural sensation after having been the focus of attention for months, sometimes even years. To go from being the golden couple to being just like everyone else can be a bit strange.

The fallout

As well as falling back to earth, you can also suffer from 'marriage movies'. Even people who have happily lived together for years suddenly find they are in conflict. This is often because they have conscious or unconscious ideas about how being married works, like a film playing somewhere in their heads of every marriage model they have seen from Doris Day films to their own parents. Even if you think this isn't the case with you, you should talk through how you expect things to change. Most people find they have new expectations, as they wouldn't have chosen marriage if they didn't expect it to transform their situation in some way. It can be as simple as feeling more committed, in which case maybe you expect your partner to reorder their priorities.

Hopefully, you have discussed all the key issues before now, but, even so, you should have a good chat about your expectations. Are you going to keep your joint wedding account? How will you divide your assets as a married couple? (Lots of people have their own homes before they marry nowadays; will you put them in joint names?) Do you want children? Do you even have a time frame for having children and is it the same?

Ways to keep it going

Everyone has their own ideas on how to keep love alive, but there are some techniques that most experts agree on. Make sure that you keep your own friends and pastimes so that you have new things to bring to the relationship; it may be tempting to spend all your time together but for most people that becomes more difficult as time goes on. Everyone needs to have somewhere to let off steam.

Many couples feel that avoiding arguments is a sign of success, for others a screaming match where anything goes can be an everyday occurrence. Both can be harmful in their own way, from storing up resentments to making spiteful accusations, but the main key for any couple is finding a way to express themselves, that both are comfortable with, when dealing with conflict. Part of being close means that you can say things to each other that

---

Here's an idea for you...

Good spouses never forget an anniversary. So, here's a list of the traditional gifts. Add it to your diary so you'll have no excuse for forgetting...first, cotton; second, paper; third, leather or straw; fourth, silk or flowers; fifth, wood; sixth, iron or sugar; seventh, wool or copper; eighth, bronze; ninth, pottery; tenth, tin; eleventh, steel; twelfth, silk and fine linen; thirteenth, lace; fourteenth, ivory; fifteenth, crystal; twentieth, china; twenty-fifth, silver; thirtieth, pearl; thirty-fifth, coral; fortieth, ruby; forty-fifth, sapphire; fiftieth, golden; fifty-fifth, emerald; sixtieth, diamond; seventy-fifth, second diamond

you couldn't to other people, but this sometimes means that courtesy can slide – 'please', 'thank you' and 'can I make you a cup of tea?' will go a long way to keep you both feeling appreciated. And keep reminding yourselves that there's more to taking care of each other than just stopping the joint account from becoming overdrawn.

What else makes your relationship different to the others in your life? Your sex life. This can often suffer in the run up to the wedding as you have so much else going on and can often be too stressed or exhausted, but it is one of the key factors that makes your relationship special. Your honeymoon can be a great opportunity to reconnect on this level before you get back to your normal life.

Change – the big challenge

Hopefully, you will spend the next 50 years in a state of bliss. A big part of this is allowing each other to change. Be realistic: the disco monster you married can't always be relied upon to get the party started when they've had little sleep thanks to your new baby. Don't tie people into the person they were at twenty, unless you can guarantee that you haven't changed a jot since you met; not even your underwear. (Which, in itself, could be grounds for divorce.)

47. French kissing in the USA

Long-distance relationships can be legendary. Too often, they're lacklustre. Whether you're working on opposite sides of the country or living in different continents, we'll save your relationship from long-distance doldrums.

Even the strongest relationships can crumble if one of you is away working, serving with the armed forces or in prison. How can you keep your love alive until your next joyful reunion?

She's leaving home

Unless you met your soulmate at an airport just hours before both jetting off in different directions, you'll probably have some time together before doing any long-distance loving. Sorry, but you do have to talk about your impending separation. It's tempting to avoid it, but most problems happen when there are misunderstandings. If you secretly expect your partner to 'surprise' you with spontaneous visits or pick you up from the airport, unless he's telepathic you're going to feel let down. You also need to work out how you'll communicate across time zones and other barriers. A videophone may be a viable and attractive option. How about a weekly emailed photo diary? Maybe it's time to get blogging? Or invest in a home DVD recorder, to send clips and comments in the post. On a more practical note, it can save a lot of hassle if you work out a household budget, especially if the main earner is working away. Staying in touch over distance is

> **Here's an idea for you...**
>
> Make a tangible reminder of your relationship for your partner – a tape or CD of 'your' songs, a personalised photo album or a framed photo of the two of you.

expensive and needs to be factored in. Worries strain relationships, so the less hassle, the happier you'll be together. In long-term relationships, people tend to get a bit dependent. If this sounds familiar, swap skills. If you both know where your fuse box is, how to clean out a U-bend or check the car oil level, you're less likely to panic when you're home alone. And we know it sounds morbid, but we suggest making wills. All that travel cranks up your chances of a premature trip to the undertaker.

Wish you were here

After saying goodbye, don't put your own life on hold until your partner's back. Go out, enjoy yourself and maybe bring back a souvenir to share with your other half when he returns.

Parcels and packages are terrific treats and a wonderful way to share things with your partner while she's away. How about posting a book you've just enjoyed or a disposable camera with a little note: 'I'd love to see the view from your window'?

I just called to say I love you

If you're slavishly predictable, your partner might feel short changed, but with a bit of invention, you'll be irresistible. Why not vary your communication methods and style: a playful email today, an erotic text message tomorrow, perfumed love letter at the weekend, quirky quips on an unusual art card midweek. As well as planned communication, be spontaneous. If you've agreed to phone every Friday, call on Sunday night one week too, just to say 'I love you'.

Help, I need somebody

Never call in a crisis. We know it's counterintuitive, but consider this: the roof's falling down, there are rats in the basement and you've locked yourself out. You're right to reach for the phone, but call the locksmith, roofer and rat-catcher, rather than your lover. It might make you feel better, but there's not much he can do in Sydney if you're suffering in Sussex. He'll just fret, which could strain your relationship. Instead, call him when you've sorted it out, and rather than ranting about your problems, rave about your solutions. Sassy independence is sexier than needy misery. Whatever your gender, be a fixer and mender.

Reunited

How much time it takes to readjust to being together can come as a shock. You're used to making decisions alone and suddenly need to compromise and do things jointly again. So if your life feels invaded by a relative stranger, don't panic. Find some time to chill out and share stories and experiences.

> ### Defining idea...
> **'I wish that you were here or that I were there, or that we were together anywhere!'**
> ANONYMOUS

157

48. Bewitched, bothered and bewildered

Flirting with the milkman? Exchanging glances with your guitar teacher? Daydreaming about running away with your husband's best friend?

Fancying someone else is not, in itself, a bad thing. A frisson of safe excitement can brighten office life and casual flirting makes a mundane journey or chore a lot more enjoyable. The danger, if there is one, is located at home. Almost imperceptibly the passion and sparkle that once existed in your domestic life can leak away like water from a punctured paddling pool and re-emerge elsewhere. You might have seen it yourself: people who are the life and soul of the party or public bar becoming bores or bullies behind their own front doors.

The trick is to find ways to keep the flame of passion alight with your partner. Early excitement needs to be replaced by a more sustainable fuel before the flame flickers and dies. But how? Start by soul searching, followed by discussions with your once nearest and dearest.

People and relationships are complex. Working out exactly why you – or, indeed, anyone – does anything is nigh on impossible. There are, however, clues. Good detective work might not lead you to the truth, but what you discover about yourself along the way might be helpful.

So you find yourself thinking obsessively about someone at work. Your 'look but don't touch' rule might not have been broken, but there are dangers. You need to ask yourself a number of difficult questions: what is it about this person that has so captivated you? Is it his youth and ability to make you feel younger/ wiser/ brighter/ funnier/sexier? Are things going on at home that make you feel pushed out, taken for granted, bored or boring and unheard?

You cannot rule out sheer lust: a new kid on the block, and especially one who makes you feel like a Greek goddess, can have an unsettling effect on you. Likewise changes in circumstances can also rock the boat. Promotion, a new colleague who you see more of than your husband and opportunities for foreign business trips might put previously undreamt-of temptation your way and into the equation. These are not excuses and should not be used to justify yourself to anyone, just information to help you understand what's going on between your ears and legs. If you feel you're the only member of the household who washes up, cuts the grass or ferries the kids to judo training and Dan in the Works Department takes your mind off these issues, you might have a better idea of how to redirect your frustration.

The daily grind, work stresses and money problems can all push people away from their partners, making them more likely to succumb to a stranger's seduction. There are times in relationships when eyes (and hands) are more likely to wander: after the birth of new baby, when you're raising a young family, the so-called midlife crisis, when the last of your children has left home and approaching retirement.

Here's an idea for you...

Long-term love can survive short-term crushes, as long as they're not kept secret. If there's someone you fancy, tell your partner. It isn't your boyfriend pointing out the other man's buckteeth and hairy back that kills your interest, but the fact it isn't a private passion.

159

In other words, times of change and turbulence. It is hardly surprising that so many people put off confronting these sorts of milestones. Sitting down together, anticipating difficulties and working out ways around them is a more constructive way forward.

How to avoid temptation

Build self-esteem People often have affairs to feel better about themselves. If you've been made redundant, the drudgery at home is only punctuated by arguments about money and you feel nagged, pulling a new partner makes you feel successful at something and desirable again. But only in the short term.

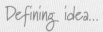

Defining idea...

'While the forbidden fruit is said to taste sweeter, it usually spoils faster.'
ABIGAIL VAN BUREN, American advice columnist

Face problems when they arise Dealing with the root of small problems as they arise prevents a lot of bother later.

Cultivate emotional intimacy You both need to say how you feel to understand each others moods and outbursts. If things feel fiery, take time out to cuddle up.

49. All by myself

If your relationship is feeling a bit flat, it doesn't mean you need to find someone else, just the person you've been living with all your life: you.

Films, TV and pop songs brainwash us. Love, they assert, is all you need. Find the girl or boy of your dreams and you'll live happily ever after. What tosh. If you look to your lover to fill aching gaps in your life you'll inevitably be disappointed in him or her and your relationship. Overdependence and enmeshment breed contempt and self-hatred. A little absence really does make the heart grow fonder. Doing a few things alone makes you a more interesting partner, with more experience and adventures to share when you are together. Think of time apart as fertiliser to cultivate a mature relationship. This way, when you are together, it's out of choice, rather than neediness or dependence.

An air of mystery

Develop a side your partner doesn't know or fully understand and they'll become curious and interested. People with an air of mystery, a strong identity and a range of interests are more attractive. Spend time alone productively and you'll bring skills and knowledge to revive your relationship. Time alone provides space to indulge in activities that don't interest your partner. If you hate football and he hates shopping, why drag a sulking 'soul mate' with you to the game or shopping centre?

Here's an idea for you...

Find something you love and do it often. It might be going inline skating, performing at a poetry open mic or having an Indian head massage. Think back to how you enjoyed yourself when you were single. Just because you are in a relationship doesn't mean you have to put away your paintbrushes, ballet pumps or flute.

To give your relationship added vitality, bag a regular night just for yourself. If there's just the two of you, you might be able to have a regular weekday night, but if you've got young children, you'll probably have to eke out a monthly me-date. Your goal is to have fun – be it with friends, trying new activities or being pampered. So do what you fancy: beginner's belly dancing, intermediate jam making or a relaxing aromatherapy massage.

Feeling unfulfilled in your relationship? Easily annoyed, irritable or resentful? Try making more time for yourself. Whatever they say in the movies, only you can bring what you want into your life. The more needs you can meet yourself, the more likely you are to have lasting love. If you're sick of being a couch potato, get active. And if your partner panics at the prospect of Pilates, train for that marathon on your own.

Just because your partner doesn't share your religion doesn't mean you have to ditch your beliefs. You might find attending weekly prayers at the synagogue or going to a lunchtime meditation group strengthens your spirit and nourishes your relationship with a committed atheist. The same is true for politics. If you don't go on an anti-war march because your boyfriend calls it namby-pamby, you'll hardly feel at peace with him and might give him his marching orders. Go alone. His friends or family will probably be delighted to have him to themselves for an afternoon.

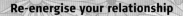

You don't have to go out to make the most of your solitude. Being home alone has much going for it. You can fart and not say sorry. You can listen to 'your' rather than 'our' favourite music and eat what you like, when you like. Sometimes we love something for the same reasons that our partners hate it. Jilly likes the *Sound of Music* because it's sentimental and makes her feel hopeful. Jim hates it because it's sentimental and makes him feel sick. Watching it together doesn't enhance their relationship, but watching the sing-along version on her own makes her more forgiving when he staggers in worse for wear. When you're home alone, you can gossip on the phone or even book plastic surgery online without worrying about what you partner will think; or soak in a candlelit bath until your skin is blue and wrinkled. Reading with your partner is companionable, but we prefer reading alone: you can rustle newspapers, walk around every few pages to digest a thriller, feel really scared or laugh out loud.

Defining idea...

'Ideally couples need three lives. One for him, one for her and one for both of them together.'
JACQUELINE BISSET, actress

50. Reach out and touch

Words are great, but your fingers can reach places language never can. Here's our eulogy to non-verbal communication and tactile tantalisation.

We crave touch. The warmth and affection of another human being is a reward in itself. We all need strokes, emotional and physical. When did you last reach out and touch the person you love?

Let your fingers do the talking

The finest touching is a sensual conversation. When you next touch your partner, wait for a reply before touching further. So if you stroke her cheek, wait until she squeezes your arm before running your finger over her eyebrows. Between people who are attracted to each other, just brushing fingertips can send shock waves. Try making little circles with your fingertips on your partner's palm or inner elbow, or the nape of his neck. Do this at mundane times, like waiting for a bus or in the supermarket check-out queue. Then next time your partner is waiting for a bus without you, he'll realise that it's just not as much fun as when you're there. A cunning piece of prestidigitation.

Hugs

We use hugs to express lots of things, like 'hello', 'I'm sorry' and 'I hope you feel better'. Other hugs are good for comforting or making your partner feel warm. Therapist and relationship guru Virginia Satir believes we all need four hugs a day for survival, eight hugs a day for maintenance and twelve hugs a day for growth. There are three types of hug, but only one hug hits the spot.

> **Here's an idea for you...**
>
> Next time you see your partner, touch before speaking. If he's in the kitchen washing up, sneak up behind him, slide your hands round his tummy and cuddle up. When she comes home from work, give her a long hug instead of firing questions or filing complaints.

The quickie
A quick grab and let go, which may be punctuated by a couple of air kisses and mwah, mwah noises. This hug's for theatrical luvvies.

The A-frame
Huggers interlock arms and may touch shoulders, but there's no physical contact any lower down. This one's reserved for spinster aunts.

The full body
Wrap your arms around each other, touching from the tops of your heads down to your toes, and bump tummies in the middle. Breathe together, snuggle and sigh. This one's the real deal.

The science bit
When non-sexual touch is neglected, we become belligerent and dejected. But why does touch make us feel so good? After prolonged touching, the hypothalamic area of the brain, which controls the fight or flight response, slows down and your body's natural euphoria-inducing chemicals – endorphins – soar, while the stress hormone

cortisol dips. Massage has extra benefits as it promotes deep muscle relaxation. Neck massage has been shown to reduce depression, improve alertness and help people sleep more soundly. When you're being touched by your beloved, your mind associates all these good feelings with them, leaving you feeling loved up and secure. If you're going through a difficult time, try to keep a hand or another part of your body in contact with your beloved. It will help you feel united.

I knead you

Hippocrates, the Greek grandfather of medicine, believed daily massage with essential oils was the key to health. We find it unlocks all sorts of sensuous pleasures and possibilities. Massage is a fantastic stress-buster, but it can also excite or invigorate. Before you switch your partner on to massage, switch off your phone. The deeply satisfying sensation is enhanced when the massage oil is heated a little. Immersing a bottle of essential oil in hot water until it reaches body temperature is ideal, but if you haven't got time, warm some oil in your hands first. Camomile and lavender are said to be calming, whereas ylang ylang is reportedly an aphrodisiac. Once your partner is relaxed and comfortable, work some oil into his skin. To really bliss your partner out, start with gentle, stroking movements to relax and sooth, before applying gentle pressure in places that feel tense or knotted. Change speed every now and then and try moving your hands in little circles, spreading the oil up to the earlobes and down between the toes. Take care not to miss out elbows or tickle when you massage foot soles. We suggest you leave pummelling and hacking to the pros.

Defining idea...

'Touch is important for survival itself. We're meant to be touched. It's part of our inherent genetic development.'
ELLIOT GREENE, past president of the American Massage Therapy Association

51. Bedroom eyes

Want a really raunchy relationship? You need a bedroom to match. We'll help you create a retreat from the rest of the world, a haven from household hassles, an oasis from office stress.

It's hard to pursue private passions if you're tiptoeing round the laundry basket or in danger of upsetting a Reader's Digest mountain. Makeover your bedroom, then make out in style.

What does your bedroom say about your relationship? Is it warm and inviting? Dramatic, with no-holds-barred colour? Fresh, clean and confident? Or cluttered, messy and stuck in another era of your lives?

Turn your bedroom into a boudoir. For a bedroom that's vibrant and exhilarating, commanding yet calm, the trick is to think sassy, not trashy. Think wrought iron four-poster bed, crushed velvet scatter cushions and antique candelabras rather than black PVC sheets, red light bulbs and mirrors on the ceiling. And not a hint of chintz.

Exploit the position of your bedroom. For instance, if it's south facing, avoid heavy curtains and opt for lighter billowy drapes to enjoy opaque morning light seeping into your lives as you wake. If you've only got a small room, cultivate a cosy, intimate feel with intense colours and quirky lanterns.

Here's an idea for you...

If you're not able to do a major makeover just yet, keeping your bedroom tidy and clutter free is a good start. Once you've exiled the junk, put a vase of fresh flowers on the bedside table, display a couple of photos of the two of you and treat yourself to some new bed linen.

If you yearn for a room that's decadent and enticing, go for an ornate style, with voluptuous velvets. Whatever style you choose, crisp cotton bed sheets are essential. Some people like the thought of silk, but you'll find your partner slipping away from you. For sensual bliss, think textures and layers. Could you put velvet, silk or fur throws over those crisp cotton sheets?

Pastel colours teamed with silver and white accessories create a dreamy and tranquil haven. You might like to hang some vintage wallpaper, or a modern imitation. Either way, pick out one or two key colours and use them in your soft furnishings. Jazz up junk shop finds with distressed paint techniques, or show off a sexy dress on a tailor's dummy. Antique hatboxes or designer luggage are glamorous storage solutions. A chest of draper's drawers makes a stunning showcase for lingerie and linens.

If you think boudoirs are all about Barbie dolls and candy floss, forget it. Your bedroom doesn't have to be toe-curlingly frilly or feminine; boudoirs can be butch. How about painting the walls with manly denim and silver stripes, or deep Moroccan blues to match mosaic-topped bedside tables, accessorised with Moorish mirrors? Or for something more fiery, why not take inspiration from the Arabian Nights? Spice-coloured saris, which you can buy in a specialist sari shop or online, come in a fantastic range of colours and lush fabrics. Use them as throws over the bed. Draw inspiration from the jewel colours of the Far East and paint one wall in deep cerise, scarlet or fuchsia. If you paint the other walls a lighter shade, it will stop them closing in on you. Or go gothic, with black framed pictures and mirrors, and tall, ornate candlesticks. But no gargoyles or you'll end up with a bedroom that's more Hammer House of Horror than period allure.

Makes scents

Use smell to carry the theme through. Scented candles, oil burners or incense can all be utilised to float soothing scents around your boudoir. Next time you wash your bedsheets, add a few drops of lavender oil to the rinse cycle.

Animal magic

If you're a wild tiger or glamour puss at heart, scatter some fake animal fur print cushions or invest in a pretend leopard rug. Don't take it too far though. The leopard print posing pouches are best left in the joke shop.

Sounds good

If you don't have music piped into your bedroom, keep a basic CD player close to the bed, with a few favourite albums to hand. It doesn't need to be all-singing and dancing, but a continuous play button comes in useful.

Light up your life

You already know a neon strip light is a bad idea and probably already have pink-toned light bulbs in your bedroom. But for a magical night, nothing compares to the glow from a candlelit chandelier.

> Defining idea...
>
> **'It doesn't matter what you do in the bedroom as long as you don't do it in the street and frighten the horses.'**
> MRS PATRICK CAMPBELL, actress, wit

52. Maybe the va va voom can work for you

We all know that lust doesn't last; but passion can. Before you have a fling, try to put the zing back in your marriage. It can be done.

No one thinks it's strange that a middle-aged man is still as passionate about his football team as he was as a boy, or that a woman gets as excited as a girl every time she goes on a shopping spree. That's seen as normal. But feeling passionate about a long-term partner is viewed as unusual, something rare and even a little strange. It doesn't have to be like that.

We almost expect not to experience passion in a marriage after a certain amount of time has passed; to think it's normal to be more interested in stroking the dog than each other. And if we expect something to happen, then it quite frequently does. As long-term married couples we are programmed not to be passionate. That is often the reason why so many relationships go stale before their sell-by date. Of course, no one expects you to be lusting after each other like love-struck teenagers, but a marriage without sex can be unhealthy and destructive.

Television would have us all believe that sex is a romping, steamy roller coaster of a love-fest, best had between two beautiful people under the age of thirty. And if it isn't like that, well then it's probably best not to bother and to do some gardening instead. That's nonsense. Sex between real people can take many guises, and if you're on that roller coaster, then great! But if you're not, don't give up. A ride on the charming, slower and slightly old-fashioned carousel can be just as enjoyable and far less stomach churning than the big dipper. The secret is finding out what's good for both of you.

So, how do you do that? You've stopped making love, the cat sleeps closer to you than your partner and you vaguely remember last having sex only after going mad on the sweet sherry a few Christmases ago. Now you're talking about divorce. After all, the postman has started to look more appealing than your husband, especially the way his muscles ripple when he lifts his sack. And the woman in the greengrocer's handles the root vegetables in a way that makes you weak at the knees.

Here's an idea for you...

Send a text message saying 'I love you and I miss holding you. I would be so happy if we could make love tonight, and I hope this makes you happy too.' Of course, it has to be in your own words and something you feel comfortable with, but the message should be open and simple. A raunchy email or text can be just what you need to put the va va voom back in your relationship. It has the trademarks of dating and therefore associates all those feelings of excitement.

If your own partner feels as exciting as a trip to the supermarket, maybe now is the time to move on, cut your losses and see if you can recapture the va va voom with someone new. But if you feel even the faintest tingle when you look at your partner, then it's worth trying one more trip to the fairground before you sign on the dotted line and finish it for good.

Let's talk about sex

Have you ever talked about sex with each other? Or was sex something that came so naturally to start with that there was no need to talk then, and now you don't know how to approach the subject? Well here's how to cope, even if you'd rather walk around Tesco naked than talk about sex with your partner – especially as talking about divorce seems an easier option.

Remember that easier isn't always better, and there are always alternative approaches to every problem. Just think about the number of ways we have to communicate today: phone, fax, email, text messaging, even the good old-fashioned letter. And it doesn't have to be complicated. Sometimes, especially if there has been a long gap since you last made love, long, involved explanations and accusations can just get in the way.

Good with words? Then what about the traditional romance of a letter? If not, then this is where the simplicity of an email or text message can really help. You may be thinking this seems cold and shallow, but if you really can't talk about it face to face you need a catalyst to get the dialogue started. What have you got to lose? Once you're talking face to face, your ultimate goal of *doing* something else face to face is much more achievable.

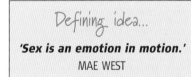

Defining idea...

'Sex is an emotion in motion.'
MAE WEST

Be brave – get talking before you start walking. Try having your discussion somewhere outside the bedroom. Remove the pressure from the situation. Open some wine, or take a walk together, but always make sure your partner feels safe, special and loved.

53. Boiling point on the sea of love

Affairs? Betrayal? Boredom? You've reached boiling point. Maybe it's a slow move towards separation, or a complete shock that your marriage is bubbling over. Take a look at precisely why your marriage might be melting.

We all claim we know that marriage won't always be easy. But are we ever really prepared for some of the storms that we'll encounter on the sea of love? Probably not.

Sailing the stormy sea of love

When we say we'll be together no matter what, we tend to be in the first bloom of love, or at the very start of our married lives together. We feel that our love is strong enough to weather any storm and we'll work through any situation together.

But every boat, from a little dinghy to a supertanker, needs constant maintenance, fuel and care to save it from sinking, as well as realistic expectations about its durability. Even the most beautiful, powerful, unsinkable cruise ship in the world went down after its first bump, didn't it? Maybe suggesting the iceberg that sank the Titanic was a bit of a bump is a slight understatement, but you get the point. Awareness, forethought and constant monitoring of what's up ahead is key to saving your marriage from following the Titanic down into the depths.

Many people have asked, 'What if the ship's designers hadn't been so cocky about the unsinkable nature of their ship? What if they'd placed more life-boats on board? What if they'd had a better look out system than a tiny man in a little crow's nest in a lot of fog?' But then life is full of 'what ifs?', and the same is true of marriage. If you are considering divorce, then the reality is that your marriage is sailing very precariously on a stormy sea. It's time to check if you can stop it sinking before you swim solo for the shore.

Bubbling over

So, is it possible to bring certain situations down to a gentle simmer before they boil over? Well, it depends what has brought things to the point of break-up and whether you have the desire to fix the damage or not.

The most common cause of a relationship coming to an instant crisis point is infidelity. Is it even possible to save the marriage if you've been unfaithful and your spouse has found out? Well the first thing to do is ask yourself the questions: why did you do it and was it a one-off fling or a full-blown affair? Be honest with yourself. Once you've discovered the reasons behind

Here's an idea for you...

If you've found out that your spouse wants a divorce and you're in shock, it's time for some damage limitation. You must limit the distress before it causes you any irreparable damage. First off, allow yourself to cry and shout out the worst feelings of pain and betrayal; don't try to keep them inside. Then call someone, a friend or family member, to come and sit with you. Arrange time off work to cope with your shock privately and to organise any practicalities. Let your work know it's a personal crisis and if you have children, inform their school. Most importantly, take some time to come to terms with the news before you jump to any hasty decisions. Think things through carefully and talk any plans through with someone you trust.

your infidelity, you may well discover underlying problems, which you either want to fix, or you don't.

An affair is possibly the major cause of marital break-up. It contravenes the basic premise of marriage – sexual fidelity. Once the affair is discovered, the bond of trust between husband and wife is severely damaged. However, an affair needn't mean that the marriage is doomed. It will take a great deal of courage and commitment to work through the hurt and distrust which is the legacy of infidelity, but it can be done if both partners want it enough.

Boiling points in relationships can also come out of situations that are far less dramatic, but equally destructive. Perhaps you're just bored. It's common to become bored with your spouse, your house, your life – suddenly you want some excitement, some passion. You want a divorce! But is this really about your spouse's shortcomings, or is it about you?

Maybe if you were to change yourself first, to find some new challenges and ease the boredom, you might begin to feel differently about your partner. Talk about the situation, state how you feel, and see if there's any way you can get what you crave and stay within your marriage. Understanding of the deeper reasons behind these issues can be vital if you want to change your course from due north to divorce.

Defining idea...

'Divorce is probably of nearly the same date as marriage. I believe however that marriage is some weeks the more ancient.'
VOLTAIRE

54. Men! How to influence your Martian

You love him – you really do – but he is such a pain at times. You need to learn how to be brilliant at influencing your boyfriend.

Because so much appears to be at stake, we sometimes do and say crazy things with the men we love, which can of course often have dire consequences later.

Women the world over will identify with these perennial sources of frustration. Why, oh why, does he …

- Not make an effort with his appearance when you go out?
- Never tidy up around the flat?
- Leave you to do all the food planning?
- Show no interest in the films you would like to see?
- Talk so much about other girls – especially the very pretty ones?
- Talk about you (often rudely) behind your back?
- Refuse to talk about marriage and children?
- Make cynical comments about the self-help books you read?

As for the targets of these gripes, they no longer try to say anything to defend themselves or improve matters. As far as they're concerned, that's just an express train to argument time.

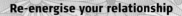

Actually, it's not so bad because you can view that list as a list of symptoms – and the majority of those symptoms can be boiled down to just one or two causes. It's a similar deal to having flu. You feel awful, your legs ache, your nose is running, you've got a sore throat, and a temperature. Those are the symptoms, but the root cause is the flu. What we need to find here is the root cause of what's getting to you: that's what we need to work on. So here it is, split into two points.

Point 1

Remember when you had 'the talk' – yes, the one about sex. Maybe it was at school, maybe with friends or maybe, horror of horrors, it was with your parents. It was useful in the end. But funnily enough, generally nobody gives you 'the talk' about relationships. Here it is.

Men and women are different – very different. You know that. That's what makes relationships such potential fun, but we do need to work with that difference rather than against it.

To be politically correct we spend a lot of time avoiding saying it, but the sexes do not conduct themselves in the same way. That doesn't stop us

Here's an idea for you...

Identify some changes you want and the influencing you need to do – getting a longer term perspective on this relationship, what his real views on children are, etc. Then think how you could make progress. Bear in mind that the one thing that will work is talking. You need a decent conversation: one quality conversation and it could all be 'sorted'. So, when do you have your best conversations? When you are both relaxed; when you've got a bit of time; when there are no distractions such as football on TV? Choose that time. And don't try to 'sell' the idea of talking. Many men will see 'the need to talk' as 'psycho-babble'. Just get the conversation going by starting in their arena. Try it: you'll be amazed at how easily it works.

Defining idea...

'How can a woman be expected to be happy with a man who insists on treating her as if she were a perfectly normal human being?'

OSCAR WILDE

wanting and ensuring men and women get equal opportunity, equal support, etc. However, we will only get on well with each other if we recognise, respect and value that difference. And this is the key foundation that is essential to good influencing.

Here's the bottom line: your boyfriend is highly unlikely to think and respond like you and others of your sex. Ever!

Point 2

No change will happen unless you are communicating and respecting the differences between you. Communication will start if you can talk to your man about his interests and embrace the fact that he ticks differently. Yes, he does go on about cars a lot, but that's what interests him. So, try to show an interest in his interests and don't judge. Then, guess what: he'll start talking, and not just about cars. And then when you are talking you can introduce some of your own points.

55. Wedded bliss

Been together for a long time? Yep, so long you've given up trying to change your other half. Well, that's not good for marital bliss.

Whatever we do as the years roll by, we shouldn't ever give up on our partners. Even after all this time, your husband will still be easy to change – no, not for a new one!

Okay, there are some things that five years into your marriage you think: "Well, those things will never change now." And fifteen years in, you're thinking: "My fault – I shouldn't have accepted that in the first place." Think again because that's not so. A great marriage needs regular reinvention to keep it fresh and keeping on sorting out these kinds of issues does exactly that. Regular influencing is a great way to a healthy marriage.

The thing you've got to get out of your mind is that because it has been like this for a long time (and that's a relative term, of course: it doesn't really matter whether we are talking five, ten or fifteen years, or even longer), it's therefore fixed; it's stuck and you're doomed to put up with it. 'Long time' does not equal 'can't change'. Individuals change all the time. It's certain you've changed a lot over the past ten years, so why can't two people agree to make combined changes after all this time? They can.

Here's an idea for you...

Fix a regular time every week or so for you both to get out of the house, get away from the kids, forget the email and go somewhere where you can talk. Become adults again. Here are a few suggestions. A very relaxed meal in a nice local pub or restaurant. A walk in the park. A long coffee in a village café. A drive in the car and a sit in the car park overlooking the beach. You get the idea. If you wanted to, you could decide to do something different each time so that even planning your 'time out' becomes an enjoyable shared experience.

Once we've got that mental block out of the way – i.e. change is possible – we need to think about what the best approach is.

Firstly, give a bit of thought to the change we really want: what do we really need to influence? Is it actually that he reads the newspaper at the breakfast table or that you never seem to talk any more? Is it actually that she's always out at various committee meetings or that it seems impossible to go out to a film or the theatre like you used to? So trace back the symptoms to the cause. Remember that many areas that require influencing revolve around money or sex (or both) but they are usually the symptom not the cause.

Here's the big idea: keep talking. Once you have identified the real issue (e.g. not planning for retirement) and not been distracted by symptoms (e.g. money arguments), then you need to talk it through and agree a plan. That can only happen if you have time to talk.

Whatever happens: keep talking. Never ever lose 'the thing' that keeps you talking. And don't just talk about the shopping or the kids' school reports: talk about you – fundamental stuff – in a non-rushed environment. We can't tell you how or when but we are betting you are intelligent enough to do that. So make it happen.

It's all about maintaining the emotional bank account. We all have one, just like our financial bank account. We have them with each other. The question is, are we making loads of deposits into the account (by being polite, being responsive, being helpful, being loyal) or are we making undue numbers of withdrawals (by being judgemental, rude, talking behind their backs)?

If we make plenty of deposits, the relationship can take the occasional withdrawals. But if it's been all withdrawals, the occasional deposit has little impact. Makes sense, doesn't it?

Defining idea...

'[A] husband who can cook is not at all the same thing as a husband who can shop, prepare, and assemble ingredients, and clean up the mess after the great burst of creativity.'
MARY-JO FITZGERALD, Marriage and the Male Animal

56. Love not war

Fighting with your partner can cause you a lot of pain and misery; learn how to stop.

Being right isn't as important as being loving so put down your cudgel and find a flower to throw instead.

Most healthy relationships have ups and downs and sometimes you have to fight your corner. If your husband gets insanely jealous every time you even speak to another man, you have a problem. If your boyfriend refuses to be seen out in public with you and wants you to keep your relationship secret, you have a problem. If your boyfriend thinks he prefers your brother to you, you definitely have a problem. The point is that there are some situations that are deal-breakers but the rest is about compromise, compromise, compromise.

The best way to learn to compromise is to step into your partner's shoes. Do it by thinking for a minute about how the situation looks from his or her viewpoint. Imagine for a second that you're your boyfriend's lawyer and you have to make a case for his side of the argument. What were his motives for doing what he did or saying what he said? It may seem a bit of a convoluted and strange exercise but really try to imagine how you'd argue his case. Not your case. His case.

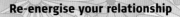

Oftentimes you'll find that the reason people do and say hurtful things is not because they're being malicious but because they can't see how they're hurting you. So, instead of fighting as though you were faced with an adversary, you should try to honestly express what you're feeling and – this is very important – say explicitly what they can do or say to make it better.

Here's an example. Suppose you have a row that starts because you feel cold and your husband feels hot. You see his refusal to turn on the heating as evidence of him not caring for you. He, for his part, doesn't see why you can't just put on more clothing, given that he would feel extra hot if the heating was on. Perhaps he thinks you don't care about his comfort either. Something small like this can quickly escalate into a horrible argument where both of you are convinced that the other person is in the wrong. A good way to deal with it would be for you to say 'I feel like you don't care about me when you refuse to turn the heating on. I need reassurance in the form of a warming cuddle that this isn't the case.' At this point your husband will look at you as if you've gone crazy.

> *Here's an idea for you...*
>
> **The next time you have a fight with your partner, write them a letter. You don't have to send it (in fact you probably shouldn't), you don't even have to read it back to yourself but write all your feelings down on paper anyway. This should dissipate some of the rage you might be feeling. Once you've expressed all your feelings of anger and righteousness, take a fresh piece of paper and write a love note to your partner that only says what you like about them. Send that one.**

You'll have two choices in front of you then. You can either return to argument mode or you can laugh and fetch a cardigan or blanket to warm yourself up in. The first choice is a quick way to ruin your mood and your evening. The second choice will probably result in your husband also laughing and turning the heating on, even if he has to sit around in Bermuda shorts to cope.

Defining idea...

'*Make sure you never, never argue at night. You just lose a good night's sleep, and you can't settle anything until morning anyway.*'
ROSE KENNEDY, Matriarch of the famous Kennedy political dynasty

The way to steer yourself out of an attitude of anger and resentment is to treat your partner with the same compassion you'd show for someone with whom you weren't in a relationship. I mean, think about it; if a friend of yours was visiting and had issues with the temperature of your home, would you insist she just put up with it? Probably not, as a good host you'd check she was OK and make adjustments to make her as comfortable as possible. Why do we think that it's OK to not have the same consideration for our partners?

57. Lost that loving feeling?

When you've misplaced your mojo, it's a drain on your physical and emotional resources.

Reconnecting is important because when you're not having sex, and you don't know why, you're missing out on one of life's great energisers.

It's a lot easier than you might think to drift into a disaster situation in your relationship, where you're with each other but not *with* each other. Luckily, it can be just as simple to reconnect.

Step 1
Are you out of sync? Might you as well be living in different time zones for all the meaningful contact you have with one another? Do you have commitments that mean you can't be together at the same time, whether that's in the morning or evening? Children pull away a lot of the energy that you used to have for each other. Are you booking a regular babysitter at least once every two weeks and spending time together, just the two of you?

Fix it tonight
Go to bed at the same time. Some people can live in different countries and keep their love alive, but you may not be two of them. Lots of couples lose it because one partner goes to bed and one stays up playing with the remote control. Get into bed at the same time and talk to each other. See what happens.

Here's an idea for you...

Are you feeling low? In women who were mildly depressed, taking the herb St John's Wort improved their mood – and in 60% of cases, it also had the effect of boosting their libido.

Step 2

Get real. This isn't terrific or easy to do, but take a long look in the mirror – metaphorically and literally. Cast your mind back to when you met your partner. Who were you? What were you doing? That's the person your partner fell in love with, and maybe you need to bring more of that energy back into your present persona. Now, literally, look at yourself. In a big mirror, naked. If you're not quite in the buff condition you were when you met your partner, it doesn't mean they've gone off you. But it could mean you've gone off yourself.

Looking your absolute best, taking time and care with your appearance, wearing clothes (and underwear and nightclothes) that make you feel sensual and erotic can't fail to make you feel more sexual. Your partner may not notice (then again, he or she might be pathetically grateful), but you certainly will. Don't underestimate the power of the shallow and superficial.

Fix it tonight

Go through your wardrobe and chuck anything that doesn't make you look good or feel good. If it's old, tired, too comfy or unattractive, chuck it out. You may be left with three items of clothing – but you'll look and feel hot in them.

Step 3

In the words of Prince, think sexy. Think about sex more often. It's generally accepted that men want sex more than women (though I wouldn't always bet on it) and surprise, surprise, they think about it more. If you're a woman who spends more time thinking about what you're going to make for dinner than how inspiring your sex life is, it's not surprising you're not feeling like sex much. This isn't a criticism. Life is busy, but our love life should be a pretty high priority.

Fix it tonight

Remember the last time you had sex. Remember the best time. Remember how it felt the first time you really wanted someone. Remember anything as long as it's a strongly sexual memory. Stay with the memory for five minutes. And revisit it every hour, on the hour. That's who you are. Find the passionate you again.

Step 4

Now it's time to talk and ask. Ask for more love. Ask for you partner to make it a priority for them too. If he or she is too stressed or too tired, then you need to help and support each other to find time to be together and reconnect. Perhaps you need to cut something else out of your life. Maybe switching off the television is all it takes.

Fix it tonight

Couples absolutely need time alone. Decide on a date and make it happen. If you can't get a regular babysitter, ask a friend to watch the kids for a couple of hours on a Saturday afternoon or even as soon as you get home from work. Then high-tail it back to bed. If it's been a long time since you made love and you're shy, just hold each other and talk about what's going on for you and why it's got so difficult.

Defining idea...

'Women need a reason to have sex. Men just need a place.'
BILLY CRYSTAL, comedian

187

58. Unleash your sexual tiger – in just one week

You know sex would make you feel better if you could just muster up the energy to open your eyes.

Sex can be a good measure of your energy levels. The more you want, the better your energy levels as a general rule. But it works the other way too.

Sex raises your vitality, making you feel passionate and engaged with life. Boosting your libido so that you want more sex – and, yes, actually having more sex – can have a very positive effect on your energy levels.

Which is all very well, but according to one survey, one-third of us are too tired when we get into bed to do more than sleep.

This idea is based on the fact that, for many of us, it doesn't take too much to tip the hormonal balance in our favour. Working on the theory, and indeed the fact, that the more we think about sex, the more we want it, this is a one-week plan that forces you to think about sex just a little bit more. Prioritising it in your mind will make you feel sexier and jolt you out of your 'take it or leave it' stance. You don't have to actually be with your partner for the magic to work. You've just got to consciously think about sex a little more.

Remember, you don't have to believe in it, for it to work ... just do it!

Seven days to total fulfillment

Monday – Hop into the shower together
You may not have time to act on it, but getting lathered up together will get you thinking about sex, and that's a start.

Tuesday – Have breakfast in the garden
University of California research shows that libido is increased by 69% if you spend an hour a day outside. Start clocking up your minutes.

Wednesday – Buy apple strudel for dinner
Or any pudding that has cinnamon in it. The Smell and Taste Research Foundation in Chicago found that the smell is such an aphrodisiac that it increases the flow of blood to the bits that matter!

Thursday – Text your partner
Couples need to keep touching to release regular doses of oxytocin the bonding hormone. When you're away, 'virtual' strokes – with saucy or romantic texts – work nearly as well.

Friday – Order garlic bread with lunch
Garlic contains allicin, which increases blood flow to the genitals and thus improves sensation and orgasms. Aim to eat a bulb crushed into food each week.

> **Here's an idea for you...**
>
> Swap the pillows to the end of the bed and have sex upside-down. Surprise releases the hormone dopamine, which increases friskiness, and swapping ends is the very easiest way to experience sex from a surprising new perspective.

Saturday – Do the shopping

Go to www.sh-womenstore.com for some ideas. Go to www.lovehoney.co.uk or www.gash.co.uk for some inspiration. Even if you're not buying, browsing will get you thinking. And that's all you need.

Sunday – Turn up the central heating

Let your partner 'surprise' you walking around naked when they least expect it. It will give them a shock – let's hope a pleasant one –but the point is, it will get them thinking.

It is self-evident that by thinking about sex more you're going to be more likely to be in the mood that night. Someone who is thinking about chores, work and all they have to do the next day is naturally not going to be as up for sex as someone who has allowed a few frisky thoughts to interrupt their routine. 'Making it different' is another simple way to keep it fresh between you. Try sleeping in front of the fire, in a tent in the garden, in the spare room. A little willingness to experiment can work wonders on your sexual energy levels.

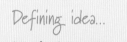

Defining idea...

'I'm too shy to express my sexual needs except on the phone to people I don't know.'
GARRY SHANDLING, American Comedian

59. Sleep is the new sex – honest!

I know a woman who tried to convince her lover that the really happening people were giving up sex in favour of sleep. But he wasn't buying it and neither am I!

It's not of course the end of a relationship if you go some time with a lacklustre or indeed non-existent love life. Every relationship has its down-time. But the major worry with the tiredness reason for avoiding sex is that it gains a weird sort of reverse momentum. Keep using tiredness as an excuse and before you know it, total inertia has set in. What you need is a two-pronged attack.

First prong – Get over yourself

Having sex when you're tired can start off indifferently and get a whole lot better. And even if it doesn't, I'm firmly of the camp that believes that in a longstanding relationship, indifferent sex is better than no sex. At least you've got something to work on.

If you're of the aficionado brigade who unless sex is a multiorgasmic garden of delight would rather not bother, then you have to negotiate this with your partner. Make definite dates when you're going to do it. Make sex that day your priority. See it as a red-letter event.

Here's an idea for you...

If sex usually takes place just before bed and is generally rushed and unsatisfying because you're both knackered, make a weekly tryst for sex where you go to bed early and enjoy each other. Therapists agree that this 'appointment system' is one of the easiest ways to ease you back into a good sex life.

Second prong – Reorganise your workload

This is anecdotal, based purely on my experience of knowing a lot of couples in their thirties with young children and having no sex. At the root of it is usually resentment on the part of one partner towards the other. Usually the woman is resentful of the man. She is usually working, even if only part time, and doing most of the childcare too. Women who have given up work to look after their children tend not to be as resentful, but they feel that their men don't appreciate all that they do.

Who does the most after a hard day's work?

This quiz gives couples a quick visual reference of who does more around the home. Tick the sex of the partner who most often undertakes a particular task. This test can be an eye-opener for couples that think they have a pretty equal relationship. If it's not so equal, you have to take steps to delegate or equalise your workload, or your sex life is unlikely to get back to normal any time soon.

Getting the children ready for the day   M ☐ F ☐
Making breakfast   M ☐ F ☐
School run   M ☐ F ☐
Supervising homework   M ☐ F ☐
Dealing with childcare   M ☐ F ☐
Getting children ready for bed   M ☐ F ☐

Supermarket shopping	M ☐	F ☐
Cooking evening dinner	M ☐	F ☐
Paying bills	M ☐	F ☐
DIY, organising repairs	M ☐	F ☐
Cleaning	M ☐	F ☐
Taking out rubbish	M ☐	F ☐
Buying children's clothes	M ☐	F ☐
Washing and drying clothes	M ☐	F ☐
Dishwasher loading	M ☐	F ☐
Gardening	M ☐	F ☐
Organising social life	M ☐	F ☐

> *Defining idea...*
>
> **'He said, "I can't remember when we last had sex." And I said, "Well, I can and that's why we ain't doing it."'**
> ROSEANNE BARR

You might be reading this and thinking, 'I'm the major breadwinner, I work my butt off and can't do childcare too.' But you'll have to find some compromise for the sake of your relationship. You need to talk openly about how you divide your joint workload, give each other the space to have a life as an individual and find time to spend as a couple. If you're reading this and thinking, 'Who needs a blinking quiz to tell me I do it all?' Then stop and examine your martyr-syndrome. Yes, you've got one. At all costs, you have to get rid of it or 'I'm just so tired' will sound the death knell for your sex life.

Overprotective parents take note: someone else can very well look after your children. Your relationship with one another can't be tended by anyone else but the two of you.

Workaholics take note: pop your clogs tomorrow and someone else will fill your job/role/career by Monday morning. No one else can take your place in your relationship.

60. When your sex drives are out of sync

Looking for a mate? Choose someone with roughly the same sex drive. Oh, sorry, you thought you had.

Every relationship goes through periods when one person wants sex more than the other – you're exhausted but your partner has one thing pretty obviously on their mind or vice versa.

Any of the following familiar?

'I just don't want sex any more'
This doesn't mean that you're always going to dread sex or that you won't regain your libido. There's nothing wrong with you either. What's far more likely is that your priorities have shifted and something else – job, kids, financial worries – is draining all your juice. Or it could be that for you sex is a demonstration of your closeness, but you feel distant from your partner: 'We're miles apart, but he/she still wants sex.' If you're one of those people who when single always preferred having sex with someone you had a connection with, why would you change because you're in a long-term relationship? But as we all know, in a long-term relationship, you're not always completely in tune mentally with your partner.

Whether you're stressed or feeling distant, the solution is the same. Get closer. Talk to your partner and explain how you're feeling. Spend time holding each other. Create spaces in your life to do this. Switch the TV off and cuddle up in front of the fire. Go to bed half an hour earlier for 'duvet time'. Spend time being physically and emotionally close and eventually you'll want sex more often. It might not be great at first, but eventually you should reach a place where your libidos are more closely in sync again.

'My partner doesn't want me anymore'
Are you sure that this isn't more that they don't want sex at the same time as you? It's truly astonishing to me the number of men who report being hurt and resentful following repeated rejection from a wife who falls asleep by nine-thirty most nights. Yet after a minute of careful questioning, it turns out they've never made the mental leap between her exhaustion and the fact that while he's lying in front of the telly, she's more often than not pottering around folding clothes, loading the dishwasher or tidying up the day's debris. You have to be equally well rested for your libidos to get back in sync.

> *Here's an idea for you...*
>
> **The defining difference between couples having lots of sex and couples having virtually none is often a sense of playfulness. Play strip poker. Play Twister. Play doctors and nurses. Go to the cinema and have a snog. Do anything that means you have fun and you'll almost inevitably rekindle passion.**

Defining idea...

'I am open to the guidance of synchronicity, and do not let expectations hinder my past.'
DALAI LAMA

Don't hassle your partner for penetrative sex. Do hassle them for physical intimacy. You don't have the right to demand sex from your partner, but in a loving relationship, you are entitled to expect physical comfort and cherishing. And the latter makes the former a hell of a lot more likely. Increase physical intimacy, have just a little more sex and wait out your partner's lost libido. With patience and (loving) perseverance, you can help them find it again.

61. Tantric sex

Not just a load of old joss sticks.

If you've absolutely had it with your partner's idea of foreplay being a quick tap on your shoulder and a hopeful expression, then it's time to go Tantric.

To the student of Tantra, sex is sacred, a means of accessing your spirituality and a way to meditate, transcend your problems and reach a happier more blissful state. For those of us who don't have the time or inclination to study Tantric sex in any great depth, it can still add a lot. It teaches sex is important, and by clearing time to undergo a few of the simpler rituals you declare to each other 'Hey, our sex life is a priority.'

Tantric sex teaches you to concentrate on your lover and on the sensations that you're feeling. Forget the orgasm. The journey not the arrival is what's important. And for that reason alone, Tantra can be liberating and mind-altering, even if you don't get into it the whole way.

Ritual one: create a 'temple of love'

A really simple method of foreplay is to make your bedroom a sensual haven quite different from the rest of your home. You don't have to opt for lurid leopard prints and black walls – unless you like that, of course – but take a long look at your bedroom as if seeing it for the first time. Does is say 'love', 'passion', 'excitement'? Is it a room devoted to the two of you?

197

Here's an idea for you...

Try dreaming of rainforests, droning music, an overflowing bank account...once you're out of Sting-world though, Google 'Tantric', but set your porn filter to 'Kill'.

First, think about what's in the room. Would you say that the television contributed to improving your love life? Unless you mainly use it to watch porn, probably not. Perhaps you spend more time watching it than talking to each other. If you want to keep the TV, find a scarf to cover it as a mental signal that you're switching off from the outside world. Similarly, ban work paraphernalia – piles of clothes waiting to be ironed, family photographs, anything that takes your attention away from each other and onto your responsibilities. Repair and clean tatty or old furnishings. Clear away clutter. Throw open the windows and let some fresh air circulate. This room is a reflection of your relationship – it's where you spend the most time with each other. It should sparkle.

Finally, create a love altar. Find a picture of you both together that symbolises the best of your relationship. When you look at it, you should feel warm and compassionate towards your partner and strong as a couple. Place it in a nice frame where you can see it easily every day. Keep fresh flowers next to the photograph and candles – anything that you have to tend regularly and pay attention to – as a physical reminder that your relationship needs similar care and tending. Make sure there are soft lights in your bedroom and soft music to hand, comfortable cushions or duvets that you can sink into, and a bedroom should always be comfortably warm so hanging around with few clothes on doesn't make you shudder.

None of this is genius level, but think of your and your friends' bedrooms. How many have been designed with sensuality, luxury, comfort and sex in mind? Your bedroom should be a place that's welcoming to both of you, so that you look forward to hanging out in the only place where most couples can be truly intimate and private with each other.

Ritual two: think yourself in love

Tantric sex depends on visualisation to build sexual energy. As your lover begins to caress you, feel how much they love you. Imagine their love for you flowing from their fingers and hands and nurturing you. Melt into their embrace. When they kiss you, feel that with each kiss they are showing how much they love you. Imagine the sexual energy that you are creating between you is visible as a red or pink light emanating from your genitals and surrounding you like a force field of love. As your partner touches you, imagine that your arousal is growing like a great wave of light. See it as fire or energy emerging from your deep pelvis and adding to the force field surrounding and supporting you. As you begin to have sex, imagine the energy passing upwards from the base of your spine to your heart and feel this energy as love around your heart – feel it as joy – and imagine it reaching out and surrounding your partner's heart. Then, as you get more excited, imagine the energy being drawn upwards and flowing out through the top of your head.

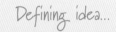

Defining idea...

'The relation of a man to a woman is the flowing of two rivers side by side, sometimes mingling, then separating again, and travelling on. The relationship is a life-long change and life-long travelling.'

D. H. LAWRENCE

That's the way to enlightenment, but it takes a bit of practice. Look on the bright side, with all that visualising going on at least you won't be thinking about who's doing the school run tomorrow.

62. Pressure – it's not a dirty word

Or rather, if you're doing it right, it can be.

For most, sex is the main course of lovemaking. Oh, OK, for most, sex is more of a quick snack. But for times when (to push the meal metaphor to the limit) you want to feast on a banquet of love, there is massage.

You don't need to be self-conscious about massaging each other. It doesn't have to be of a professional standard because what you lack in technique you can more than make up for by what is called 'loving intention'; your total focus on your partner's relaxation and pleasure will do lots of good.

First, select your oil. You can buy massage oils premixed or create your own blend by adding eight to ten drops of oil (or a mixture of oils) to three dessertspoons of a base oil such as almond. Good oils for sensual massage are geranium, which is uplifting and grounding; lavender, which is relaxing and soothing; sandalwood, which is warming and encouraging; and ylang ylang, which is sensual and erotic. Burning the same combination of oils as you massage will heighten the experience for your lover.

Choose a warm, comfortable place in your home. Put on some gentle music and lower the lights. Take a bath or shower together. The masseur (or masseuse) should dress in light comfortable clothes and make their lover comfortable lying on their front.

Take some oil – and you should have liberal amounts to hand – and warm it between your palms. Then start working the oil into your partner's back. Use firm gliding strokes over the large muscles of the shoulder blades, then work down the sides to the base of the spine and then work upwards using the balls of your thumbs to apply pressure on either side of the spine. The secret of applying pressure is to channel the strength of your body through the balls of your thumbs. Lean into your lover's body but apply pressure only to the meaty parts of the body (but not the belly). Don't apply pressure on hard bony areas.

Continue with sweeping movements alternated by gentle pressure across the back, buttocks and the back of legs. Use long strokes along the arms and gently pull at each finger in turn. Try different pressures. Use fists to apply heavier kneading movements to the buttocks. Apply very light blows across the back. Then alternate with gentle fingertip stroking.

Don't worry about your technique, just concentrate on your lover's body and giving it pleasure. Ask for a little feedback. For example, does your partner want a gentler or firmer stroke? But don't talk too much. Allow your partner to relax into the massage.

Ask your partner to turn over. Holding their head steady with your knees and massaging their face is particularly relaxing. Don't apply heavy pressure to the stomach. Brush but don't directly touch their genitals – the oils may irritate

Here's an idea for you...

Maintain skin-to-skin contact throughout the massage. Cup one hand on your lover's back while you pour more oil so that the back of your hand maintains this contact.

sensitive areas. Anyway, the point is to build sensual pleasure for you both, not necessarily to move onto sex. Judge how your partner feels. Are they giving the impression that this is turning them on? Or is it so relaxing that they want to curl up in your arms and sleep. If you're not sure, ask them, and don't let your wishes come through either way. Making it clear you expect sex in return for giving massage isn't considered sporting.

Short cut to bliss

If you don't have the time to indulge in a full body treat, give a foot massage instead.

Bathe your lover's feet. A few drops of peppermint oil in a basin refresh instantly and keeps things fresh for you. Then ask them to sit while you kneel at their feet, with a towel over your knees to cradle each foot in turn. Massage oil over one foot. Apply pressure through your thumbs systematically all over the soles of the feet. Concentrate particularly on the fleshy parts of each toe in turn and gently pull and rotate each one. If you're feeling particularly loving, wipe the oil from your lover's nails and give them a pedicure (men, too). Men, painting your lover's toe nails means she remembers your heavenly foot massage every time she catches sight of her tootsies – an easy way of garnering brownie points.

Defining idea...

'To lovers, touch is metamorphosis. All the parts of their bodies seem to change, and seem to become something different and better.'
JOHN CHEEVER, American Writer

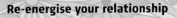

63. Are you sexually mature?

It is big and it is clever.

I've got a theory about what happens when couples are no longer connecting sexually. That theory goes something like this...

Men and women may enjoy casual sex in much the same way, but when it comes to the long haul – the big relationship where the expectations and desire of each partner is that it lasts for the foreseeable future – different attitudes towards what constitutes closeness can develop over the years. I'm going to generalise like crazy, so you two might not conform to this pattern, but on the whole women seem to show their love through emotional closeness and need their partner to show them that he loves them through emotional closeness – talking, discussion, showing empathy (that means picking your socks up off the bedroom floor in case you were wondering). However, men, on the whole, show their love through physically doing something – earning money, cleaning the car, sexual contact. Sex, not discussion, is their way of showing love and feeling loved.

Men don't place enough value on emotional contact, and women don't place enough value on physical contact. That's fine when things are going well, as both partners 'put out' for each other. But if a change happens in their lifestyle and one partner withdraws the contact the other needs, they get caught up in a vicious cycle. He isn't encouraged to extend emotional closeness to her while she's withdrawing physical contact from him, and she in turn can't understand how he can expect her to have sex when they're barely grunting at each other and he

Here's an idea for you...

Remember the old saying about walking in another's shoes if you want to understand them? When your partner has upset or irritated you, make a real effort to understand why they behaved in that way. Still confused? Make them explain what's going through their head. Silence is the worst thing you can do.

spends entire evenings watching TV. Their sex life at best is mediocre, sporadic and unsatisfying. And it stays that way.

This is the pattern of the sexually immature couple. They might have shagged like stoats in their youth. They may have more sexual experience than Peter Stringfellow and Jordan combined. But sexual experience has nothing to do with sexual maturity.

Signs of sexual maturity

You don't wait for sex to just happen
You make sex a priority. You go to work when you're tired. You call your mother when you're stressed. You feed the kids when you have a headache. Sexually mature couples give sex the same priority they give other important things in their lives. They at least remain open to the idea of having sex at any time. They trust that their lover will find a way to turn them on.

You know the importance of doing it differently
Not least because your relationship, your body and your life won't stay the same. Being prepared to change the way you have sex prepares you for the inevitable changes that will occur in your life. It's something that brings you respite when life gets messy, joy when life gets dreary, and comfort when illness or death leave their scars on your psyche. Sex with your loving partner is where you go when you want

to celebrate life's happiness, and it's where you run to hide from life's hurts.

You use sex as a way to show your partner that they're loved

Reaching out to your partner helps you avoid passive–aggressive games. You don't let just one person always initiate sex because that means the other has the power to refuse or withdraw. Sex can become a punishment or reward and if this is your relationship, that's a dangerous place to be, because both of you will end up hostile or resenting each other for different reasons.

> *Defining idea...*
>
> **'The highest level of sexual excitement is in a monogamous relationship.'**
> WARREN BEATTY, a man who should know

You actively think of how you can use your sexuality to make your partner happier

This isn't just about giving your partner orgasms. Sex is a gift. You sometimes do stuff for no reward. Lots of people find it really difficult to make a gift of themselves. Even when they push themselves to sexual extremes in an effort to keep the spark between them alive, their relationship isn't intimate enough to maintain all the emotional intensity that scary sex throws up.

You try for each other

And by reading ideas like this you let the other person know it. Continually being prepared to come out to bat for your relationship is as loving as it gets. Congratulations.

64. What's your lovestyle?

Learning your lovestyle can help your love life, but not as much as learning your partner's lovestyle.

A psychologist called John A. Lee interviewed hundreds of people and concluded that there were a number of different ways of 'being' in a relationship. Understanding this makes it a whole lot easier to keep your sex life on course.

Lee's book *Lovestyles* can supply a definitive quiz to help you recognise you and your partner's lovestyle but this short version could give you some clues. Select the style or styles that seem more like you and your mate.

Are you eros?
❀ You see someone across a room and just 'know' they're for you.
❀ Sexual feelings are important – love is central to your life.
❀ It's hard for you to find the right one – you're choosy.

Are you ludus?
❀ You hate to be tied down to events in the future with a partner.
❀ In the past you have been accused of being emotionally immature or commitment-phobic.
❀ You find loads of different types of people attractive.

Are you storge?

✿ Love will fade but you can live with a friend for life.
✿ Love is the basis of a strong community for you.
✿ When you're good friends with someone, sexual problems can be resolved.

Are you mania?

✿ To you being in love is synonymous with anxiety, even obsession.
✿ You're capable of losing weight, sleep and sometimes your sanity when you're truly in love.
✿ It takes a long while for you to recover from a break-up –
inevitably you're the dumped not the dumper.

Are you pragma?

✿ You have a shopping list of criteria that you expect your partner to fulfill.
✿ You believe you can master any goal with common sense including a succesful relationship.
✿ You'd never end up with someone who didn't fit in with your ambitions for your life and your social group.

Eros lovers have an idealised physical image of their lover. But equally they believe they are on the planet to love one other person unstintingly – they've just got to find them! They stay loyal as long as romance is high on the agenda. If you're with an erotic lover, don't forget romance.

> Here's an idea for you...
>
> **Your lovestyle can vary depending on whom you're with – it's worthwhile thinking why you were, say, an erotic lover in one relationship but pragmatic in another. Are some characteristics helping or hindering your present relationship? Should you swap?**

Ludus lovers are often frustrated with aspects of their lives and are unwilling to commit themselves in a love relationship. A pure 'ludus' will be concerned about causing hurt and warn lovers in advance that commitment is going to be shaky to put it mildly. Some are less scrupulous. Ludics avoid seeing the partner too often at the beginning of the relationship and even if they marry, there will often be distance and secrets. Love is a banquet and they want to try it all. This drives erotic and manic partners mad and their attitude bores and scares ludics.

Storge lovers often grow up in supportive families and communites. They expect lovers to be 'special' friends. Storgics do not become preoccupied with love but in a long term relationship they get very possessive if their love (their status quo) is threatened and will fight tooth and nail to retain their lover. If the commitment isn't there, sexual interest palls. Love is not an end in itself; it's part and parcel of their life or it doesn't work.

Mania lovers are the potential stalkers in the pack. They expect love to be dificult and all absorbing and for them it is. They are jealous and possessive. It's a rare person who long term wants a manic love and it's no surprise that they are almost inevitably abandoned.

Pragma lovers are the opposite. They don't fall in love with people who don't 'fit' in with their lives, plans and goals. They disdain excessive emotion and jealous scenes but they do appreciate signs of commitment. They'd like to have a love relationship but not if it means sacrificing peace of mind and their comfortable life. Most suited to living alone if it came to it so beware if your partner is pragmatic – don't rock the boat too much.

Be healthy
and energised

When it comes to health, it really is a case of 'we don't know what we've got 'til it's gone'. But by making a few straightforward changes we can feel energised and well today, and have the confidence that we are doing all we can to ensure long-term health and a lifelong sense of well-being.

Do you feel as good as you look?

1. Do you sleep at least 7 hours a night on average?
2. Do you eat red meat more than three times a week?
3. Do you drink at least 1 litre of water a day?
4. Do you add salt to food?
5. Are you a non-smoker?
6. Do you live or work on a main road?
7. Do you eat five fruit and veg a day?
8. Do you drink more than four cups of coffee or tea a day?
9. Are you at your ideal weight?
10. Could you do with losing at least half a stone?
11. Have you got the energy to do everything you want in a day?
12. Do you feel guilty about how little exercise you do?
13. Can you touch your toes?
14. Are you a bit stiff with random aches and pains?
15. Do you enjoy a glass of wine or a beer most evenings?
16. Do you drink more than one glass most evenings?
17. Do you visit your doctor at first sign of a problem?
18. Do you put off medical, dental or optical problems until you really can't avoid them?
19. Do you see headaches or stomach aches as possible symptoms of stress and take measures to calm down?
20. Do you watch TV as your main form of relaxation?

Score 1 for every odd number you answered 'yes' to. Subtract 1 for every even number you answered 'yes' to. (It helps to use your fingers!)

If you scored **between 4 and 10** you take average to good care of your health. Check out the even numbers to which you answered 'yes' as a clue to how you can fine tune it. Idea 66 might appeal to take your health onto the next level.

If you scored **between –3 and 3** you could do with some help. Although you do go some way to improve your health there are obviously areas for improvement which will help you feel better and healthier as you get older. Check out 76 and 79 if your diet and lack of exercise is a concern.

If you scored **–4 or less** it might be time for a reality check. Your health is way down on your list of priorities, but let's face it, what could be more important? Start at idea 65 and work your way through this section. You'll feel better for it, honest.

65. What's in what?

Which foods should you target for good health? Here's a quick guide to what's in your food.

The key to a great diet is variety. This will ensure that you get a broad spectrum of nutrients – vitamins and minerals for everyday health.

A nutritional rainbow

The rule of thumb is to eat as many different coloured foods as possible throughout the day. Coloured food is full of nutrients – look for reds, greens, yellows, oranges and all the colours in between. These will give you antioxidant vitamins that can protect you from disease. A broad spectrum of vitamins and minerals is really important.

I'm not going to go through every vitamin and mineral here, but I'd like to highlight the B group of vitamins, which are very important to our nervous system. They're found in a wide array of foods, but particularly in grains. I'd also like to highlight vitamin C, which is found in berries, citrus fruits, tomatoes and potatoes. Of the minerals, a key one to top up on is calcium, which is found in almonds, sesame seeds and vegetables (that's where cows get their calcium from to provide calcium-rich milk). Among other things, we need calcium for bone and teeth formation, as well as nerve and muscle function. Zinc is another top mineral as it's

Here's an idea for you...

Why not try a rotation diet? It doesn't have to be overly complicated. Choose a different grain for each of the five working days. So, Monday might be your wheat day, Tuesday your oat day, Wednesday your rice day, Thursday your millet day and Friday your rye day. Try to consume just the allotted grains on each of these days. In this way you'll be automatically varying your diet.

essential to most bodily functions, including fertility and brain function. Zinc is found in shellfish, lentils, pumpkin seeds and eggs. Before we leave this lightning tour of vitamins and minerals I'd like to mention selenium, another mineral worthy of top billing. Selenium is another antioxidant and it may help prevent cancer. It's naturally found in wheat germ, tomatoes, onions, broccoli, garlic, eggs, liver and seafood. If you want to know more about vitamins and minerals and where to find them, a great book worth investing in is *The Optimum Nutrition Bible* by Patrick Holford. It's a good, easy and informative read.

So, why do we need vitamins? Well, they're essential to life. They contribute to good health by assisting the biochemical mechanisms in the body and help metabolism. They're considered micronutrients, as the body needs them in tiny amounts to make everything run smoothly. Vitamins work with enzymes to make functions work in the body. There are two main categories: water-soluble vitamins, which must be taken into the body daily, and oil-based vitamins, which can be stored (these include vitamins, A, C, E and K). Minerals come in different forms. The major minerals, such as calcium, magnesium and potassium, form part of the structure of bones and organs. These are needed either in high milligrams or even gram quantities on a daily basis. Then

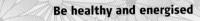

there are the trace elements, which are important for biochemical reactions in the body. Become deficient in any of these and eventually some part of your body will begin to grind to a halt.

Variation in the diet is the key to expanding the possibility of a wide choice of vitamins and minerals. Due to modern methods of transporting and storing food, even the freshest food can be nutrient deficient. Mineral levels in food are decreasing at an alarming rate because their soils are becoming depleted. You may wish to supplement your diet with a good multivitamin and mineral supplement. A qualified nutritionist will help you make a good choice.

> Defining idea...
>
> **'Nurture your mind with great thoughts.'**
> BENJAMIN DISRAELI

66. Get organic

With more and more headlines screaming at us every day about unsafe food, is it any wonder that we're turning to organic food in our droves? But is it worth it?

From pesticide residue in pears to mercury poisoning from tuna, it's no wonder we're unsure about what's safe. But aside from this, we're turning to organic because of the taste. Remember how tomatoes should taste? Quite simply, like organic ones.

Production means prizes

Farmers have been under a huge amount of pressure to increase productivity, but at a cost. Many nonorganic fruit and vegetables contain a wide range of weedkillers, pesticides and fertilizers to increase food production. Fruit and vegetables also have to look perfect for supermarkets to accept them. Gnarled or pitted products are simply not accepted. But what effects do these chemicals have on human health? It seems that we know that pesticide residues can cause anxiety, hyperactivity, digestive problems and muscle weakness. Children are particularly vulnerable, as their immune systems aren't fully up and running and their comparatively small body mass means that chemicals are more concentrated.

And it's not just fruit and vegetables that we have to worry about. The biggest risks and the biggest worries come in the form of meat products: crazy cows, potty pigs – it's no joke. The many years of intensive farming in crowded conditions has reaped a whole host of health concerns. It's just not possible to crowd animals into such tight spaces without using industrial strength chemical agents to get rid of the threat of spreading disease.

Feeding on demand

We're so used to having exotic fruit and vegetables out of season and on demand that at first it's difficult to accept that we can only get organic fruit and vegetables that are in season. Of course, a lot of organic food is produced abroad and flown to our supermarkets and this makes it more available, but vitamins and mineral content is lost if food has been on a long journey. It's therefore much better to buy locally produced products if you can. Many supermarkets are cottoning on to the fact that organic means *big* business. But remember that just because it says its organic on the packet, it doesn't mean that it's better for you, especially if it has been processed. Once organic products have been turned into a crisp, cake or biscuit, for example, you'll have more or less the same concerns attached to the conventional versions of these foods: high sugar and fat. So don't be had!

> *Here's an idea for you...*
>
> If you can't afford to go the whole organic hog, then prioritise. The government advises that carrots, apples and pears should be peeled as they absorb insecticides through the skin, which could make them unsafe. Buying organic could be a better option. Conventionally farmed salmon are treated with pesticides to prevent mite infestations and there are fears that the chemicals become concentrated in the fish. And choose organic milk and beef, as 'normal' cows are in some countries treated with hormones and other growth promoters.

Expect the inspection

The term 'organic' is defined in law and can only be used by farmers who have an organic licence. These farmers have to follow guidelines on how to produce food to organic standards and they're inspected regularly to make sure that these standards are being met. Visit www.soilassociation.org to find out the ins and outs of organic certification in the UK.

Defining idea...

'Organic farming delivers the highest quality, best-tasting food, produced without artificial chemicals or genetic modification and with respect for animal welfare and the environment, while helping to maintain the landscape and rural communities.'
PRINCE CHARLES, a big fan of organic food

Do I buy organic foods? Yes, and I think it's worth it. I always make sure that any meat, eggs or fish is organic and I get organic fruit and vegetables when they're available. I have a box delivered to my door. You'll probably find details of an organic home delivery company at your local healthfood shop. I'm now very aware of what fruit and vegetables are in season. And instead of looking in a recipe book and going out to buy what I need, I simply look in the box and create my menus around what I'm given.

67. Superfoods

What exactly are superfoods? Comic-book heroes with a mission to save the world?

In their own small way superfoods are indeed our own personal superheroes, as they're foods that have beneficial effects on our health.

Often the best way to get the best from these superfoods is to juice them so that their goodness is easy to absorb. Let's run through a few of the top superfoods that you could incorporate into your juicing repertoire. Well, 'a' is for apple and unsurprisingly apples are a number one superfood. In fact, the well-known herbalist Maurice Messegue once said, 'If you could plant only one tree in your garden, it should be an apple tree.' So, now you know. Apples contain plenty of vitamin C, and the pectin in apples helps keep cholesterol levels stable. Pectin also protects us from pollution. On top of all this, the malic and tartaric acid in apples help neutralise the acid by-products of indigestion and help your body cope with dietary excesses.

Beetroot was used in Romany medicine as a blood-builder for patients that looked pale and run down. Don't overdo it though, as beetroot is such a powerful detoxicant that too much could be a strain on your system. Broccoli is another big super hero. It has been demonstrated in a number of studies to have a protective effect against cancer. And yet another superfood is the humble carrot. Carrots are so rich in betacarotene that a single carrot will supply a whole day's worth of vitamin A requirements. Carrots are also a number one cancer protector.

Here's an idea for you...

Consider taking superfoods in powder form – you can get a day's worth of vegetable requirements in one drink. The only downside is that they have an 'interesting' earthy flavour, but don't let that put you off. It could be my imagination, but I swear I feel a definite zing when I drink mine every morning! Check out www.gardenoflifeusa.com or www.kiki-health.com.

A great ingredient to add into a juice is a little bit of ginger. Ginger is anti-inflammatory, helps colds and flu and chest congestion, and has been used for centuries as a remedy against sickness and nausea. Another great additive to a juice is parsley, which is full of vitamins A and C and bursting with manganese, iron, copper, calcium, phosphorous, sodium, potassium and magnesium. It acts as a blood purifer.

Although I've picked out just a few here, most fruit and vegetables are of course superfoods. Each and every one has some benefit to our health. Sometimes there are surprises – a kiwi, for example, contains twice as much vitamin C than an orange. And pineapples have both an antibiotic and anti-inflammatory effect. Mother Nature is simply amazing!

Squeeze me!

So how can you obtain the amazing health benefits from superfoods? Why not try your hand at juicing? Some people think this is a better way than vitamin pills to get your nutrition, as juice is easy to assimilate into the body and it's in the natural form the body can recognise. If you're serious about juicing, invest in a really good juicer like a Champion Juicer (www.championjuicer.com). Further juicers can be found at www.wholisticresearch.com.

What health bonuses do you get by juicing? Well, fruit and vegetable juices are absolutely packed with enzymes, which are vital for digestion, brain stimulation and cellular energy. They're also packed with phytochemicals, which are linked with disease-busting properties. Juice is also a concentrated supply of nutrients, which juice you up with energy! And as if this wasn't enough, juices help to balance acid and alkaline in the body – over-acidity is the root cause of many health problems. Stress also produces a lot of acid compounds in the body and juices help to neutralise these.

Juicing is the number one weapon in your detox armoury. Detoxing isn't a solution to every health challenge, but it can have a powerful effect on cleansing the body and establishing a foundation for health.

Defining idea...

'One that would have the fruit must climb the tree.'
THOMAS FULLER, by the time you've bought the fruit, cut it up, juiced it, drunk it and cleaned the juicer, you've certainly 'climbed the tree'

68. Eat fat

Shops are full of low-fat everything, from cookies and cakes to yoghurt and tofu. In fact, the body desperately needs fats, but only the right kind will do.

Fat has practically become a four-letter word, certainly a feminist issue and definitely public enemy number one. But the new thinking is that fat is your friend – so embrace it. There's one small catch – you must make sure that it is the right kind of fat.

We have a complex about fat. So ingrained is the message of how fat clogs up our arteries, increases our apple-shaped girths, sends our risk of heart disease soaring and is linked to the hooded claw that is cholesterol. The expression 'a moment on the lips a lifetime on the hips' was probably specifically invented for this fat phobia.

The impression given by health writers in the 80s and 90s was that fat was definitely public enemy number one. There were well-meaning diet gurus writing books telling us to avoid it at all costs. However, all fat was not created equal and as we are finding out to our cost, avoiding all kinds of fat is detrimental to our health.

Oil in its unprocessed form is highly perishable and before man moved en masse into the towns, oil used to be sold fresh door to door. Although this is hard to believe nowadays due to the highly processed yellow cooking oils available in supermarkets, if oil wasn't kept cool it would go off and be rancid in a matter of days. The advertising boys have managed to persuade us that we should go for the polyunsaturated or cholesterol-free oils, but these oils have often been refined very highly using high heat and bleaches that strip them of any nutritional value and may in fact make them unstable and potentially toxic.

The chemical building blocks that oils are made up of are called fatty acids, and the fatty acids that are essential to human health and cannot be manufactured by the body are called essential fatty acids or EFAs. As their name would suggest, these oils really are essential to human health and without them we'd be on the fast track to degenerative disease.

EFAs have a more than magical effect on our health and wellbeing. Our skin is waterproofed with oil, and our hormones and brains work with it. In fact, the brain is more than 60% fat, which makes the insult 'fat head' actually quite a compliment. The list of essential fats' great benefits to humankind is really quite impressive. They improve skin and hair condition, aid in the prevention of arthritis and lower cholesterol levels, and that's just for starters. They're also helpful in terms of heart disease and eczema, they reduce inflammation in the body and help in the

Here's an idea for you...

You probably get enough omega-6 as the Western diet tends to be omega-6 heavy, but you could get extra from nuts and seeds – grind some (sesame, pumpkin and sunflower) in a coffee grinder and add them to your morning cereal. To get enough omega-3, up your oily fish quota (salmon, herring, mackerel or sardines). If you're vegetarian you could add a flax seed oil supplement your diet. There are hundreds of good supplement companies, but you could try the widely available brand Solgar (www.solgar.com).

transmission of nerve impulses in the brain. Your body is made up of tiny individual cells, each one crying out for EFAs to make the machine of your body operate. On top of all this, EFAs may help to reduce the likelihood of getting a harmful blood clot.

The two basic groups of EFAs are omega-3 and omega-6 groups. Omega-6 is found mostly in raw nuts, seeds, legumes and in unsaturated oils such as evening primrose oil or sesame oil. Omega-3 is found mainly in fresh deep-water fish, some vegetable oils, flaxseed oil and walnut oil. You mum was right, fish does make you brainy!

Having said all this, the one thing you don't do is cook with essential fats as they're highly unstable. The heat destroys the fatty acids and worse it results in dangerous chemical agents called free radicals, which sounds like something out of *Star Wars*. Better to cook with olive oil, which isn't an essential fat, but a monounsaturated fat that takes higher temperatures to damage it.

Defining idea...

'May understanding of health be the starship of the next generation. May the worship of disease die with us.'
UDO ERASMUS, oil guru and clearly a fellow *Star Wars* fan

The Fat Guru

The guru of fats is someone by the name of Udo Erasmus who knows all there is to know about oils and what they do for you. In his book *Fats that Heal, Fats that kill*, fats are examined in some considerable detail. He says that EFAs should be consumed in a ratio of about 3:1 to 5:1 for omega-6 and omega-3 respectively. Reality is that nowadays we consume a ratio of 10:1 to 20:1. We're cruising for a bruising in health terms as our bodies struggle to use the wrong ratio of fuel to power our system.

69. Water babies

Seventy per cent of the planet is covered in water, and when we're born 70% of us is water too. It's cool to be wet, so why aren't you drinking enough of the stuff?

There are life forms that can live without oxygen, but none last long without water. So why do we pay so little attention to it?

Do you know what constantly amazes me? People who go to a posh restaurant, spend a fortune on the meal and then think they're being clever by asking for a glass of tap water. Granted, some places seem to charge more for water than for wine, but is this a smart way of saving money? Most tap water tastes disgusting. I realise that this is my personal opinion, so do your own survey. The most unpalatable glass I ever had was in England's rural Oxfordshire. It was like drinking part of a swimming pool. Even London water tastes better despite, so legend has it, having passed through eight other bodies first. However, is changing to bottled water the solution?

Bottled bliss?

Bottled water isn't always the purest water. In fact, it might actually contain more bacteria than the tap version. Most tap water, however, will contain a cocktail of contaminates, most commonly lead, aluminium and pesticides. Also, the labelling on bottled water makes it far from clear in terms of what you're getting.

Here's an idea for you...

If you find 2-litre bottles of water too intimidating, try the small ¹/₂-litre bottles instead. If you're not used to drinking masses of water, increase your intake slowly by just one ¹/₂-litre bottle a day at first. If it feels like trying to rehydrate hard-baked earth after a drought, add some lecithin into your diet as this will help make your cells more permeable to water.

Generally, water can be called natural mineral water, spring water or table water. Mineral water is generally from a pure, underground source, where the rocks and earth have naturally filtered it. Spring water also comes from a filtered underground source, but does not have to be bottled on the spot. Table water is definitely the dodgiest dude of all as it's the least defined and could be a mix of water including tap water so unless you really like the design of the bottle you could just be wasting your money. Watch out for artificially carbonated table and spring water as this can rob the vital minerals in the body by binding to them. Also, look at the proportion of minerals – remember that salt (sodium) will dehydrate the body slightly.

Every now and then, there'll be a TV programme featuring blokes turning into women or male fish turning into female fish. Scare stories aside, the point is that we're being continuously exposed to xeno-oestrogens (foreign oestrogens) in our environment and these can have a feminising effect on our bodies. One source of these foreign oestrogens is through plastics – the worst thing you can do is leave your water heating up in the sun in a plastic bottle. So, blokes shouldn't simply blame their boobs on beer (although alcohol also has feminising effects, but that's another story!).

Water works

What are the best choices then? Well, one cheap solution is to get a filter jug, which removes the bug-busting chlorine element. The carbon filter also takes out some minerals, so another top tip is to change the filter at regular intervals to prevent manky old ones from leaching bacteria back into your drinking water. The jug should be kept in your fridge.

Another option would be to have a filter attached to your tap so that water is continuously filtered or you might want to consider the more expensive, but definitely superior, reverse osmosis systems which separate the water from the other elements that are contained in it. This is what NASA developed for its astronauts (you don't want to think about why they're filtering water!).

Defining idea...

'Water, water, everywhere, Nor any drop to drink.'
SAMUEL TAYLOR COLERIDGE, The Rime of the Ancient Mariner

70. Get your nutritional act together

You've made the brilliant decision to take your health and nutrition into your own hands. Now what?

Put some solid systems in place to ensure that your good intentions actually get done. There's nothing more stressful than hundreds of 'I shoulds' running loose in your brain, like 'I really should buy fresh stuff instead of ready meals.'

My first tip is to write all these Shoulds down somewhere so that you can quit worrying about them. Break your Shoulds into sections, such as Diet Shoulds, Exercise Shoulds and Stress-busting Shoulds. Give each Should a priority rating from one to three and tackle the high scorers first. So, if 'I should stop having nine cups of coffee a day' is more of a priority than 'I should stop eating that extra square of chocolate a day', score it as a three and make it something you'll tackle this month. Only aim to take on three Shoulds a month – too many and you won't do them. Get the high-scoring ones under your belt before you take on the lower scorers.

Choose a day to start the healthy new you, but don't make it a Monday as it's always too depressing to start something at the beginning of the week, especially as the weekend is so far away. Take just one month at a time and say to yourself you'll stick to it for that month. In this way, you won't feel that what you're going to do will be forever. If you think that something is forever, you tend to rebel against it and are less likely to stick to it.

Once you've got rid of all the old packets of food that are lurking around in your cupboards, it's time to go shopping for the basics. You'll need some of the following essential cupboard starters to get you going:

✿ Organic porridge oats and millet
✿ Rice milk – just for a change!
✿ Brown rice, quinoa (a wacky kind of grain) and wheat-free pasta
✿ Almonds, brazil nuts and cashew nuts
✿ Pumpkin seeds and sunflower seeds
✿ Oatcakes and rice cakes
✿ Tahini and houmous
✿ Extra virgin olive oil
✿ Tuna in olive oil
✿ Lentils and chickpeas
✿ Tinned tomatoes, sweetcorn, butterbeans and artichoke hearts
✿ Dried herbs, pepper, tamari (a kind of wheat-free soya sauce), olives, pesto, bragg liquid aminos (a bit like soya sauce)

Here's an idea for you...

First go through your cupboards and throw out everything with unrecognisable ingredients on the back of the pack. The general rule is get rid of any ingredient that comprises more than three syllables as this usually means that it's a chemical ingredient that might not be a healthy option. You don't have to actually throw food away, just give it to less healthy friends who don't care that the ingredients are in a kind of chemical Greek.

These are only suggestions, of course. You'll probably want to add other stuff and take away anything you don't like.

Also, load the fridge with plenty of fresh vegetables. Ones that keep are broccoli, cauliflower, red cabbage and cabbage. Frozen vegetables can be useful too, so get some peas and spinach in.

Defining idea...

'Be prepared.'
SCOUTING MOTTO, if you have all you need in place, then your changes will stick!

I once had a client who asked me why I'd put tuna in olive oil on the list. This is simply because I really hate tuna in brine, which I think tastes like dry old bits of wood. But hey, each to his own! If you like tuna in brine or are worried about the extra calories the oil will add, then brine it is. Likewise, anchovies. If there's one thing I detest it's anchovies, but if you like them then by all means add them to your cupboard basics.

71. Check it out!

Ever fantasised about making an appointment with your doctor and saying, 'Check everything out, please'?

Getting a health all-clear is a great way to motivate you to maintain a healthier lifestyle in the future.

Regular health checks are essential if you want to live a long and healthy life because you've got a much better chance of curing many serious diseases – including cancer – if you catch them early. Unfortunately, doctors have neither the time nor the resources to run random tests for every patient, which leaves you with two options. You could opt for one of the many screening packages on offer from private health companies (which can be costly). Alternatively, there are many self-checks you can easily do at home which can help you assess whether you do really need to see your doctor for further investigation.

The first check is to find out if you're overweight or obese. Obesity is linked with a host of diseases such as cancer, diabetes and heart disease. To check if you're in the healthy weight range, calculate your body mass index (you'll probably need a calculator). First, measure your height in metres. Multiply this figure by itself (e.g. 1.5 m × 1.5 m). This gives your height squared. Now measure your weight in kilograms. Divide your weight by your height squared. This gives you your body mass index. A healthy figure is 20–25. A BMI of 25–30 is overweight; 30–40 is obese BMI, and above 40 is very obese. (If you don't want to do the maths, there's a BMI calculator on www.cyberdiet.com.)

Here's an idea for you...

If you don't know what your cholesterol level is, make an appointment with your doctor to get tested this week. Alternatively buy a cholesterol self-test from pharmacies which involves taking a small sample of blood from your finger tip and placing it on a test strip. Results are then compared to a colour chart in three minutes.

If you are overweight, it's worth considering a diabetes test. The average person lives with diabetes for sixteen years before diagnosis – by which time the disease may have caused heart and kidney damage. You're more at risk if you have a family member with the disease, you're over fifty or overweight. You can buy a self-test for diabetes cheaply at most pharmacies, but be sure to follow it up with a medical appointment if it's positive.

Next, listen to your heartbeat. Heart disease is a massive killer, but you don't need to book in for an ECG (electrocardiogram) to check out your heart – simply observe what it's like after physical exertion such as climbing stairs. See your doctor if your heartbeat is irregular, or takes a long time to come back to normal.

If you've no idea what your blood pressure is, now's the time to find out. Hypertension, or high blood pressure, is the biggest cause of stroke or heart disease so it could be worth buying a digital blood pressure meter from pharmacies.

Women over fifty are routinely invited for a mammogram every three years. But more than 90% of breast cancers are found by women themselves. The key is to be aware of what's normal for your breasts – don't get obsessive about checking them, but feel for any lumps once a month or so when you're in the bath or shower. And make sure you report anything unusual, such as nipple discharge or puckering of the skin of the breast, to your doctor.

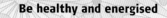

Don't skip your smear test. A smear test checks for cell changes on the cervix which could, if left untreated, lead to cervical cancer. Women aged between 20 and 64 should have a smear test every three to five years, although you may be tested more regularly if you have shown any signs of abnormal cells in the past. Men, meanwhile, should see their GP for a prostate test if they suddenly start peeing more frequently.

Checking your health doesn't have to be just another chore – it can even be fun if you rope in a partner. How about an all-over massage, with some mole checking thrown in? Look out for moles which have changed shape or colour, seem bigger, bleed or are itchy. Some men are also more than happy to take over checking their partner's breasts and also prefer their partners to check their testicles for unusual lumps that may be testicular cancer. Any excuse, eh?

Defining idea…

'Be careful about reading health books. You may die of a misprint.'

Mark Twain

72. Detox and thrive

Detoxing: who needs it?

Answer: every single one of us. We need detoxing so badly that our bodies are actually hard at it 24/7, 365 days a year, without a break.

You know you need a spot of extra detoxing if you're tired, if you have big bags under your eyes, if you feel headachey, if you're constipated, if your periods are a real pain, if your stools are smelly and your breath not-so-fresh, if your eye-whites aren't white and your tongue is heavily coated.

Just what does all this detoxing remove? It's the normal wastes created in-house by day-to-day living, plus the toxic polluting chemicals we take in with our food, our drink and even the air we breathe or fill our homes with in cleaning, cosmetic and toiletry products.

Start by cutting down on the toxic load: alcohol, nicotine, coffee, fizzy drinks, too much sweet, fatty, additive-loaded food and household or cosmetic chemicals. Drink six to eight glasses of water – preferably filtered – every day. And discover a team of herbs that have been used for centuries for cleansing and detox. In medieval times, country people would make up 'spring drinks' from herbs sprouting young, fresh and green in the hedgerows – dandelion, nettles and that sticky, clinging stuff cleavers. After a winter diet of stodge and salted or dried foods, these spring drinks supplied a badly needed boost of tonic and cleansing phytochemicals. 'A course of dandelion treatment in the spring,' wrote the modern French herb enthusiast Jean

Palaiseul, 'will tone up your whole body, cleansing it of the waste matter deposited by the heavy clogging food of winter.'

Much of your body's garbage ends up in your urine, filtered by your kidneys. Nettles stimulate both kidney and bladder function, and they're rich in cleansing, nourishing minerals too. Both dandelion and nettle come high on any herbalist's list of cleansing, detoxing herbs today.

Cleavers boosts the efficiency of your lymphatic system, that efficient drainage network that helps remove toxins from the body, and it's good news for the skin too. Herbalists include it in prescriptions for acne, eczema and psoriasis, as well as arthritis and gout.

Here's an idea for you...

The French obsess about the health of their livers, and if you eat in any French bistro in the springtime, you will find their favourite dandelion salad on the menu: salade de pissenlit. Snippets of bacon are fried until crisp, a little vinegar is swished around the pan, and then its contents are poured over a dish of the sharp-tasting fresh young leaves. A very enjoyable way to do your liver a bit of good.

Croatian herbalist Dragana Vilinac formulates herbal blends and tinctures for one of the UK's most popular herbal suppliers. And when I asked her to suggest an effective mix of detox herbs, I was not surprised to find both dandelion and nettle in it, as well as burdock – 'an esteemed blood cleanser and digestive stimulant,' she explains. Here's her formula: burdock root, 5g; dandelion root, 5g; nettle root, 5g. Put them in a pan with 600ml of water, bring to the boil, cover the pan and simmer very gently for fifteen to twenty minutes. Take it off the heat, leave to steep for another fifteen minutes, then strain and drink a small mugful three times daily. This trio of roots, she explains, will enhance the elimination of wastes, help offload toxic wastes and calm any inflammation. Stock up with the ingredients from a herbal supplier, and give yourself a two-week course, cutting down on caffeine, alcohol and junk food at the same time, and drinking plenty of water.

Dragana also suggests another version, for occasional use, which is quicker and easier to prepare. Leaves are milder medicine than roots, so: dandelion leaf, 5g; nettle leaf, 5g; cleavers, 5g. 'This will help protect the body from the accumulation of excess fluid around the waist, under the skin, in the lungs in the form of phlegm, in the bladder,' she says. To brew it, mix the herbs, put 2 teaspoons in a mug of boiling water, steep for ten minutes, strain and drink.

Nettles, cleavers and dandelion can all be gathered wild in the spring but make sure they haven't been sprayed, either with pesticides or by a passing dog. Pick only the youngest and freshest ones, and eat them lightly steamed.

Defining idea...

'Health is not a "gift" but something each person is responsible for through his or her own daily effort.'
HIDEO NAKAYAMA, Japanese dermatologist

In German folk medicine, the seeds of the impressive milk thistle were used for jaundice and other liver complaints. Modern researchers have found that it can actually protect and regenerate liver cells, good news for overworked, hungover livers. Take a ten-day course of it. Women on the contraceptive pill, or those who are pregnant or breastfeeding, should avoid it, though.

73. Time of the month

Periods don't have to be a pain.

Enlist some herbal allies to help end those monthly miseries.

In a normal healthy woman, eating a good diet, periods should be no big deal. But if the bleed is excessive or prolonged, if it happens in between periods or if there's unusual pain in the pelvic area then or after sex, get yourself checked out by your doctor. If your GP finds nothing you should worry about, try some appropriate herbal help.

If there's one herb that really is specially for women, it has to be *Vitex agnus castus* or chasteberry, usually known just as vitex. Men have been warned off it for centuries by its reputation for suppressing their sexual urges, leaving women free to exploit its extraordinary hormone-regulating powers. Hormones out of sync are responsible for a lot of the grief in periods, and legions of modern women have learned to be thankful for vitex.

Two large surveys carried out in Germany studied its effect on 1542 women suffering from PMS over twenty-three weeks. In 90% of cases symptoms such as headache, sore breasts, mood swings, anxiety and restlessness were completely relieved. Improvement usually began within three to four weeks of starting treatment. (Don't take it, though, if you're on the contraceptive pill, HRT or if you're taking prescription drugs.)

When cramps are so bad that you can hardly drag yourself through the day, try something soothing. US herbalist Rosemary Gladstar suggests a hot ginger poultice. 'Make a pot of strong ginger tea by grating fresh ginger and adding it to cold water. Bring it to a low boil and simmer (with the lid tightly on) for ten to fifteen minutes. Allow it to cool just slightly. Dip a clean cotton cloth in the tea and wring out any excess liquid. Put a dry towel over the pelvic area and then place the hot poultice over it. Cover it with a thick towel, leave it on till it begins to cool, and repeat till the pain is eased.' Drink a cup of warm ginger tea sweetened with a little honey; at the same time add rosemary. That'll help ease the cramps, too.

In traditional Chinese medicine, dong quai or Chinese angelica is prescribed for almost every female complaint in the book, from menstrual cramps, irregularity and weakness through to menopausal problems. It's a warming, comforting herb, specially useful when you're feeling low and fragile. It's often combined with cramp bark – the name is self-explanatory. US herbalist Michael Tierra suggests combining equal parts of angelica, cramp bark and chamomile, plus a little grated fresh ginger root, for a calming and warming tonic for such times. Put 25g of this mix into a pan with 600ml cold water; bring it to the boil and simmer for fifteen minutes, then strain and drink hot. Dong quai should be discontinued a week before your period starts, as it may stimulate bleeding. And don't use if you are on blood-thinning drugs.

Contraceptive pills, incidentally, deplete many essential nutrients in women taking them – including zinc, magnesium, vitamins C and E and vitamin B6. Try to make up these deficiencies in your diet: eat more nuts, seeds, wholegrains, green vegetables and take a good vitamin and mineral supplement as extra insurance. If you feel your diet is inadequate, take one of the special supplements aimed at women.

The EFAs – essential fatty acids – are especially important. They are found in oily fish, and one EFA in particular, gamma-linolenic acid, or GLA, is supplied by only three to four plants, among them the lovely evening primrose, whose seeds are rich in the stuff. This EFA helps regulate hormone balance in the body, and controls the production of certain compounds called prostaglandins which may be responsible for a whole slew of PMS symptoms including mood swings, depression and – in particular – the extreme breast tenderness that some women experience. So striking is the relief it can give for this symptom that doctors in the UK are allowed to prescribe it to sufferers. Look for a good brand (the market is awash with cheap ones) and take 500mg once or twice a day.

Finally, plants that can influence human hormonal states are powerful medicine. If possible consult a herbal practitioner who can fine-tune a herbal prescription to your specific case.

Defining idea...

'...the body normally runs its affairs very well indeed: a good medicine might therefore be one that gently nudges it back on track when it becomes disrupted.'
SIMON MILLS, author of *Woman Medicine: Vitex agnus-castus.*

74. Winter woes

Few of us get through winter without a single cold.

But with a little herbal help you can arm yourself against infection, stop a starting cold in its tracks or, at the very least, limit the damage.

There's usually a moment when a shivery, chilly sensation warns you that a cold is on its way in. That first shiver is a sign that the viruses are already multiplying, and the battle against a cold is won or lost at this stage.

Top of any herbalist's list of great anti-cold herbs is garlic, famous in folk medicine across the planet for its protective and immune-boosting powers. It's also been more closely scrutinised by scientists than any other medicinal plant. Take the fresh cloves in heroic quantities and that cold won't stand a chance. Some friends of mine chop up and eat two or three fat fresh cloves in a thickly-buttered sandwich at the first shiver of a cold or flu – and they haven't had a cold since they started doing this some six years ago. However, lots of garlic can be an irritant to a sensitive gut, so experiment with smaller quantities first.

Dozens of studies have demonstrated the power of echinacea to prevent, or at least diminish, the force of an oncoming cold. Once again you need to take it at the very first sign of symptoms – and in high doses. The test of a good strong echinacea is that it makes your tongue tingle a bit. If you're especially prone to colds and other bugs making the rounds in winter, consider taking echinacea in a lower dose throughout the season; it's not true, though widely believed, that you need to take regular breaks while doing so. The company founded by Swiss naturopath Dr Alfred Vogel, who pioneered the use of echinacea in Europe, makes a tincture from the fresh plants organically grown in its own gardens, as well as a chewable tablet form, handy for the desk drawer or for travel.

Elderflower is another tried and tested country remedy for colds, especially when combined with peppermint. Put a teaspoon – or a tea bag – of each in a mug, fill with hot water, strain and drink hot at an early bedtime. You'll probably sweat the cold out overnight and have a sound, sweet sleep.

Here's an idea for you...

Onions, close cousins of garlic, share many of its wonderful healing powers. You could exploit both in this recipe sent to my husband by a friend in Angola: he swears it will see off both cold and flu bugs in short order, especially if you take it at the first suspicion of either. Peel and chop up an onion and a fat clove of garlic. Put them in a pan with the juice of a lemon, a dessertspoonful of honey and a mugful of water. Bring to the boil and simmer very slowly, covered, for forty to fifty minutes. Drink it red hot and, if you're feeling really chilled, add a spot of dried chilli powder.

For true kitchen medicine, here's a great spice-rack remedy from herbalist Dee Atkinson. Take a teaspoon each of dried sage, rosemary and thyme, put them into a teapot and add a pint of boiling water. Infuse for ten minutes, then strain and drink hot throughout the day. Another great spicy warmer-upper is ginger, which is also wonderfully stimulating: it's revered throughout the East for its many healing powers. Hot ginger tea could be your first line of defence against a threatened cold. To make it, grate a chunk of peeled, fresh ginger root into a mug, add a pinch of cardamon, fill with boiling water and infuse, covered, for ten minutes. Alternatively, add a pinch of powdered ginger to hot lemon and honey.

Defining idea...

'A family is a unit composed not only of children, but of men, women, an occasional animal, and the common cold.'
OGDEN NASH

75. Waterworks

If you keep getting bouts of cystitis, the bugs that are responsible are probably becoming resistant to antibiotics.

Use herbs to clear up the infection, soothe the inflammation and help guard against further attacks.

Go to the doctor if you're running a fever, experiencing serious pain in your bladder or lower back, or noticing blood in your urine. They could indicate serious kidney problems.

Meanwhile, here are tried and trusted herbal remedies for urinary tract infections (UTI) – and one new star. That's cranberry, of course, the shiny red berries most of us only see as a sauce for festive roast turkey. But cranberry was a North American folk remedy for bladder infections long before scientific researchers took a close look at it. Now we know that cranberries contain a compound called arbutin. Once it enters the urine, arbutin splits into other compounds, one of which, hydroquinone, has a direct antiseptic action on the kidneys, the urinary tract and the bladder. Hydroquinone also plays a neat little trick on those E.coli bugs: it stops them anchoring to the wall of the urinary tract and, instead, they are washed away with the urine. In clinical trials, even drinking a commercial, highly sweetened cranberry juice helped clear infections. You can also buy unsweetened – very tart and rather pricey – cranberry juice, or tablets containing concentrated cranberry

Here's an idea for you...

Why keep cranberries for Christmas? They're a superfood in their own right: no other fruit is higher in wonder-working antioxidants than the cranberry. While they're in season, stew them with apples, add them to frozen *frutti di bosco* mixes for great winter puddings or throw a small handful in the juicer along with half a dozen carrots and chunks of peeled raw beetroot for a wonderful tart pink pick-me-up. You'll be protecting yourself from urinary tract infections at the same time. And while they're in season and cheap at your greengrocer, why not toss two or three packs into your freezer?

extract. You can also add dried cranberries to a dried fruit compote. There have been some reports in the press about cranberry causing problems, but there's lots of really good research backing up its benefits for UTIs, so give it a try.

Bearberry, a close plant relation of cranberries, is one of the first remedies a herbalist would think of in treating this problem, and an ingredient in almost every herbal remedy for cystitis on the market. Guess what? It's arbutin at work again, plus other plant chemicals that will work to soothe, tone and strengthen your urinary tract, as well as seeing off those *E.coli* bugs.

Buchu is yet another herbal standby; its leaves contain bacteria-killing oils which will help clean up your urinary tract. It's especially useful when urinating causes a painful burning sensation, and marshmallow can be helpful here too, soothing and calming inflammation. Make up a herbal mix of buchu and marshmallow leaves and use it for a tea to be drunk three times a day while the infection persists. To make the tea, put a good teaspoon of the herbs in a mug, fill it with boiling water and infuse, covered, for ten minutes. Then strain and drink hot.

Infection weakens your urinary tract, which makes it much more vulnerable to further assaults. If this is the case, take a couple of doses of buchu from time to time as prevention, and give yourself a long course of a good herbal tonic. My favourite is a Swiss-made mix of healing herbs called Bio-Strath. Lemon balm, chamomile, elder, lavender, sage and thyme are among the herbs in this useful mix. In a number of clinical trials, it has proved its ability to boost resistance, raise energy levels and lift the spirits. It's prepared as a pleasant-tasting liquid: a couple of good glugs a day over four to six weeks will raise your resistance and improve your general health.

Defining idea...

'**Bladder infections are common in women: 10–20% of all women have urinary tract discomfort at least once a year, 37.5% of all women with no history of UTI will have one within ten years; 2.4% of healthy women have elevated bacteria in urine – unrecognised UTI.'**
JOSEPH PIZZORNO, MICHAEL MURRAY and HERB JOINER-BEY, in *The Clinician's Handbook of Natural Medicine*

76. How to eat

Yes, yes. You've heard it all before. You are what you eat. But the truth is, very few of the people who complain of being tired are eating enough good-quality fuel to stay healthy, much less energetic.

There are usually reasons (let's be kind and not say excuses). We know what we should eat but ... life is so crazy, we've been ill, we've no time ...

Some energy-boosting ideas will help even if you continue ignoring the basics, but if you don't eat well past the age of twenty-five it's near impossible to achieve everything expected of you.

On the other hand, follow the basic rules below and you will almost certainly start to feel better. All foods are equal in one way. They are broken down for fuel, but your body can use some of that fuel more easily than others. The sources the body finds it easiest to access are: fruit, vegetables, wholegrain bread, pasta and rice, because these are easy to convert into glucose. Glucose combines with oxygen in the cells to become ATP (adenosine triphosphate), which is stored and used as needed. If this carries on normally all is well and we have enough energy; when it goes wrong, we are lacking in energy.

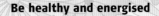

Three ways the energy supply can be disrupted

- ❀ Energy production is powered by vitamins – in particular the B vitamins and coenzyme Q10. B vitamins are relatively easy to get in the diet, but our ability to take up coenzyme Q10 diminishes as we get older. These nutrients are also destroyed by alcohol or smoking.
- ❀ Without oxygen, the glucose can't be used by the cells. Poor respiration, poor circulation and damaged blood cells (anaemia) all affect our energy levels.
- ❀ Some carbohydrates are *too* effective at creating energy. Refined carbs such as pasta, white bread and doughnuts are converted so quickly that if the body's given a huge dose of them – and let's face it, that's how it often gets these foods – it gets a bit overexcited, panics, and stores the sugar – and these stores are what make us fat. Our bodies are really good at this because those whose ancestors weren't good at it didn't tend to make it through famine.

So how do you use this information?

Follow these rules. They are simple, but don't underestimate how difficult it is to change habits, especially when it comes to food. Take it one step at a time.

The best piece of advice on changing eating habits is one that numerous nutritionists have given me – don't think of *cutting out*; instead focus on *adding in*.

Here's an idea for you...

Keep a food diary to see how, what and when you eat ... and, most importantly, why. This pinpoints situations when you find it hard to stick to the 'rules' and other habits that might be sabotaging your energy levels.

A six-week plan to transform your energy levels

Each week concentrate on adding in one habit. You can do them all at once but, if you find eating regularly and well difficult, take it one week at a time.

1   Eat breakfast. Every day. No excuses.
2   Eat lunch. Every day. No excuses.
3   Start snacking. Never go longer than three hours without eating. Regular healthy snacks mean you don't overeat at meal times. Since eating huge amounts at mealtimes can deplete your energy – about 10% of your daily energy intake goes on digesting what you eat, and a big meal means you're doing it all at once – snacking is less stressful for your body. It also keeps your blood-sugar levels stable so you have a constant flow of energy throughout the day.
4   Add in energy-giving carbs. Eat a fist-sized portion of wholegrain carbohydrate at every meal because it supplies B vitamins and doesn't get broken down too fast; for instance, wholegrain pasta, brown rice, oats or wholemeal bread (around two slices); Wholegrain contains fibre and fibre slows down release of the sugars in carbohydrates into the bloodstream. This means a slow release of energy throughout the day.
5   Add in energy-giving protein. Eat a deck-of-cards-sized portion of protein at lunch – and if you really want to see a difference in your energy levels, have some at breakfast too. That means meat, fish, eggs (×2), cottage cheese, cheese, tofu.
6   Drink enough fluid – about one to two litres a day – not including alcohol or strongly caffeinated drinks.

77. Why you need to move

Do you feel tired a great deal of the time? Do you need a couple of cups of coffee to start functioning? Is the only time you feel energised when you're worried, nervy and tense?

That's not normal. What is normal for your body is to move. Regular exercise gives you natural vim without having to resort to caffeine and adrenaline to get anything done.

Imagine an end to swinging between jitteriness and lethargy. Understanding how your body makes energy will help you understand why the need for movement is just that – a need, a necessity. Without it, you can't be energetic.

When you run for a bus, your heart beats faster and more blood rushes round your body. You need more oxygen, so your lungs start to work faster. The essential transfer of oxygen into your cells, and carbon dioxide from your cells, happens at a faster rate. Inside your cells, the mitochondria (energy factories) are producing ATP, your body's fuel (if your body is a car, ATP's the petrol). It's produced from glucose in the cells. This is anaerobic exercise. You can't work anaerobically for too long, because there is a limited amount of glucose, but the more you exercise anaerobically, the better your body gets at it (and the more likely you are to catch the bus). When we run out of glucose in the cells, our body starts exercising aerobically – producing ATP from stores of glycogen and glucose held in reserve in the fat cells of the body. And again, the more ATP you produce, the better your

Apply the 'talk test'. The intensity that you're aiming for with cardiovascular exercise is such that you'd be able to hold a conversation with a friend while you exercised – but it wouldn't be easy. Make it your initial goal to exercise at this level for about ten minutes each session. When you get to the level where you could only blurt out one-word answers to a question, or you might collapse – you've gone too far.

body gets at doing it. By exercising you train your body to be more efficient at producing energy when you need it.

What happens without that boost of oxygen to the cells? Without the stimulus to produce more ATP, our bodies become sluggish and lethargic. If we're not getting the boost from oxygen, we start relying on other things that raise our heart rate in order to get an energy surge to carry us through the day– notably stimulants like caffeine and nicotine.

Exercise's benefits to your body are legion, but when it comes to energy, it means you will have a constant flow of energy to achieve everything you need to achieve easily and calmly. Your dependence on artificial stimulants will diminish. Your concentration will also be more focused. According to a study in the journal *Medicine and Science in Sports and Exercise*, the physically fit scored highest on memory and intelligence tests and were more creative.

But you know all this. What you may need is an attitude turnaround because the problem, research shows, is that we don't perceive exercise as a life-enhancer, but as yet another energy-sapper, draining yet more of our precious time. Exercise is one of the first things to go when we feel under pressure. In fact, it should be one of our priorities. When we're stressed, we produce adrenaline. Exercise burns it off, allowing us to calm down and deal with the pressure.

A three-step plan to get you moving

1   Every day – let your body out to play

Movement is play for your body. Every day give it a little of what it needs to be happy. It doesn't matter if walking up the stairs is as much as you can manage; walk up the stairs today. And tomorrow aim to walk up the stairs twice. Or go for a few stretches while you're watching TV. Or race your kids to the end of the street. Start small and build up the expectation that you will move every day – just as you would brush your teeth.

2   Every second day – feel your heart beating

Exercise that doesn't set your heart beating fast is still good for you but to start the energy-boosting process, you want to feel your heart beat, which means your lungs expand. This is cardiovascular exercise – and it includes walking, running, cycling, swimming and dancing. It doesn't include most forms of yoga, weight lifting or Pilates. If you are not used to exercise or have been run down, walking briskly for just five minutes a day is enough to aim for at first.

3   Keep going for six weeks

For most of us, with anything new, we will give up within three weeks. But if we can keep going for six weeks, we have the makings of a habit – something that, even if we slip for a while, we will return to because we like how it makes us feel. That's easier with a written plan of when and what you'll do. I urge you to keep it simple – start with just following steps 1 and 2 here for six weeks.

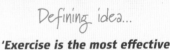

Defining idea...

'Exercise is the most effective anti-ageing pill ever discovered.'
National Institute of Health, USA

78. How to get enough sleep

The answer's simple – make like a great big baby.

Welcome to the nanny state. This is where we come over all strict. But it's for your own good, you know …

Lack of sleep is a growing problem, and like all health writers I've written thousands of words on the subject of getting a good night's sleep. I've interviewed most of the country's top sleep specialists. And what did I learn? That possibly treating yourself like a baby is the best thing you can do. Babies have to learn to go to sleep themselves. Most of us (but not all of us) learn this – but some of us (many of us) forget.

How much sleep is enough? The standard advice is that there is no 'right' or 'wrong'– it's what's right for you. So when people like Madonna say they can get by on four hours sleep, it's possible, but not desirable.

For the great majority of us who have normal working hours, aiming to get to bed by midnight and sleeping for at least six to seven hours is the bare minimum we need simply to restore our bodies after a hard day. Most of us would do better getting to bed significantly earlier and aiming for eight solid hours. Latest research is nudging towards nine hours a night as optimum. So if you're in the Madonna camp, thinking that you're doing pretty well on four or five, it's worth re-examining.

Here are four lessons we can learn from babies:

Babies need a lot of sleep

And so do most grown-ups, whether they like it or not.

Are you shaking your head and thinking you'd love to sleep more, if only you didn't keep waking in the middle of the night? Most people I know who can't sleep have tried everything that their pharmacist and doctor can suggest. Or they are self-medicating with alcohol. But that's doing nothing to deal with the original problem. Are you working long hours (and that includes housework)? Under huge mental strain? For the record, stress is the number one reason according to The American Psychological Association for short-term sleep problems such as frequent middle-of the-night waking and insomnia. If you know that something is keeping you awake at night, your only solution is to resolve the stress in some way.

Babies are good at recognising what's keeping them awake and getting it dealt with so that they can get back to sleep

Most grown ups aren't. But without resolving stress, and cutting the strain they're under, they'll never get enough sleep.

Then there are stimulants. Research shows that caffeine drunk before midday can still affect your sleep that evening. All of us, ideally, should be having our last cup by noon, and those who are sensitive should cut it out altogether or limit themselves to one cup of caffeine at breakfast. Alcohol knocks you out and then causes you to wake up in the early hours of the morning. Any sort of screen can knock you off your sleep pattern. I know one woman who was chronically sleep deprived for two years before she made the connection between checking her emails just before she went to bed and waking up worrying about work at 3 a.m.

Babies need a restful routine, like a warm bath and a bedtime story before bed

And grown-ups like a warm bath and a bedtime story before bed too. Grown-ups who are drinking, partying, emailing, watching TV, chatting with their mates on the phone or in other ways keeping their brains active could well get too stimulated to sleep. What they need is a relaxing ten minutes in the tub and a nice, quiet read.

Babies sleep best in a dark room

So do grown-ups. We evolved as a species to sleep in almost total darkness. Even a small amount of brightness can be strong enough to enter our retina even when our eyes are closed. This sends a signal to the brain that upsets the internal clock. Light in the hallway, shouldn't enter your room, turn the digital alarm clock to the wall, don't fall asleep with the TV on. Blackout curtains are recommended if your streetlights are bright.

Defining idea...

'There are two types of people in this world: good and bad. The good sleep better, but the bad seem to enjoy the waking hours much more.'
WOODY ALLEN

79. How to start exercising when you really don't want to

Exercise is the one thing that will boost your energy levels faster than anything else. But what if you just can't get started?

Here is how to get started and stay started.

Research shows that when life gets busy, exercise is one of the first things to get bumped off the schedule. But before you berate yourself for your lack of sticking power, it's good to remember that, even for professionally fit people like personal trainers, exercise is cyclical. There will be times when it gets pushed to the sidelines. However, for those who have learned how much exercise helps them cope with a busy life, the gaps before they start exercising again are likely to be shorter than for your average Joe. If you've never exercised at all, this idea aims to get you to a stage where you too know that the benefits are so great, it isn't worth going without it for too long.

This idea is equally suitable for those who have never exercised regularly, and those who used to, but have lapsed. If it's too easy for you, ratchet up a gear, or jump some steps – but beware. Research has shown that there are two reasons that exercise programmes fail:

❀ we don't see the results we want (that's dealt with below); or

❀ we set our expectations too high.

It's far better to do a little and stick to it until you have the exercise habit than go nuts, join a gym, write an ambitious exercise programme and then give up completely after a couple of weeks of failure to keep to it.

Decide on your goal

If you've never exercised before, or haven't for a long time, please start with a modest goal. If it's ten minutes of activity a day – that's brilliant, as long as you are confident you will do it. Aim to visit your local pool once a week, then three times a week. Aim to swim once a week, and walk round the park once a week. Aim to do a yoga class on a Saturday morning.

You gotta have a plan

You need to make a schedule where every week you are aiming to do a little more, a little more frequently until you are exercising for around three to four hours a week – enough to get you out of breath for most of the time. That could take a year, but don't think about that now. Stick your monthly schedule on the fridge. At first your goal should be just to stick to your weekly plan. Once you've got the hang of it, you can make your goal bigger, such as: run round the park, undertake your local fun run, cycle to the next town then cycle back.

If you are very exhausted, very unfit, have been ill or are very overweight, all you might be able to manage is walking up the stairs. Fine. Make that your goal: to walk up stairs three times a week, then five times a week, and so on from there. Aim for cardiovascular exercise to begin with, that gets your heart beating, because that's the type that will give you energy fastest.

When I've not exercised for a while, here is my programme.

- ❀ *Week 1.* Walk slowly for five minutes, walk briskly for five minutes, walk slowly for five minutes. Aim to do that for three days a week.
- ❀ *Week 2.* Aim to do the same five times a week.
- ❀ *Week 3.* Walk slowly for ten minutes, walk briskly for ten minutes, walk slowly for ten minutes. Aim for four times a week.
- ❀ *Week 4.* Walk slowly for five minutes, walk briskly for twenty minutes, walk slowly for five minutes. Aim for five times a week.

Then I start running for blocks of time. Eventually, I'm running for most of the time and I'm doing it every second day.

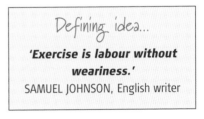

Defining idea...

'Exercise is labour without weariness.'
SAMUEL JOHNSON, English writer

80. NAFH or naff?

That's Non Allergic Food Hypersensitivity to you and me – the new name for food intolerance. But many people swear that their once rock-bottom energy levels picked up after they sorted out a food intolerance.

But at the same time a whole lot of rubbish is talked about food intolerance, too. So how do you work out if avoiding a certain food might be the answer to your lethargy and irritability?

For a while, it seemed everyone I know was looking exhausted, fiddling with a lettuce leaf instead of eating dinner, and eschewing tomatoes because of their acidity. It is almost standard advice from alternative therapists to blame NAFH for the epidemic of ill-health and tiredness sweeping the country. Since one in four of us will at some time consult some form of alternative therapist, an awful lot of us are going to get the idea that we've got intolerances to certain foods.

But is it all a load of rubbish? Just another way of being 'funny' about food?

Conventional medicine does not have much truck with the notion. Your GP understands food allergy and that's a very different beast. With food allergy, you eat a food that you're allergic too – shellfish, peanuts, strawberries – and within minutes, you get very ill indeed. In fact, in the worst cases, if you're not pumped full of drugs, you could die. On the other hand, food intolerance is nothing like as dramatic. It's characterised by extreme tiredness. Symptoms might include diarrhoea and other chronic gut problems, migraines, headaches, rashes and bloating. The highest figure for NAFH is 45%; sceptical doctors say that figure is more likely about 5%. The trouble is, we don't know the exact mechanisms. The immune system is almost certainly involved but we don't have any reliable tests or cure.

Another sticking point for those sceptical of intolerances is that they are often to the most natural, pure foods. But this shouldn't be such a surprise. The truth is that nature isn't here for our benefit – it's here for its own. Cow's milk is meant to feed little cows. Plants don't want to be eaten which is why most taste vile and some are poisonous. Even those that are desirable to eat – fruits – simply use us as 'carriers' of their seeds but, just so we don't get in the way of their propagation, they have evolved to pass through our system very quickly (most fruits are mild laxatives).

So, intolerances are likely to be towards simple foods; they are also more likely to be towards foods we eat a lot. We are omnivores and can eat more or less anything. That's because back when we were hunter-gatherers, the picky eaters didn't tend to make it through the winter. Our species developed on a diet that was varied not to

> *Here's an idea for you...*
>
> **Even if you don't have an intolerance, eating a more varied diet will boost your energy levels as it gives you a wider variety of nutrition. Substitute soya milk for dairy at one meal and rye bread, oats, porridge or brown rice for your usual pasta or bread. If you feel more energetic after such a meal, consider substituting more often.**

say disgusting. According to Allergy UK, the cause of intolerances is likely to be that we rely too much on one kind of food. Here in the UK we eat more wheat and milk, and that's what we're more intolerant to; in the States they are much more allergic to corn than here; in the East there have been cases of intolerance to rice.

Defining idea...

'**Part of the secret of success in life is to eat what you like and let the food fight it out inside.**'

MARK TWAIN

The easiest answer? Boost your immunity

A decreased immunity in the gut affects the microflora of the gut. Food is less well absorbed, and the lining of the gut can become irritated. This becomes dysbiosis. This leads to food allergies and food intolerances. According to one commentator, dysbiosis is found in up to 85% of food intolerances.

Taking probiotics can boost the good bacteria in your gut and boost your immune system. (The Common Cold Centre recommends it as a way of guarding against colds.) Eat live natural yogurt or take a probiotic supplement such as acidophilus. You need to take a good quality product, however.

81. Dump the Marlboro man

Why cutting out smoking is the single most important thing you can do for longer life.

You may well be tempted to skip this chapter if you're a smoker. Who needs another lecture? You need positive encouragement to help you give up – and here it is.

You know very well that smoking causes cancer and heart disease. It's written on every packet. And anyway, you're going to give up soon. Just as soon as you're over this stressful period at work...

You're probably well aware that if you're a smoker, you can expect to die seven years earlier than your non-smoking friends. The 4000 chemicals in tobacco smoke accelerate the furring-up of the arteries associated with lung cancer; with every inhalation you take in massive amounts of free radicals, which attack the DNA of your cells. One day, you may not have enough antioxidants to stave off the damage and cancer could take hold somewhere in your body. You know all this – most smokers actually overestimate the health risks, according to one study.

The saddest thing about this highly addictive and dangerous habit is that many smokers don't enjoy it most of the time. OK, that first cigarette in the morning, or after a meal, can taste pretty good, but after that it's never quite the same. So you light another, hoping that the next one will be better. Then the next one.

Here's an idea for you...

Put some forward planning into the next time you give up. Choose a date a few weeks in the future and put it in your diary. (Avoid 1 January whatever you do!) If you smoke at work, choose a Saturday or Sunday. If you work in a non-smoking office, you might find it easier to pick a work day. Try to anticipate tricky situations and have a plan of action in advance. Drinks after work for a colleague's birthday? Tell them you can only stay for an hour – then leave before the craving (and the alcohol) takes hold. And write a list of positive benefits of not smoking (for example, I'll find exercise much easier, I won't have to spend hours standing outside the office and people's houses in the cold and rain, I can stop feeling anxious about cancer) and read it whenever you feel your motivation wane.

It's time for some positive pep talk and a pat on the back. Yes, you read that right. Smokers are essentially nice people with a nasty habit. It's time to stop haranguing you and treating you like public enemy number one. So here is some good news for smokers!

❧ Have you tried to quit before and failed? Congratulations! You're one step closer to giving up for good. The average smoker quits ten times before finally managing it long term. So the more times you quit, the more likely you are to quit for good. Never give up giving up!

❧ People manage to quit *all the time*. A lot of people are non-smokers. You could be one of them.

❧ You've got a lot to look forward to. Within weeks of giving up, you'll have an improved sense of smell and taste. Now, imagine what a kick you're going to get from standing by the seashore and taking a great big breath when you've kicked the habit, and going to your favourite restaurant and really tasting how fantastic the food is...

❀ The French and the Japanese smoke more than the British and Americans do, yet suffer from less heart disease and less lung cancer. This suggests that a diet high in antioxidants can help stave off the damages of smoking. Trouble is, studies have shown that smokers on average eat less fruit and vegetables than non-smokers. Maybe eating a healthy diet when you're a smoker seems like rearranging the deckchairs on the Titanic, but eating a healthy diet is more important than ever. Aim for up to ten portions of fresh fruit and vegetables a day to get your maximum antioxidant protection and give your body the best chance of staving off the ageing effects of your habit.

❀ There are hundreds of people out there willing to help you give up. Don't go it alone. Ask your pharmacist about nicotine patches or gum. Try hypnotherapy and acupuncture. Ask your doctor to refer you to a smoking cessation clinic. It's a serious addiction so take a serious approach to giving up.

Defining idea...

'It is not the strongest of the species that survive, nor the most intelligent, but the ones most responsive to change.'
Charles Darwin

82. Think before you drink

Let's not get too hysterical about alcohol. But let's think about it.

No one's saying 'give it up'. But if your energy levels aren't high, it's one of the obvious energy drainers.

Alcohol (any old alcohol, not just wine) does your heart good. Probably not quite as much as is claimed. For instance, women can only expect the benefits of alcohol to kick in after the menopause, and even then, more than one or two drinks a day is probably detrimental, rather than beneficial.

Having said that, there is even some evidence that it could do your energy levels good. A Spanish study of nearly 20,000 adults found that drinking moderately meant increased sense of wellbeing and less sickness than teetotallers.

But once you get over that moderate one or two into three or four, the bad side kicks in. Less oxygen reaches your cells because alcohol causes dilation of the blood vessels. You could become dehydrated – alcohol is a powerful dehydrator. And your liver has to work hard to metabolise it if you drink to excess.

Then of course, there's the danger of hangover.

The pounding headache of a hangover is down to dehydration. Even a very slight thirst means you have already lost 1% of your body's fluid and two cups of water are needed to replace it. When you reach hangover levels of dehydration your body is

screaming for pints of fluid. Alternate a glass of still water with every alcoholic drink.

Milk thistle is a natural detoxifier that helps the liver to function optimally. Take the herb before and after drinking alcohol.

Handling alcohol on a daily basis

Let's face it, being a teetotaller is very hard in our society. For some of us, it's harder than others. I know one journalist who, when he's with his work colleagues, actually pretends to be a reformed alcoholic so no one forces him to drink. 'I just couldn't hack the amount that some of my colleagues drink and remain functioning. I don't know how they do it.' This isn't a bad strategy. He's happy to drink at home with his wife – just not with what he calls the 'booze monsters'. Here are some strategies that might help.

> **Here's an idea for you...**
>
> **What's your drinking rate? Your liver can process one unit of alcohol an hour. Stick to that and fill up with water for the rest of the time. You'll find you feel more in control, you may never have a hangover again and you'll have more energy the next day.**

- ❀ Alcohol cuts down on oxygen and this leads to tiredness – both mental and physical. Don't slouch over your pint. Breathe deeply. This is a lot safer now that more pubs are banning smoking.
- ❀ Carry *Nux vomica* – a homeopathic remedy that stops nausea and headaches.
- ❀ Fruit juice is your best friend: it is full of the antioxidants that help strengthen the liver; fructose increases the speed at which the body metabolises alcohol; and vitamin C is a natural energiser.
- ❀ Watch out for high-sugar drinks like sherry and alcopops. The sugar means they're absorbed into the blood stream faster and eliminated more slowly, so you get more drunk faster – and stay that way longer. Brandy, oaked Chardonnays and young red wines may also be high in compounds called

congeners that are hard on the body, and take more energy to metabolise.

✿ Eat before you go out – it will cut down the effects of alcohol and save you calories too. If you're full, you're less likely to get drunk, or to become a victim of 'the munchies' and start scoffing nibbles to keep going. I've followed the advice of nutritionist Amanda Ursell, who told me to eat beans on toast as a stomach liner, and it works excellently well – not filling you up too much, but minimising alcohol's bad effects.

And if it all goes wrong?

Give your liver a makeover. This will help you recover your energy the day after, faster.

Take 600–1000mg of milk thistle throughout the day. This strengthens the outer membranes of liver cells. Research at the Cedars-Sinai Medical Centre in LA shows that, if you take milk thistle in the days before a big drinking session, it reduces hangovers.

Take 1200mg of N-acetyl-cysteine. This dose was reported by the *New Scientist* to completely banish hangover symptoms.

Take 75mg of vitamin B complex, 500–1000mg of vitamin C and 2 g of evening primrose oil before you go out, and repeat the morning after. This may help reduce the effects of hangover by replacing destroyed vitamins.

83. Good morning, sunshine

Here's the simplest yoga routine, that's been energising people for thousands of years.

Time spent mastering this move could be one of the best investments you make in terms of energy.

One reason its fans love yoga so much is that it gives them energy. This specific effect on energy levels has been backed up by research. The *Journal of the Royal Society of Medicine* reported on the effects on participants' mood and vitality in three groups of volunteers: some did relaxation exercises, some visualisation and some yoga. Those doing a 30-minute programme of yoga reported an increase in both mental and physical energy. They also reported a lift in their mood. They were more alert; the other groups reported feeling more sluggish and less happy.

You don't have to do much yoga to benefit. The 'Salute to the Sun' is just that – it's meant to be carried out while facing the rising sun. But wherever you do it, it's specifically designed to increase your energy. That said, this is a brilliant way of starting your day: it releases tension, limbers up the body after sleep and stimulates circulation before your day.

If possible, do this outside, facing the sun, first thing. Failing that, your bedroom's fine. Stand straight and tall, feet bare and about a foot apart. Hold your hands, pointing upwards, in front of your chest as if you were praying.

1   *Inhale* and lift your arms straight above your head, stretching backwards a few centimetres so that you feel a stretch across your front.

2   *Exhale.* At the same time, bend forwards from your hips so that your hands are on each side of your feet. You may have to bend your legs slightly at the knee until you get more flexible.

3   *Inhale.* At the same time, place your right foot behind you as far as you can. Then place your left foot there too, so that your hands and feet are supporting your body.

4   *Exhale.* At the same time, lower your knees to the floor, then your chest, then your chin. You should look as if you are about to do a press up.

5   *Inhale.* At the same time, slowly straighten your arms and arch your back from the waist so your chest is lifted off the floor.

6   *Exhale.* At the same time, push back onto your knees, tuck your toes in, then straighten your arms and legs so that you make an inverted V, standing on your toes.

7   *Inhale* and step between your hands with your left foot.

8   *Exhale* and step between your hands with your right foot.

9   *Inhale.* At the same time, slowly return to the standing position.

Now repeat. Take your time to learn how to do this properly. The breathing is important. But with practice you should be able to do this between 10 and 20 times in a minute. The more you do it, the more energy you gain. Once you've got the hang of it, swap the leg you lead with from stage 3 (right first, then left) – but I found it helped to get the hang of it one way before I started mixing it up.

One result of all the upward and downward movements, say yoga adherents, is that they strengthen the adrenals, those glands that we depend on for energy and which are overworked by stress. The 'Salute to the Sun' is a marvellous, instant tonic but taking up a regular class and beginning your own practice, as it's called, will benefit you more.

Does yoga deliver? I've met some yoga practitioners who weren't as relaxed, enlightened and serene as they thought they were. But I've never met one who didn't look fabulous. So that's a nice secondary benefit.

Defining idea...

'I got into yoga late, when I was 38 or 39. I wish I'd started earlier.'
STING

84. Energy black spots transformed

Reframe your world. In even the most energy-draining situations, we can find a potential source of pep.

Some bits of the day just make us feel bad. Here's how to turn them around.

You hate getting up

Research has shown that pressing the snooze button doesn't actually make you less tired. An extra ten minutes – even an extra hour – doesn't refresh you. By getting up when you wake up, you reclaim time – and that is energising. Incapable of getting up? Instead of pressing the snooze button, try stretching. Think of a cat. Many animals have a good stretch before they rise to get their muscles stretched and warmed up and get oxygen into their blood stream. It will work for you too.

You hate your commute

See your commute as a chance to really get moving. There is nearly always some way you can make your commute to work more active. Walk to work. Or get off a stop early and walk a little of the way to work. Or walk up the escalator. Or walk up some of the stairs to your office. This will underline to your psyche that you are an active person, pursuing your vision of your future, energetically and dynamically. Play your own music on the way to work, if you don't already do so.

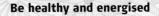

You hate the way your working day disappears and you feel you've achieved nothing

Use your lunch hour productively. Too many of us, even if we take a break from our desk, don't differentiate our lunch hour from the rest of the day when we're a wage slave. This hour is *your* hour. Make it a habit to do two things for yourself every lunch hour that will boost your energy – one you don't want to do, but will make your life easier, and one you do want to do, that will cheer you up. Make a phone call you're dreading, pay a bill, draft your CV – these are dull, but getting them off your list will make you feel better. Plan your next holiday, eat some chocolate, go for a walk – these are energising, and just for you. Reclaiming your lunch hour will mean every day has something positive in it.

> Here's an idea for you...
>
> **Eschew the lie-in. Research shows that catching up on sleep at the weekend knocks out your body clock and will lead to you being even more tired in the following week. As far as possible, go to bed and rise at the same time each day – it makes you less tired in the long run.**

You hate waiting

All those moments hanging around waiting at the check out, waiting for the train, or for the kettle to boil, or for the lift, can be put to use. Run over your goals and plans for the day. Think of the next challenge (whether that's a difficult phone call, exercising or facing someone you're not keen on). Run through the scene in your mind, imagining it going as well as possible and how you'll feel afterwards. 'Dead time' is usually filled with fantasies – often negative fantasies of all that could go wrong. Instead, start having positive fantasies that boost your confidence and energy. Or do some pelvic floor exercises – a toned pelvic floor means better orgasms for both sexes.

You hate Barbie

Kids sap our energy by demanding attention, usually when we don't want to give it. The single best piece of advice is to give them that attention wholeheartedly. Becoming engaged in what children are interested in can be remarkably relaxing to the adult brain. Instead of begging for a couple of minutes to yourself to read the paper, help your child dress Barbie, complete their jigsaw or win at their computer game when they want you to do it. You'll find that two minutes of your attention will energise you and mean they are satisfied enough to leave you alone. The point is that if you have children you *do* have to spend time looking after them. So, personally, finding a way to make it relaxing and energising even when I'm overworked and stressed out really helps. When you're bathing the children, feeding them or dressing them, try to sink into their world, their level of interest, rather than having your mind racing with what's next on your agenda.

You hate hangovers

Nights out with friends are relaxing and essential, but have you noticed how rubbish you often feel the next day? A meal out, lots of booze, smoky atmospheres – no wonder. Suggest you see your friends in a different environment – a movie, a walk, a sauna or a night in a sushi bar (go easy on the sake) should make you feel better the next day rather than worse. If your friends like the pub and that's it, reduce your alcohol intake to one drink every second round.

85. Get in the raw

Eating more raw food – we're talking carrots rather than chicken – is a well-documented route to raising energy levels.

The most famous raw food proponent was Dr Max Gerson. He started off by using a raw-food diet to cure his own migraines, then other people's migraines.

Then he moved on 'up' the disease ladder until he became famous for his treatment of cancer. Gerson believed that the starting point of all illness is an imbalance between sodium and potassium. His theory was that eating raw fruit and veg (which are loaded with potassium) increases oxygen uptake by the cells and mobilises white blood cells to fight disease. This results in better health and vastly improved energy.

Most doctors wouldn't agree with this, but then they wouldn't disagree that, as a nation, we'd benefit from upping our fruit and vegetable consumptions. Personally, I once followed a 100% raw food diet for a month and felt marvellous on it after just a few days. I had energy to burn and seemed to achieve much more completely effortlessly. But it is a huge faff at first and can take over your life. I once read a fascinating account by a journalist of living on raw juices for a few weeks in an attempt to reverse the genetic condition that would mean she'd be blind in her thirties. To her amazement, and that of her ophthalmologist, her sight improved during her experiment, but she found the effort of juicing vast quantities of vegetables every day too high a price to pay. She couldn't leave her home, shackled as she was to her juicer.

Here's an idea for you...

What puts people off juicing is that the preparation and clean-up after takes longer than drinking the juice. The secret is to gather all the ingredients of your juice together and fill your sink with soapy water before you start. Chop and clean in one shot. When the juice is made, pop the dirty bits straight into hot water to soak while you sip your juice slowly. Soaking immediately makes clearing up much quicker.

The writer and alternative-health guru, Leslie Kenton, is a devotee of raw food. Her realistic recommendation is for a diet that is 75% raw and 25% good-quality cooked wholegrains (brown rice, wholemeal, organic bread). At this level of raw food intake, she believes you get all the health benefits, including an increase in vitality. She has written extensively on how to transfer to a raw-food diet.

You would have to be very motivated to move over onto even a 75% raw-food diet. Another option is to gradually introduce more raw foods into your normal diet. What you will probably find is that, as you eat more raw food, you will enjoy the 'clean' taste and find that you are gradually including more healthy, less processed foods. It goes without saying that the gurus of raw food insist on organic: where that's not possible, scrub all produce thoroughly under running water.

Some ideas that are easy to instigate

✿ Eat a bowl of salad leaves a day – rocket, lettuce, basil, parsley, watercress. Experiment with different types. Grate a little carrot or apple over your leaves, or add some homemade vinaigrette, balsamic vinegar or olive oil.

✿ Start every meal with raw food. For breakfast, fruit; for lunch, fruit or a salad; for dinner, salad again. It is an easy way to up your five fruit and veg, and as a side effect it should help you lose weight: research showed that those who ate a small salad before dinner ate less at the meal and lost weight effortlessly.

✿ Buy a juicer. Vegetable and fruit juices give a concentrated shot of vitamins and minerals, and they are easily digested. Recent research shows that drinking fruit and vegetable juice three times a week slashes the risk of Alzheimer's disease by 76%. (The Gerson Diet, incidentally, recommends ten huge glasses a day.)

✿ Make your own coleslaw. One of the very easiest ways of including more raw food is to grate half a cabbage, a couple of carrots and an apple into a bowl and mix up with a minimal amount of mayonnaise. Or better still, skip the mayonnaise and soften the slaw with your own homemade vinaigrette sweetened with a little honey. This tastes so good that commercial coleslaws will soon seem too cloying.

> *Defining idea...*
>
> *'Everyone has a doctor in him or her; we just have to help it in its work. The natural healing force within each one of us is the greatest force in getting well. Our food should be our medicine. Our medicine should be our food.'*
> HIPPOCRATES

86. Eat breakfast

If you don't, you're missing out on the number one trick for combating energy loss.

I'm evangelical about this one. If you're tired, and you don't eat breakfast – that's probably the reason.

I'm not a person who likes to eat in the morning, but years of talking to nutritional experts brainwashed me. They all said it was vital. I started. My energy levels soared, specifically my mental focus. The difference in concentration is so fundamental that now, no matter how frantic my morning, I won't drive unless I've eaten breakfast.

This has turned me into a breakfast fascist. If I were an employer, I wouldn't care about the standard of a potential employee's CV if they wouldn't promise to eat breakfast each morning. They may not realise it, but they are certainly not performing to their full potential, even if they think they are.

The best fuel combination is a carbohydrate and protein breakfast. Carbohydrate releases energy quickly (it gives you the boost to run for the bus), but protein releases energy for longer (it will help you clinch the deal during that tricky pre-lunch conference call). If you eat carbs alone in the morning or nothing at all, your body may well crave more carbs at 11 a.m. – hence the dreaded doughnut run that wreaks such havoc with your figure and your idea of yourself as a person in control of their life. So remember. Carbs good, bit of protein essential. Here are some ideas:

OK breakfast

Bowl of non-sugary cereal (Shreddies, All-Bran) with semi-skimmed or skimmed milk. Piece of fruit or good-quality juice.

How to make it better

The milk provides some protein, but not much. Nibble on a little hard cheese or cottage cheese, or have a slice of cheese on wholewheat toast to get some more protein in there.

Better breakfast

Porridge with plain yogurt and a handful of seeds and dried fruit and/or a teaspoon of honey to sweeten.

How to make it better

Again, try the cheese thing, or a handful of nuts on top of the porridge. You may find that the yogurt does enough to fill you up. It does sometimes for me. But not always. Which is why you should build up to the ...

Best breakfast

- ✿ Scrambled eggs on wholegrain toast.
- ✿ Mackerel or kippers on wholegrain toast.
- ✿ Smoked salmon and cream cheese on wholegrain toast or bagel.
- ✿ Omelette with cheese, tomato and mushrooms.

Here's an idea for you...

Try this heart-boosting smoothie, which fulfils all the criteria. Mix half a pint of ice-cold semi-skimmed or soya milk with a banana, a pinch of cinnamon and two teaspoons of fish or flaxseed oil. Throw in a handful of soft fruits such as raspberries, blueberries or strawberries. (Out of season, you can buy frozen packets of these in supermarkets.) Sip, with a handful of nuts.

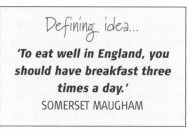

How to make it better
Add a piece of fruit and you're set to go.

My favourite breakfast

My friend Lynn Osborne, a gifted acupuncturist, gave me two nutritional tips – green tea and drinking chicken soup for breakfast. A bowl of homemade chicken soup is a marvellous breakfast on a cold morning – on any morning. Protein, vegetables (for carbohydrate) and filling without being fattening. You can throw in some noodles if you feel like it. You feel light and full of energy. Use your own recipe or try this one. This makes enough for five bowls. Keep half in the fridge and freeze the other half until later on in the week.

Buy yourself a special breakfast bowl. Enjoy your soup as you drink it. Think of China – calm and peace (which is, of course, where Lynn picked up the habit during her training).

Sauté one chopped leek and one chopped onion in a little olive oil, then add a minced garlic clove and cook until they are transparent. Add three chopped potatoes, one chopped carrot and 1¼ litres of chicken or vegetable stock, plus a handful or two of cooked, shredded organic chicken. Throw in a pinch of nutmeg, grated ginger or horseradish if you like. Bring to the boil and then turn down the heat and simmer for fifteen minutes or until the potatoes are cooked. Add a handful of greens – pak choi, spinach leaves, curly kale, watercress – and continue to simmer until these are just cooked. I like mine chunky but you could liquidise yours if you prefer. Add pepper. I don't use salt, and if you do, try to cut down.

87. Let in the light

Most of us have heard of SAD – Seasonal Affective Disorder – but are less aware that there are millions of people affected by the 'sub-syndrome'.

They don't have SAD, but they feel exhausted all winter.

Before electricity, everything changed for our ancestors during the winter months. Lack of daylight affected every part of their lives. Now we can work and play round the clock; the lack of light need never impinge on our 'lifestyle'.

But that doesn't mean that lack of daylight doesn't have a profound effect on us.

Normal electric lights can't replace daylight as far as our bodies are concerned, which explains why millions of us suffer symptoms of SAD unwittingly. And lack of energy is one of the biggest symptoms.

Around one in twenty of us suffer from SAD, which can involve severe depression. But what's amazing is that so many of us don't realise it and a far, far larger number are believed by experts to suffer from a milder form without ever knowing it. And lack of energy is the clearest symptom of this 'sub-syndrome'.

❀ Do you dread the winter months?
❀ Do you feel lethargic during the months of November to April for no apparent reason?

Here's an idea for you...

Have your morning cuppa outside if at all possible, or next to a bright window. Research on sheep in the Western Isles has led scientists to believe that SAD is related to levels of melatonin, the hormone that induces sleep. We need daylight to 'switch off' melatonin after a night's sleep, and getting outside as soon after you wake (as long as it's light, of course) may help.

✿ Do you tend to put on weight in winter?
✿ Do you find it near impossible to get out of bed in the morning when it's dark outside?
✿ Do you find you are more paranoid or self-doubting in winter?
✿ Do you feel more anxious in winter?

Answer yes to two or more and there's every chance you could be affected by SAD.

The further north you live, the more likely you are to be affected by the lack of light. One study has shown that those in the north-east of Scotland have a higher level of SAD symptoms than average, and it is likely that depression in winter gets gradually more likely the farther north you live, as the light available diminishes.

What can you do?

Stage 1

Get outside for half an hour a day during the winter. Make it a habit of going for a walk at lunchtime, but since sunlight is so precious in the UK during winter, if at all possible, think about dropping everything, making your excuses and getting outside as soon as the sun comes out, whatever time of the day.

Stage 2

If you still feel blue, St John's Wort has been proven to help with the symptoms of SAD. It is not suitable for those on some other medications including the Pill and some heart drugs. It is also helpful in combating the comfort eating that goes along with mild depression.

Stage 3

Investing in a light box, which supplies doses of strong white light as you work, or sit in your home, could well be answer. A study published in the *American Journal of Psychiatry* found that light therapy was more effective than Prozac in treating SAD: 95% of its users reported that it improved their condition. In general, 85% appear to benefit from light boxes and see an improvement within three to four days of treatment of around two hours a day. Specialised light boxes can be found on the internet, but lights are now readily available on your high street, at chemists and health shops. For milder cases there are 'alarm clocks' that wake you gently and gradually in the morning with light rather than ringing.

Stage 4

If depression is a problem, the group of anti-depressants that work best are the SSRIs (Selective Serotonin Reuptake Inhibitors). Older kinds such as the tri-cyclics tend to make you feel more lethargic and tired, so they aren't the best option if you are already tired.

Defining idea...

'Do not anticipate trouble, or worry about what may never happen. Keep in the sunlight.'
BENJAMIN FRANKLIN

88. Supermarket savvy

Turn your supermarket shop into an energy-boosting adventure.

Live a little – eat more! Choosing from a wide variety of foods will boost your energy. (And changing your variety of crisp doesn't count.)

The average person eats only around twenty different foods. How dull is that? Nutritionists say we should eat from the widest variety of foods possible because, unsurprisingly, that will result in getting the optimal number of nutrients. You should be looking to make your choice from between 60 to 70 different foods on a regular basis!

There are two advantages when it comes to your energy levels in mixing it up.

1 You will be eating a cornucopia of energy-boosting nutrients.
2 You will render your shopping trips a lot more interesting.

The nutrients that are vital for energy are the B vitamins, vitamin C, magnesium, iron and chromium. Shopping with the following lists in mind will ensure you're topped up with all of them.

The top 10 multi-taskers

To make it really easy when you're shopping *add three of these a week* to your shopping trolley and mix it up: select another three next week. They have been chosen to supply a good mix of B vitamins, magnesium, iron and chromium – the nutrients especially crucial for energy release.

- ❁ Bran flakes – packed with iron, B vitamins and vitamin C.
- ❁ Beef – iron, chromium. (Liver is another good food for supplying the energy nutrients.)
- ❁ Wholegrain rice and bread – B vitamins and magnesium.
- ❁ Chick peas – magnesium and iron.
- ❁ Oats – vitamin B and magnesium.
- ❁ Sardines – magnesium and iron.
- ❁ Quorn – loaded with one of the key B vitamins.
- ❁ Turkey – vitamin B12 and iron.
- ❁ Nuts and seeds – mix and match different types for 'broad spectrum' cover. Pumpkin seeds are a particularly good source of iron.
- ❁ Rye bread – good for iron and B vitamins.

Here's an idea for you...

Stick to the perimeter of your supermarket like glue. Almost always, the 'real' food is focused on the outside of the store, the junk in the middle aisles. Leave your trolley at the end of the aisle when you go to buy cleaning fluids and pet food. Having to carry junk food back to your trolley makes it less likely that you'll pick them up in the first place as it's a lot harder than just tossing them in.

Twelve cracking vitamin C sources

Choose three a week, on top of your usual foodstuffs. Mix them up. These all supply more than 20mg per 100g of food: blackcurrants, bran flakes, Brussels sprouts, cabbage (raw has double), cauliflower, citrus fruits, kiwi fruit, mango, raw red and orange peppers, raspberries, strawberries and watercress.

Six top snacks

These combine the all-important energy combo: protein with carbohydrate. Stock up with enough of these so that when you need a between-meal pick-up, you can reach for a snack that will fill you up without sending your blood sugar soaring (which leads to a slump in energy later). Some of these are a bit odd at first, but just try eating one of these snacks mid-morning and mid-afternoon, and you'll be amazed at how satisfying they are.

- ✿ Two oatcakes with peanut butter
- ✿ Nuts – a good handful maybe with a few raisins or sultanas
- ✿ A stick of celery spread with cream or cottage cheese
- ✿ Slices of apple spread thinly with peanut or other nut butter
- ✿ A vegetable juice with a few nuts on the side
- ✿ A boiled egg and a couple of rye crispbreads or a slice of rye bread.

Other great energy foods to add to your shopping list on a regular basis

Eggs (protein/vitamin B); pumpkin seeds (a great source of zinc); mackerel (best source of omega-3, which is the wonder nutrient of the moment, and also a great source of protein); bulgur (a good source of slow-releasing carbohydrate for long-lasting energy); Marmite (good for B vitamins); basil (beloved by herbalists for its uplifting qualities); artichoke (rich in vitamin C and magnesium); beetroot (high in vitamin C, magnesium, iron and B vitamins); kale (packed with iron and B vitamins); lentils (loaded with magnesium); celery (has special phytochemicals that are good for energy and improving mood).

89. Makeover your metabolism

Want to have more energy and lose weight? Yes? Then read on.

Strap a couple of laptops round your middle for the day and you'll soon find just how draining carrying around that extra 10lbs can be.

If you're overweight, losing a few pounds will help your energy levels. But how do you do it without feeling more drained? Try this; it's called calorie cycling. Versions of it have been around for years, but for some reason it isn't trumpeted by the slimming industry. Maybe because it works.

The reason I like it is that it is realistic. It takes into account that none of us can stick to a diet all the time. Of course, some people do spend their lives on a diet – stick-thin celebs are the most visible example. But if they ever slip up, they will balloon overnight because constant starvation has lowered their metabolic rate – the rate at which they burn off calories – to that of a vole.

Which brings us back to calorie cycling, because it works on the principle that by mixing up your calorie count, your metabolic rate stays on its toes, so to speak. Your metabolic rate doesn't drop as you lose weight; in fact, it revs up. It's thought that dieting suppresses production of an appetite-regulating hormone, leptin. High leptin production means a high metabolism; reduced leptin means metabolism goes down and your appetite goes up. This mechanism helped our Stone Age ancestors cope with famine. Now it just makes us fat.

How does calorie cycling work? Simple. You diet for a few days, then for one day you eat pretty much what you like. There is evidence that it works. Research done by the National Institute of Health in the States discovered that when healthy young men restricted calories and then binged, their metabolism rose by 9% on the morning after their binge day. It's thought binge days 'reset' leptin production. Below are some ideas. For more sophisticated diet plans and more *advice read The Rotation Diet, The Warrior Diet,* Eating for Life and The Abs Diet. (Don't follow any diet without your doctor's advice if you have a medical condition or suspect you could have one.)

The hard-core version

This version means you eat lightly during the day (but frequently), and more at night. You further mix things up by dropping most carbs for a couple of days, then adding them back in. The advantage is that you are never more than three days away from a pudding.

Eat unlimited amounts of fruit and salad during the day, with eggs as your only protein. (I strongly advise having a boiled egg for breakfast or, if you're like me, you'll keel over.) At night, eat unlimited amounts of vegetables with a large-ish palm-sized piece of protein – beef, chicken turkey, fish, or tofu. Don't eat any starch or sugars.

Follow this for two days, then switch to one day of eating much the same but, after you've eaten your evening meal, have some carbohydrates – a roll, a baked potato, some pasta or rice and a dessert, too, if you like. You must eat the protein and vegetables first because the theory goes that you should never eat starchy carbohydrate foods on an empty stomach. The sugars are rapidly absorbed into your bloodstream resulting in a blood-sugar spike and release of insulin, which encourages your body to store excess energy as fat. Eating non-starchy carbs such as vegetables, and protein beforehand slows down the absorption of sugars.

Defining idea...

'The doctor of the future will give no medicine but will interest his or her patients in the care of the human frame, a proper diet and the cause and prevention of disease.'
THOMAS EDISON

The straightforward version

Eat around 1700 calories for four or five days. Eat around 2000 calories for one day. Eat 1700 calories for four or five days. Eat around 2000 calories for one day. You get the picture. Don't do this for more than a month – it's low in calories.

Typical 1700 calories

- ❀ Breakfast – bowl of cereal with semi-skimmed milk and a small glass of orange juice
- ❀ Mid-morning – half a dozen almonds
- ❀ Lunch – sandwich, apple
- ❀ Mid-afternoon – orange
- ❀ Dinner – plate of chicken and vegetable stir-fry followed by a peach and a small glass of wine.

Work smarter

Part hard work, part politics — that's the formula for getting on in the work place. Unfortunately too many of us (especially women) are good at the first part of the equation and not so good at working clever, rather than just working hard. Here's all you need to know to start revolutionising your working life

Work – heaven or purgatory?

Some of us have a harder time than others when it comes to getting on at work. Make sure you're not missing a trick.

1. You walk into the lift and your CEO is there already. You:
- ☐ a. Think, 'terrific – a chance to shine'.
- ☐ b. Smile broadly, say little.
- ☐ c. Smile weakly and concentrate on not dropping your latte on his suit.

2. During conversations with someone superior to you in the pecking order, you:
- ☐ a. Look them steadily in the eye.
- ☐ b. Look them in the eye when they are talking but find it hard when you are talking.
- ☐ c. Find it hard even when they are talking.

3. Before you meet someone for a business meeting, you assume:
- ☐ a. That they'll like you.
- ☐ b. That it will go OK if you can get in the right frame of mind.
- ☐ c. That you may put them off the idea or that they may not want to work with you.

4. You think you could work on your own:
☐ a. Really well. You are the sort of person who adapts although you'd miss office banter.
☐ b. Pretty well. But it might get lonely.
☐ c. Either brilliantly or terribly.

5. Your social life is:
☐ a. Very focused around your work mates.
☐ b. Sometimes geared around work colleagues but not on a weekly basis.
☐ c. Almost totally separate.

Score 3 for every 'a', 2 for every 'b' and 1 for every 'c'.

Score 12-15

You are confident and happy in your work. But read idea 91 just to make sure that you remember that working hard at a job isn't always enough.

Score 7–11

You have the skills but there is an ambivalence about either the job or the company. Read idea 97 to see if it helps.

Score 6 or less

Maybe you've never fitted in at your present job, in which case read idea 92. Maybe you just hate your job, in which case read idea 109. It could be time for a change.

90. Handling the boss

You may think the boss holds all the cards – after all, he can fire you. But that's not the whole story. You can influence your way to what you want.

You want to work part-time. They won't allow that: apparently, it's not company policy. Yes, you can, though. That's what this idea is about.

Once upon a time, the employer held all the power. Employees couldn't do anything for fear of losing their jobs. In the twenty-first century, that's no longer true. And this isn't to suggest in the cynical sense that so much of the legal system is now stacked against the employer that you can get away with murder. No, the situation has changed in a healthy and positive way for you.

Read this carefully and believe it: there are simply not enough great employees around. Think about it: the last bank you went into – what were the staff like? How about the restaurant where you ate last week, or your daughter's school? What are the people like there? Quite.

There really is a shortage of excellent people for employers to choose from. So that's where we will start. Delay the influencing you need to do to get the change you want and start to shine like a great employee. Here's the deal: if you're a great employee, you cannot be replaced (or at least it is very hard to do so). That means

Here's an idea for you...

We know that great employees get what they want so analyse what makes a great employee. It's someone who has a 'can do' approach ('*what can we do to get this policy to work?*'), someone who is brilliant at the basics such as time management (*arrives at meetings on time*), someone who is customer service focused (*smiles and empathises when dealing with people*), someone who builds rather than destroys ('*it would have been good to have had more notice, but we didn't, so what can we do instead?*'). You're good at all of those, aren't you? Imagine what would happen if you became great at them. As you now realise, it's only one decision away.

you will be listened to and it means you have a good chance of getting what you want: you have become a fantastic influencer. Clever, huh?

No sane employer gets rid of great employees. Hence, great employees are good influencers. Start your influencing career by deciding to be excellent; deciding to be great.

But perhaps you think, 'Why should I? I am not paid enough to be excellent.' That's partly the point. Or maybe you think you will be excellent when you get the team leader's position. This is the trick most people miss: just be excellent for yourself. Nobody can take it away from you and, when you are, people want you. That's when you get listened to and you have your say.

If you're thinking you shouldn't have to raise your standards and you should simply have the right to go part-time, then you're not going to get very far with your ambition. It's the wrong mindset. If instead you decide to begin to enjoy getting better at the work and consequently do a great job, you will be recognised and you will start to get more of what you want: the corner office, then the promotion. And all without consciously influencing. It's a self-fulfilling prophecy.

Once you're an excellent employee, you'll have the boss's ear and that's when you can go for the jugular. Make sure you do it professionally, though. For instance:

❀ Get hard data for the changes you want (e.g. current salary ranges for your job);

❀ Book proper time for proper discussion and make sure you're fully prepared (e.g. to explain how the more flexible hours will help your child-care arrangements but won't alter your effectiveness);

❀ Build a relationship that fosters adult-to-adult conversation (i.e. don't allow yourself to be bullied);

❀ Respect the challenges your boss has, so fight the important battles.

> *Defining* idea...
>
> **'It is one of the strange ironies of this strange life [that] those who work the hardest, who subject themselves to the strictest discipline, who give up certain pleasurable things in order to achieve a goal, are the happiest people.'**
> BRUTUS HAMILTON, US athlete

91. Face it, you are you and they are them

Take a positive, practical but sceptical attitude to your organisation. Don't expect to spend your whole career in one organisation and don't trip over internal politics.

Are you in the right place? People are happier and work better when they can identify with the objectives of the organisation they work for.

It is hard to get up in the morning with energy and enthusiasm if you feel that your work contributes to something you couldn't care less about. Make sure you are working for an organisation that is doing something worthwhile and is likely to be successful. You are much more likely to build a career there.

If right now you're working towards a goal that neither interests you nor inspires you, you've got to make a change. It's up to you. Your career is a key element in your way of life and your general happiness; if you are in the wrong place get out of it.

You have our undivided loyalty – until it doesn't suit us

Now let's look at the other side of the coin – the organisation itself. Your organisation is probably chaotic, either all the time, or sometimes, or in places. This is both a problem and an opportunity for the career minded. This chaos means that whatever it says about looking after you and your career, your company may very well not be able to live up to its promises. Organisations, for example, have to take technological change on board if they are to survive even if it costs careers. In short, the organisation has to look after itself in a businesslike way, so you need to look after yourself in a similarly objective and professional way.

> Here's an idea for you...
>
> **It is best for your boss to think that other people believe your good ideas are his. You, on the other hand, should ensure people know that your ideas and your boss's good ideas are both yours.**

And circumstances change. A promise made to a member of staff in good faith may suddenly become impractical. In this environment the safest view to take of your organisation is that you owe it your loyal support only for as long as your objectives and the organisation's can co-exist. Career planning is now a question of a number of jobs rather than a simple progression up a single organisation. Companies don't offer jobs for life and most successful careerists will change employers from time to time. Keep an open mind and don't get so set in your ways that you get caught out by a reorganisation in which you find yourself 'Co-ordinator of Long-term Planning'. Such a post almost certainly means that you are no longer part of those long-term plans. I'm certainly not encouraging you to be dishonest yourself. But be warned that others are sometimes going to use 'their best intentions' to meet their obligations.

Career players take integrity very seriously. They do not, however, ignore the facts of the new world – the 'company man' is extinct. The key phrase now is 'fluidity of labour'.

Nurture the politician within you

It is not possible for any organisation to exist without some form of internal politics. People often have conflicting agendas and objectives. Face it. Don't make a decision on behalf of an organisation without paying attention to what the implications are for you. If company politics permeate every decision that affects your career, you should face another brutal fact: *in company politics the competition is your colleagues.* After all, this is more than a matter of survival. The Vicar of Bray played his organisation's politics well and survived, but he never made it to bishop. My Dad, watching the politics that my mother got into in a small local church, was heard to murmur, 'The more I see of Christians, the more sorry I feel for the lions.' If the Church cannot avoid internal politics and strife, what chance has a capitalist corporation?

Finally

So, it's a question of 'us and them', or rather, remembering what we have said about your colleagues, of 'me and them'. Take responsibility for your own career, and work on the basis that no one else will.

92. Know what to say to whom

A meteoric careerist can't have too much exposure to top people. Think hard about extending your senior contacts.

You happen to be in the lift with your Chairman, or a senior executive of a major customer. Make sure you know what you would say to them.

Most of us in such a situation are like rabbits caught in the headlights and blow this short window of time with small talk. There is a clue here for the careerist. But it's not just about the Chairman.

You can expand on this by dropping in on anyone. Hewlett Packard used to have a useful slogan, 'managing by wandering around'. It was a neat way of reminding managers that part of their job was to be around and meet people by chance as well as in formal meetings. I extended this to 'selling by wandering around', which meant using the same technique to cruise around customer premises making new, and preferably high-level, contacts. 'Cultivating your career by wandering around?' It's not as snappy but that doesn't mean that it doesn't work.

Plan your absences

Try to be in the office at the same time as your boss. After all, in your absence she might give an interesting and potentially rewarding opportunity to someone else. You need to know her diary so that you can plan your absences at times when she won't notice you're not there.

The clincher for how vital it is to know your boss's diary is that you will know when she is definitely far away. Believe me, there is nothing more embarrassing than being caught nosing around in someone else's files.

Obviously you want high-level exposure to things that go well. You also want cover against being held responsible for something going wrong. Short-sighted people with moderate ambitions keep a detailed record of their activities with a note of the people who supported them on the way. The more ambitious person with her eye on the big picture does it in such a way that the record can prove that others were completely responsible if it goes wrong. Don't forget to have a shredder handy if all goes well, though. It wouldn't do for you to enable someone else to take the glory.

Here's an idea for you...

If, for example, you know your boss's diary you'll know when she is going to be talking to a person you would like to meet. First, prepare. If you did get the opportunity, what would you say? So, you know what you would say; now engineer the opportunity to say it. The best way is simply to breeze in. 'Oh, I'm sorry I didn't realise...' 'That's all right,' says your boss, 'Come in and meet Lord so-and-so.' She will probably add more in terms of a quick description of what you do for the organisation, and that is your moment. 'As a matter of fact, Lord so-and-so, I've been thinking that we ought to have a brief word on...' Brilliant: a new contact – put it in the address book.

'It's not how you play the game, but who you get to take the blame' goes the rhyme. This is the business version of the Olympic spirit. If you're involved with high-level operations it's generally not a good idea to be closely associated with failure. Stay clear of the firing line unless there are massive Brownie points for effort as opposed to achievement.

> *Defining* idea...
>
> **'There is no stronger way of building a career than "working the corridors".'**
> Richard Humphreys, serial chairman

There is another way of looking at this if the cock-up is really huge. A person in charge of a substantial development project spent £50 million of his company's money on it and was, towards the end, powerless to prevent it having no impact on the business at all. The entire sum was completely wasted. Asked into his boss's office he pre-empted the inevitable by saying that he knew he was there to be fired. 'No way,' said his boss, a very aware woman, 'Now that we have spent £50 million on your learning what doesn't work, we are not about to throw that investment away.' It's a variant of the 'Owe your bank £1,000 it's your problem, owe it a million and it's theirs.'

93. How do I look?

Like it or not, your appearance and your health are of more and more interest to your employer. Think about what you look like and whether you are paying enough attention to fitness.

Are you fit for the purpose? It does, of course, depend. If your boss is a fitness freak you have a choice of two courses of action. Either you can join her and beat the hell out of your colleagues at squash or tennis or whatever, or you can religiously avoid exercise of all sorts. The latter makes a definite point, so think about it.

Nowadays there are myriad ways of keeping fit by working out before or after office hours. If you are a bit anti-exercise, which you probably are if you are reading this idea, look carefully at all the opportunities. You don't have to do circuit training on a daily basis to give the impression that your health is as important to you as it is to your company. Walking can do it; so can cycling, jogging or roller-skating. If, however, your only exercise is straining to get the cork out of the bottle and the occasional one night stand, you could follow nutritionist Nigel Bentley's advice and get off the bus or the tube a few stops early and walk the rest of the way. If that doesn't suit you, try sitting on a horse. That's a fine way to get some fresh air, good exercise and, for goodness sake, a bit of excitement – you're quite high up off the ground. I've found that a bit of horse riding woke me up in the morning brilliantly and was as good a cure for a hangover as any.

If there are sports facilities at work use them by all means, but don't make a big thing about it. A lot of people, maybe most people, eventually find doing gym exercises monotonous and boring. So don't make yourself a hostage to fortune by shouting off about going to the gym every day after work; your bosses will notice when you stop.

A colleague of mine, Tony, tells the story of his personal trainer. Tony is a man who could eat for his country. He puts as much passion into eating and drinking as he does into his pretty successful career. The price he pays is a weight problem. At appraisal time his boss seemed to make light of it when he said 'What about shedding a bit of weight, Tony, we don't want to lose you to a heart attack.' Tony realised that there was more to the comment than light-hearted banter, so he hired a personal trainer. The woman took her job as a trainer very seriously and went through a detailed questionnaire on Tony's lifestyle and dietary habits. Each item was scored and at the end of the questions she totted up Tony's total, read the possible outcomes and finally announced in a puzzled voice that according to her charts he was already dead.

What do your clothes say?

The advice of one of the senior telecommunications people I have trained is not for the faint hearted. She says that you should avoid looking like everyone else. If the first thing board members know about you is that you wear bold jewellery, you

> *Here's an idea for you...*
>
> **It is never a good idea in career terms to fail at anything, so don't try and do too much. For example, try using a personal trainer just once a week or twice a month. That should spur you to some effort. It will eventually be embarrassing to tell them week after week that you haven't been off the sofa since you last met.**

Defining idea...

'This is the Law of the Yukon, that only the Strong shall thrive; That surely the Weak shall perish, and only the Fit survive.'
ROBERT W. SERVICE, Canadian poet

have made your point. Some of them may not like it, but this is compensated for by the fact that they've noticed you. I was always a little nervous about the topic of appearance in my one-on-one coaching sessions with senior managers. In the end I decided that the right question to ask yourself is whether your clothes are saying what you want them to say. Back to the telecommunications woman. She always wore arty clothes – brightly coloured suits featured heavily, along with large, luxurious scarves and eccentric shoes. In the nature of the training course I had to ask the question 'What do you think your clothes say about you?' She responded, 'They say that although I have got a senior job in your organisation, you will never own me.' I couldn't argue with that.

94. Go on, give them a shock

As part of your campaign to gain high exposure to senior people, take any opportunity you can to introduce new information into the organisation.

Look at your organisation as though you were the owner.

Left to itself a company ossifies. All organisations need alert managers to tell them how the world in which they are operating is changing. And it is difficult to be sure what changes in the environment will have an impact on your particular organisation. This makes the gathering and proclaiming of new facts or statistics a fertile ground for standing out in the crowd. The aim here is to draw the attention of management to new information that might have a long-term impact. This is an area for lateral thinking. Remember, we are talking about the long term – you should be long gone by the time your predictions face a reality check.

Brilliant entrepreneurs do this stuff really well. They take, for example, something a customer said to them the other day, a project they just approved in research and development, something their teenage son said at breakfast together with a headline in today's paper and discover an insight. That's what you are trying to do here, develop the way of thinking that entrepreneurs use to plan the way ahead.

Here's an idea for you...

Look for external sources of information that senior manager will find useful. Customers and competitors are very fertile ground. Spend a bit of time today looking at information about a competitor. If you are financially inclined, compare your competitor's annual report with yours and look for major discrepancies. Now see if you can get your boss interested in going further into it.

Make sure you set aside at least fifteen minutes of every day to read relevant published material; you will find this invaluable in presenting yourself. Reading technical papers, or even just the dailies, will help you to start to detect new and useful facts at an early stage. A rich vein for this type of information is the technical section. Technological change over the last ten years has rendered hundreds of traditional skills unnecessary. When, for example, did you last see someone literally cutting and pasting a newsletter?

Look for trends, sociological and other

Send notes to appropriate people quoting sources of information such as the *Harvard Gazette* that no one is likely to have read. The conclusion that you draw from the information must give senior managers food for thought. You must lead them to some clear conclusions showing problems, preferably catastrophic ones, or opportunities, preferably big ones, in the future. The area of demographics is another dead cert. Grey people buying power, the growth of old retired people, the death rate in Russia and so on. I advocate strongly the use of real facts in this regard, but if you have to make them up make sure it is not remotely possible to challenge them.

If all else fails there is always regulation and health and safety. Find out the trends here and predict the impact on your organisation.

Gather new facts and statistics as often as seems sensible given that you are also over-performing in your day-to-day function, and you will almost certainly at some point do your organisation a big favour. It would have ossified in that area if you hadn't warned it: organisations don't spot trends. Sometimes, if the coming event is catastrophic, what you say will give them the most tremendous shock.

Health warning: Do not pull the facts and statistics stunt too often. Some people send off two notes a week. This is a mistake. You are trying to build a reputation as a person with their finger on the pulse, not as a crashing bore.

> *Defining* idea...
>
> **'Study your subject well; observe carefully your customer requirements; strive mightily to fulfil that customer need and work hard and diligently at all times.'**
> SIR GEORGE BULL, Chairman, J. Sainsbury

95. Back the right horse

You need to get noticed. Identify who is important to your progress, and get to them. Sometimes that will mean bypassing a human blockage – perhaps your own boss, or some obstructive gatekeeper who is there to keep you away from the decision maker. Here are some tactics to leap such hurdles.

Suppose, for example, that your job is to supply computer and telecommunications solutions to the finance department of your company.

Your customer and decision maker is the Finance Director, but on a day-to-day basis there will be a key person whom you meet regularly and with whom you form plans for future approval by the Finance Director. Such people can usually be divided into three categories – the Good, the Bad and the Ugly.

The Good are terrific to work with. They understand their business and they are happy to tell you all about it, so that you can come up with the best possible plan together. Cultivate such people. Latch on to their coat tails. Buy them lunch. Feign interest when they show you pictures of their family. Help them to enhance their reputations and they will help you enhance yours. They will probably be quite happy for you to talk to the ultimate decision maker should you need to, but they'll do it with you as part of the team.

The Bad are often bad because they are scared. They're scared of their boss, they're scared of making mistakes and they're probably scared of a brilliant careerist like you. They probably don't know enough about their business to really brief you on what it is they want and will probably bar you from seeing the decision maker until you have earned their trust. That is the vital element of dealing with the Bad – you have to gain their trust.

It should be quite easy for a cool careerist like you to do this. Achieve some good, high-profile results that end up on the Finance Director's desk, and make sure Mr Bad gets all the credit. But do this genuinely. If you have to, you can dump on him later by showing that it has been you and your team all along that got the results, but life is easier if you can avoid having to do this.

At the point when he trusts you, Mr Bad should let you meet his boss. There is a problem if he won't. Access to his Director is vital if you are to carry out your role. So, like it or not, you have to get to them.

Remember, 'it is much easier to ask for forgiveness than to ask for permission.' Once you have created a relationship with his boss, Mr Bad will never be in such a strong position again to get in your way.

Now for Mr Ugly. Mr Ugly is mean. He doesn't trust you, he doesn't trust his boss, he doesn't trust anyone. Quite often such people are bullies. You can't really play along

> *Here's an idea for you...*
>
> **Never ask Mr Bad for permission to go and see the decision maker. If he refuses (which he probably will), you're then in an impossible situation. If you go behind his back, then you're heading for a confrontation and the relationship will be ruined for good. No – do it first and beg forgiveness later.**

with them if they are not allowing you to do the best you can for your customer; so you have to grasp the nettle and probably cause a major stink. Funnily enough, the way to deal with them is to cause them some fear, uncertainty and doubt.

Dealing with Mr Ugly

One of my salespeople had a Mr Ugly to contend with. I had to go in to see him and explain very logically that if my salesperson could not see the boss I would have to go in myself. I then displayed knowledge of what this bloke's competitors were doing and showed him that he was losing ground by not investing enough with us. I kept him just short of blowing his top and his uncertainty made him a bit easier to deal with. Unfortunately, however, he would not keep up with technological change and buy a 2960 B from us.

He would not even talk about it. The time had come to take a big risk. We made an appointment to go and see the Director, his boss, and we specifically asked that the meeting be with him on his own. As we had hoped, the director knew there was something wrong in that part of his business and agreed, albeit with at least a show of reluctance. We were pretty nervous; this was a major knifing job on a fairly senior person in a big customer. The Director's opening was 'Now just before we get to the intriguing question of why you wanted to see me without Rob, I thought I better let you know that he has just recommended that we buy a 2960 B.'

96. Encourage everyone

**One of the best things you can do for your
career is to deliver projects to your boss on
time and within budget. Your team will deliver
when you lead it effectively. Pick the right
management style for the right situation.**

There is a spectrum of leadership styles, and you will need to adopt them all at
certain points in your working life. Your style will vary from autocratic 'do as I say'
to democratic 'consensus-seeking'.

Your predominant style will depend on your organisation, the nature of the project
and the characteristics of the team. Try not to make it too dependent on your
natural way of leading people. You need to develop more flexibility than that.

You need to show your boss that you do not just hire people who are like yourself,
but can manage anyone who you need in your team.

Consider the appropriate times to use these different styles. Obviously when the
project hits a crisis and there is no time to consult you'll have to make decisions
alone, take the risks yourself and seize control. You will get through the crisis, but
at the cost of teamwork. Try to use this style sparingly and remember that such
heavy 'push' management tends to get results rapidly but its impact falls off just as
quickly. If you want a change in performance to stick, you need to move along the
spectrum towards consensus.

Opinion seeking is further along the spectrum. Ask all the stakeholders as well as your team what they think about a wide range of issues. This 'pull' type of management builds confidence and demonstrates that you value the team's views. It is also an opportunity to go high up in the organisation to get the advice of some senior people whose experience you would like to exploit. Stakeholders love it and it spreads the risk a bit if something goes wrong.

Finally you get to the truly democratic style of management. It is essential to use this style on a regular basis. It 'empowers' the team. (Am I the only person who thinks that the buzzword 'empower' is just good, old-fashioned trust dressed up to sound impressive?) Simply encourage team participation and involve them in making decisions. Keep them up to date with your thinking and with issues that are affecting the project. There is no doubt that people blossom under such a regime; they improve and maintain performance and motivation. They also speak well of you to your boss.

Develop good team members

In most teams the egos of the individuals can get in the way of sharing suggestions. There are exceptions and they tend to be successful people. Hire them. They

---

Here's an idea for you...

If you can't admit that you can't do something, your people won't either. Encourage them to talk about those parts of your strategy they are less confident of handling. Then you can help them, or rearrange the plan to take that task away from them.

encourage openness and constructive criticism of everyone, by everyone. They tend to be laid back, good listeners and understanding of people's problems. They are terrific allies of the team leader and still liked by their colleagues in the team. As team leaders themselves they bring the best out of people. They don't manage everyone in the same way, though. Some of the team they can encourage to be musicians, and some will always be actors.

Defining idea...

'Striking amongst the musicians is their total lack of self-importance. They play a piece and then discuss among themselves as to how it may be improved. They make suggestions for each other directly, not via the director. No actor would tolerate a fellow performer who ventured to comment on what he or she is doing – comment of that sort coming solely from the director, and even then it has to be carefully packaged and seasoned with plenty of love and appreciation.'
ALAN BENNETT

97. Draw your own map

In order to get to the top you need to be seen as a strategic thinker. To get that reputation you need to do some. Strategic thinking, that is. Here's a short cut to a creating a team strategy.

The aim of this idea is simple. You are going to present a strategy for your team that is going to knock your boss's socks off and make him insist that all your colleagues copy you.

And that's the second benefit – while you're producing a first-class performance, everyone else is tying themselves in knots trying to write a strategic plan. Only you know the short cut.

The first skill involved in creating a strategy is the ability to balance short-term thinking with long-term planning. Put some long-term thinking time into your schedule. You don't have much time; you needed a strategy yesterday. And, who knows, you may need a new one tomorrow.

Once they've decided to create a strategy, most managers think they need a consultant to help them to write it. Other people think they need a facilitator to help the team with the process. From vast, and occasionally bitter, experience I believe it is better if you can to do it on your own. Facilitators have to be perceived to add value to the planning process, so they invent complicated procedures and forms. Actually all you need is some flipcharts, pens and one crucial technique.

Right, you've got your team in the planning room and agreed to do at least half a day on the plan, and another half day in a week's time. Write first on the flipchart your vision for the future. You should have prepared this earlier and checked it over with the key people in your team before the session. This saves hours, and if later it turns out to be not quite right you can change it during the time you are implementing the strategy.

Here's an idea for you...

It is a really good idea to check this analysis with a few people including, of course, your key customers. Don't be frightened to show them your analysis. If there are bits they don't like or don't agree with, it's better that you know now.

The planning techniques

Use SWOT analysis as the analytical part of the process. Ask the team: in terms of achieving our vision, what are our Strengths, Weaknesses, Opportunities and Threats. Don't get hung up on words. Get the ideas down. Remember that you are all going to be living with this plan forever. But it will evolve constantly. you don't have to get it spot on at your first meeting.

And now follows the bit where a lot of teams go wrong. You've got to get from analysis strategic goals and action plan. Give each weakness, opportunity and threat

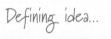

Defining idea...

'Strategies are intellectually simple; their execution is not.'
LARRY BOSSIDY, industrialist

an identifying number. (Ignore the strengths for now.) Write down the following topics: people, skills, facilities, customers and suppliers. Allocate each weakness, opportunity and threat to one of those topics. If some will not fit, choose another key word – it's unusual to need more than six or seven. Now allocate each topic to one or two team members. Send them away to work out the goals the team should set in that area and the actions necessary to achieve this. Tell them that the strengths might give some clues for the action plan. At a second meeting the following week discuss and agree the goals and actions, allocate the actions to a team member – and you have a strategic plan!

Throughout the process be prepared to question and challenge accepted norms. The really upwardly mobile careerist will fight tooth and nail before acknowledging that something the company is doing wrong cannot be changed. But watch the politics. It's a tough call, but you have to judge whether your boss's entrenched views can now be challenged by you and your team. In my experience, though, the safety-first acquiescence path is so much easier to contemplate that most people err on that side rather than taking the risk of becoming known as a doubter or, worse, a troublemaker. Courage, *mon brave*, nobody said life was easy.

Prepare to shine. You have a strategy and it is written down. Tell people about it, partly because you are trying to build your career and partly because you want to influence others towards your way of thinking. Make presentations. Sell your methodology to others so that you become the source of the company-wide strategic planning system. And then sit back and watch your colleagues suffer.

98. Changing horses mid-career

If you make a move to a new company your fellow managers there have an advantage over you. They know the ropes and how to shine in the existing environment. It is therefore a very good idea to do something early on to question that environment and change it in a high-profile way.

When you are changing employer think long and hard about why they hired you.

If you are joining at a fairly high level it is likely that the people who hired you saw you as an agent of change, for a part of their business or culture which is underperforming – new blood, new brooms and all that. If this is the case, you can afford to take a few risks in the early days.

Make a splash, why don't you?

Here's a brilliant example of making a great splash early on in a new outfit. A manager I know moved from one telecommunications company to another much larger and longer established one. He knew, from his competitive knowledge and from things said at the interview, that senior management were implementing a

> ### Here's an idea for you...
>
> **Even if you are staying put in your organisation have a long, hard think about change. What in your company really needs to be changed? Think deeply and don't be held back by things that seem to be cast in stone – nothing is. Right, if the change is within your authority, just do it. If it's not in your authority, but it wouldn't be a suicidal risk, just do it anyway. If it's too much of a risk to take on yourself, go to the person who could do it and persuade them to let you do it. Try not to give them the whole idea or they might pinch it.**

huge programme of change aimed at knocking the old-fashioned corners off those managers who had served with the organisation since the year dot.

Many of these people were accustomed to a hierarchical, rather deferential culture where seniority counted highly. They were also struggling with the idea that the customer was king. On his very first day the new boy took action using the car park as his vehicle, if you'll pardon the pun. He removed every car parking space allocated on the basis of management seniority, and reallocated the best spaces to customers only. As he was doing this he realised that some areas were not only dark but also outside the range of the security cameras. So he allocated the next best spaces nearest to the entrance to those women who sometimes or regularly worked late.

At a stroke he got the support of those of his people who felt held back by the old guard, and of the more ambitious women willing to work long hours. His action also became high profile without his having to tell a soul – the old guard did it for him: they were fuming. They sent angry e-mails to the HR department and senior managers in all parts of the organisation complaining about this loss of their hard-earned privilege. They themselves gave him the oxygen of publicity. By the end of his very first day he had a very high profile. He had sorted the resisters to change from the enthusiasts for it, and impressed on senior management his grasp of what they were looking for in terms of cultural change. Senior management congratulated themselves, modestly of course, for hiring the right person for the job.

Defining idea...

'**Most ideas on management have been around for a very long time, and the skill of the manager consists in knowing them all and, rather as he might choose the appropriate golf club for a specific situation, choosing the particular ideas which are most appropriate for the position and time in which he finds himself.**'
SIR JOHN HARVEY-JONES, former ICI chief

99. Make them agree fast

What do you want from your brilliant career? It's probably a mix of money, status, fun and finally power or influence. Let's look at the last of these, and find a way you can get agreement quickly to any proposal, big or small. This method is quick to prepare and must be reuseable.

Most managers are familiar with showing the benefits of a proposal to an audience. 'What's in it for them?' 'What does it actually do for the bottom line?' Well, we've had this dinged into us enough times during various training courses. And it's true. You are more likely to be convincing if you spell out the benefits of your proposition from the recipient's point of view rather than take the risk of allowing them to do it, or not do it, for themselves.

How about showing people 'how' to make the decision? This takes user-friendly propositions to the next level by adding another topic. So far we are all convinced that you present a proposal like this:

✿ Problem or opportunity
✿ Your proposed solution
✿ Benefits to the audience of the proposed solution

I want to add another element between the presentation of the problem and your solution – let's call it the *basis of decision*. Here are a few of examples of the practical bases of decision suggested by a seller of insurance policies to opticians:

✿ The package should include all principal business needs in one policy.

✿ The administrators of the scheme must have a lot of experience in your type of business.

✿ The insurance cover must be tailored to your business without losing its cost competitiveness.

✿ The underwriters must be first-rank UK-based companies.

Now, the salesperson could have promoted exactly the same ideas by banging on about the product she's selling. 'My product includes all the principal business needs in one policy. The administrators of my scheme have a lot of experience in your type of business.' And so on. There are two reasons why using the basis of decision approach gets better results faster in terms of persuading people that you have the right solution. The first is that it sees things from their point of view. (You often, for example, introduce the basis of decision with words like 'I understand you are looking for a solution that...' or 'Seen from your point of view you need a solution that....')

> Here's an idea for you...
>
> Take an idea you are trying to persuade your boss or your team to accept. Write down the features of your solution and then turn them into a basis of decision. Some will be dead easy because they truly have merit when seen from the audience's point of view. Some will be difficult, probably don't pass the 'so what's in it for me test' and should be discarded.

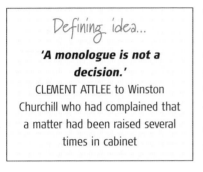

Defining idea...

'A monologue is not a decision.'

CLEMENT ATTLEE to Winston Churchill who had complained that a matter had been raised several times in cabinet

The second benefit is that you can ask if the audience agrees with the basis of decision. If you've simply dumped on them a list of product features you can't say 'Isn't that right?' because they will just say that they don't know. If they give you a positive response to your proposed basis of decision you've more or less cracked it. Just tell them that's what your solution does.

It doesn't always work

I was selling a computer to an educational establishment. They had very little money and I showed them how, if they bought a second-hand machine, they could have much more power and functionality. I took my boss's boss in to a meeting where I was hoping to close the business. I went through the basis of decision. I asked them if they agreed that I'd got it right and they did, whole-heartedly. 'Well,' said my boss's boss, 'that more or less describes our solution, so are you going to buy from us?' There was a short pause before the chairman said that there was one more thing – they didn't want to buy anything second-hand. Mmm, I'd missed that.

Finally

Like many effective techniques, using the basis of decision to get your own way is very simple. It's common sense, but it's not common practice. So it's good for your career and it gets result fast!

100. The multi-headed decision maker

In your career you'll have to sell yourself and your ideas to little committees. The challenge here is to see the situation from the various points of view of the members. Here's a way of getting many heads to nod at once.

When you go for a promotion you'll generally encounter at least three individuals. There's the senior manager whom I like to call the decision maker. Working for her is the manager to whom you will actually report, and then there's someone from Human Resources. Each of them reaches a conclusion from a different standpoint. The manager is making sure that they can trust and work with you as well as whether you are up to the job or not. The guy from HR confines himself to advising whether or not you have the skills and experience to do the job well. So what about the decision maker? She is, of course, contributing her experience to her manager; but she is also getting to know you better and deciding if you may be the sort of high flier that she needs.

The cup of coffee close (see next page) is quite fun if they agree to your returning in a few minutes. If everyone looks at you when you come back in they have gone for it. If only the chairman is looking at you and some people are having their own quiet discussion you can be sure you have more work to do or that you have lost.

323

Here's an idea for you...

What can you do in non-interview situations where you have to persuade a number of people to make a decision in your favour? Try the cup of coffee close. If it feels good and the vibrations are positive, offer to leave the group on its own for ten minutes. 'Look it must be difficult for you to make a decision while I'm here, I'll go and have a cup of coffee while you have a chat. I'll pop back in a few minutes.' Either they are going to agree to your suggestion, a buying signal, tell you it's not necessary for you to go, another buying signal, or they are going to say that it is not necessary for you to return and that they will get back to you in due course, probably a warning signal.

Preparing to impress people with different requirements

In your preparation for the interview you need to think of what each party is looking for. First of all take HR. To prepare for them you need to know the rules about grades, training and experience. They also tend to ask some pretty stock questions like 'What would you say were your main strengths and weaknesses?' If you are not familiar with that sort of stuff, check out some of the vast number of books on interview questions and techniques.

It gets trickier when you think about your potential manager. He'll get advice on whether you are up to the job, and anyway his natural leaning is towards the question of trust. Are you being sincere? Can he rely on your loyalty? Are you just using this as a stepping-stone or will you actually do the job for long enough to make a difference? To help him out it's a good idea to ask questions. It's a much better idea to ask him about the job than it is to ask HR about the pay and conditions. I know that's obvious, but lots of people do it. They even ask if they can continue with their current holiday plans, for goodness sake. Do that sort of thing after the interview.

Finally, and probably most difficult, is the decision maker. She has to think you are shaped like a bullet at the same time as the manager is getting the impression that you are going to settle down for two or three years at least. I think the best way to handle this is to make any ambitious noises at the start of the interview. Then talk for the rest of the time as though you know that you will have to stay in the job for a while to get the experience. As long as you have scored the point with the senior person up front, she will ignore what you said later if she chooses to move you on in six months.

> *Defining idea...*
>
> **'A committee is a group of people who individually can do nothing but as a group decide that nothing can be done.'**
>
> Attributed to the American humorist, FRED ALLEN

101. It's a bargain!

Negotiate for everything! Your career will benefit in two ways. Negotiating to reduce your costs and increase your sales is good for performance, and this experience helps you practice for the most important negotiation of them all – your job and salary

You better believe it, everything is negotiable. Negotiating is a part of our lives; we do it all the time. In fact we do it so often we probably don't realise that we *are* doing it.

If you have children you've probably already done some negotiation today. Imagine telling a child that anything at all is non-negotiable. Fat chance. You can learn a lot from watching children negotiate. They have no inhibitions, they are prepared to use the sanctions they have available to them and they are completely devoted to the present with no thought for the future. These are all negotiating skills we lose as we grow up.

Never go into any negotiation to 'see what they are going to say'. Prepare positively. If you're selling, look for reasons why the other person should see that your proposition has value, rather than why you should be allowed to maintain your

price. In this context negative preparation is a disease with commission-based sales people. Try it out. Give a salesperson the authority to offer a 10 per cent discount, and every deal done from that day will have the discount deducted; that's their opening offer.

Prepare all aspects, not just money

Think widely in negotiation. Look for objectives beyond, for example, price. What else could you get from the other party? Now put those objectives into priorities. You will have some objectives that you must achieve, some that you are going to work hard to achieve and some that would be nice to achieve. Now think of the other person's priorities in the same way. In fact think about all aspects of the person with whom you are about to negotiate. The more you understand them, the more likely you are to find a solution they will deem acceptable.

When you negotiate, you use your own flair as well as your company's rules. Managers like people who are entrepreneurial and who know that sometimes they need to walk over the company's normal business processes. Such entrepreneurs are regarded as good, but run the risk of upsetting others who play by the rules. Strike a balance here if you want to impress everyone.

Here's an idea for you...

Ring up an internal department who supplies you with a service and complain about their prices. You are, after all their customer. If they say that the price is company policy, go higher up their organisation. Eventually you will get to someone who can vary prices. It may be tricky to steer such a change through the management accounting systems, but where there's a will there's a way.

Defining idea...

'Nothing is illegal if one hundred well-placed businesspeople decide to do it.'
ANDREW YOUNG, US diplomat

Listening is a key skill at the discussion stage. Look at it this way. If you listen more than you talk in a negotiation it almost certainly means that you know more about the other party than they know about you. This logically leads you to a solution that suits them. You already know the solution that suits you. The opposite of listening in negotiating is interrupting. When you interrupt someone you are telling them to shut up. You are demeaning their arguments and suggesting that they can't say anything useful to take the matter forward. Imagine if you told someone in so many words that nothing they can say is important. That's the message that interrupting gives.

102. Relaxation – what we can learn from the cavemen

There's nothing wrong with stress. We're designed to get stressed. It's how we deal with it that's the problem.

Coping with stress should be simple. My central message to you can be summarised in one sentence. Get stressed – relax.

So why are we facing an epidemic of stress? The answer lies in the way we interpret the word 'relax'. Remember that stress developed in order for us to deal with danger. When faced with something that scares us (more likely nowadays to be a 'to-do' list running into double figures rather than the sabre-toothed tigers that ate our ancestors), we release adrenaline, this in turn causes the release of noradrenaline and cortisol and these three hormones together sharpen our wits, release energy to our muscles and divert resources from one part of the body to the bits where you need it most. Which is why you feel twitchy when you're very stressed and can't sit still. The adrenaline coursing through your body would have been just dandy in helping you cope with the sabre-toothed tiger but is a bit of an overreaction when your boss has caught you booking your holiday on the internet rather than working on the sales report.

Anyway. All those hormones get the job done. But then we come to the little-mentioned other side of the stress equation – 'relaxation'. After fighting off a tiger,

> Here's an idea for you...
>
> **Next time you're waiting in a queue, or for traffic lights to change or for the lift to come, see it as an opportunity for a mini-break. Take some deep breaths, feel the tension flow out of your body and your shoulders drop. People who make an effort to do this report being less stressed in a week.**

or running away from it, our cavemen ancestors would have made their way back to the cave for a little lie down. There wasn't much to do in the caves. Sit quietly, stare at the walls. Maybe draw on them. Rest and recreation, calm and peace, lots of sleep – sometimes for days. Rest is essential to repair and recover from the effect of stress hormones on our organs. That's what we learned to expect over the course of millennia.

But what do we do now after a stressful day? We are likeliest to celebrate with alcohol, a cigarette, coffee (all of which trigger another stress response). Or even worse, after a stressful situation, we throw ourselves straight into another one. This means that our bodies are bathed in stress hormones for far longer than was ever intended.

The body's hormones work in delicate balance. When the three main stress hormones are fired they affect the levels of all the others, notably insulin (which regulates sugar levels and energy) and serotonin (the happy hormone which affects mood and sleep). When they go awry over long periods of time, the results can be disastrous for our health, both mental and physical.

Which is why we start off stressed and end up stressed, fat, unhappy and unhealthy.

The solution is to build relaxation in to your life, hour by hour, day by day.

Five minutes every hour

See your day not as a long purgatory of stress but as lots of small stress responses punctuated with mini-relaxation breaks. As a rough rule, every waking hour should have five minutes of pleasure. So after every hour of working, take a minimum to do something pleasurable – answer an email, stretch your shoulders, have a cup of tea. Can't leave your desk? Spend a few minutes a day dreaming of something that makes you happy.

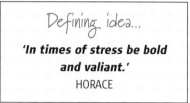

Defining idea...

'In times of stress be bold and valiant.'
HORACE

Fifteen minutes every day

Practise active relaxation – listening to music, yoga, sex, dancing. TV is passive and doesn't count.

Three hours every week

At least three hours every week should be spent doing an activity you love. It should be calming, and non-work orientated. I make it a rule that it only counts as my three hours if I can do it without make-up. In other words, it doesn't count if it involves people that I feel I have to make an effort with. You will have your own way of judging if it is truly relaxing. Be honest. This cannot be an activity that furthers your career, your ambitions, your children's friendships or your perfectionist streak.

103. Achieve the life–work balance in ten minutes

I refuse to call it work–life. It should be life–work. And that's what achieving it entails – a life-work.

Unless of course, you've read this idea.

Just a small point, but have you ever met anyone who felt they've achieved the perfect work–life balance? I've been thinking about it since lunchtime and I'm still struggling to come up with a name.

One of the most pernicious things about stress is the way we don't notice how it switches our attention away from what we value and love in life until it's too late. So here are some clues to work out if stress is stomping all over your life–work balance...

1. Do you feel like your day is spent dealing with difficult people and difficult tasks?

2. Do you feel that those you love don't have a clue what's going on with you and you don't have a clue what's going on with them?

3. Do you regularly make time for activities that nourish your soul?

4. Do you feel you could walk out the door of your house and no one would notice you were gone until the mortgage had to be paid?

Yes, you guessed it? Number 3 was the trick question. Answer yes to that one and you're probably alright. Answer yes to the rest and you could be in trouble.

In a nutshell: make sure you're putting time and effort into the people and activities that make your heart sing and it really is very difficult to buckle under the effect of stress.

> *Here's an idea for you...*
>
> **Designate Saturday 'family' day and Sunday afternoon 'selfish' time. We can usually find an hour or so on Sunday afternoon to spend on ourselves – just don't let it get filled with chores or your partner's agenda.**

But I think too much emphasis is put on the stress caused by the 'work' part of the equation and not enough placed on the stress caused by the 'life' bit. Everyone assumes that all we need is less work, more life and all would be harmonious balance. Hmmm.

Where it has gone all wrong for so many women is that they've cleared enough time for the 'life' part of the equation but not taken into account that it isn't necessarily restful or enjoyable. This is no idle observation. Research shows that men's stress hormones tend to fall when they get home whereas women's stay high after the working day, presumably because they get home to confront a dozen chores and hungry kids. Your children may be the reason you get out of bed in the

Defining idea...

'**The best and safest thing is to keep a balance in your life, acknowledge the great powers around us and in us. If you can do that, and live that way, you are really a wise man.'**
EURIPIDES

morning but you need to accept that spending time with them is not necessarily any less stressful than work – in fact, it often makes work seem like a walk in the park. More time with your kids is not necessarily the answer.

More time with yourself, very probably, is.

That old saw is true – if you don't look after yourself, you can't look after anyone else. And all it takes is just ten minutes a day.

And ten minutes of selfishness every day is enough to make a profound difference in your ability to achieve a life balance that works. Try it.

104. Crisis management

Facing the week from hell? Here's how to survive it.

Don't catastrophise

Dorothy Parker, on hearing a telephone ring, apparently drawled 'What fresh hell is this?' We've all been there. On really busy days with multiple deadlines, I've got to the stage where I'm scared to answer the phone in case it's someone demanding something else of me. Then I made a conscious decision to stop being such a victim. My attitude became 'Why fear the worse until it happens?' Every time a negative thought crosses your brain, cancel it out with a positive one. This takes practice. An easy way to do it is to develop a mantra to suit whatever crisis you're in today and that you say to yourself mindlessly every time your mind goes into tailspin. Right now, I have to pick the kids up from school in half an hour. I have four weeks to my deadline for this book and I have done approximately half the number of words I promised myself I'd write today. My mantra is 'I am serenely gliding towards my deadline and everything will get done' and every time panic hits, I chant this to myself and feel much better.

Master the only question that matters

Here's an idea for you...

Keep a time log of your working week so you finally get a realistic idea of how long it takes you to complete all your usual activities. This means you stop kidding yourself about how quickly you will perform tasks in an imperfect world – where you're interrupted frequently – and you'll reduce your stress levels hugely.

The 'best use' question was taught to me by my first boss and it is invaluable in negotiating your way through any day with dozens of calls on your time. It helps you to prioritise 'on the run', sometimes quite ruthlessly. On the morning of manic days decide what you've got to achieve that day and if anything interrupts, ask yourself 'Is this the best use of my time, right now?' If the answer's no, take a rain-check and come back to it later. So if a friend calls at work, nine times out of ten, you won't chat then, you'll call her back at a more convenient time – unless, of course, she is very upset about something, then talking to her *is* the best use of your time. Nothing else is more important. By doing this, I don't let colleagues sidetrack me with complaints about their lack of stationery, unless of course it's the best use of my time. (No, you're right, so far stationery has never been the best use of my time, but you get the idea.)

Always underpromise

A lot of stress is of our own making. Thomas Leonard, who founded Coach University, the first professional training centre for life coaches, says 'One of the biggest mistakes is to tell people what they want to hear, give them what they think they want, without thinking if it's feasible for you. You overpromise results you can't deliver without a lot of stress. And of course, if you don't deliver, not only are you stressed, *they* are, too.' Leonard's advice is to underpromise rather than overpromise. That way your friends are delighted when you turn up at the party you said you couldn't make and your boss thinks you're wonderful when you get the report finished a day early rather than a week late. Make it your rule from now on to be absolutely realistic about how long it's going to take you to get things done. And until you get expert at this, work out the time you reckon it will take you to complete any task and multiply it by 1.5.

> Defining idea...
>
> **'There cannot be a crisis next week. My schedule is already full.'**
> HENRY KISSINGER

105. Dressing for success

When you're confident and glowing this is a reflection of your state of health and mind.

Poorly turned out says, 'I don't value who I am.'
Confident dressing says, 'I've arrived and am ready to grasp life and opportunities to the full!'

You might think that your skimpy belly-baring top is going to win you that top job and set you on your personal road to riches, but remember that, with the exception of top models, most people look truly terrible in anything that exposes their love handles to full effect. In the majority of cases, love handles should be viewed strictly by appointment only.

Dressing for success is mostly about being wonderfully stylish, without looking boring or frumpy. You can still express your personality, but you also need to take in the sensibilities of who is looking at you. Think of yourself as your own personal marketing manager, with you as the product. I'm sure your mum will have nagged you about many of the ground rules: 'Clean face, clean hands and don't forget to brush your hair!'

Good tailoring

Good tailoring is everything, even if you have only a couple of good things in your wardrobe. Top them up with cheaper items that you can get away with. For example, there's no point in spending a fortune on sweaters, T-shirts and everyday trousers and skirts. There are plenty of great and cheap places to shop and you can even visit eBay (www.ebay.co.uk) and try to get designer clothes or high street stuff cheaply.

The other top rule is to make sure that you have great shoes. And polished ones at that! It's an old cliché but you are judged by the shoes you wear so anything too wacky and people might think you have a weird shoe fetish (fine if you do and you don't care who knows it of course). Make sure your handbag is a good quality one and not overstuffed. Also, have a pen and a notebook somewhere near the top otherwise when you're out to impress you might end up spending half an hour burrowing around looking for one and your success quota will plummet by 100 points. Sort through your handbag at least once a week as it's surprising how much we can manage to accumulate. I once found myself carrying a harmonica and a book called *Absolute Beginners: Harmonica* in my bag for a whole week. Hardly useful everyday items!

Your hands are important, so make sure that your nails are well cared for. Treat yourself to a manicure once a month if you can afford it, but at the very least, short, clean nails are a must. Just a word about make-up – don't overdo it! When you're

Here's an idea for you...

Get help! Most department stores have personal shoppers who will take you around the store for free. Don't feel embarrassed if your budget is small or if you're only interested in one or two items to build outfits around. That's what they're there for.

Defining idea....

'Less is more.'
LUDWIG MIES VAN DER ROHE

running out of inspiration, approach the make-up counter at your local department store and they'll give you a new look for free. My personal favourite is the Aveda (www.aveda.com) counter as they're good at giving customers a natural look rather than leaving them with a ginger tan.

If you don't know what suits you in terms of colours, you could locate your local rep for Color Me Beautiful (www.colormebeautiful.com or www.cmb.co.uk). You don't have to follow all their suggestions, but having a vague idea of what suits you might prevent you from making expensive mistakes.

It's worth buying one or two really good pairs of beautifully cut trousers. My personal favourite for trousers is DAKS (www.daks.com) who know a thing or two about cutting for the fuller bottom. Don't be tempted to buy a cheap suit. You should have at least one suit that makes you feel great and that you're proud of. Anything of good quality that makes you feel good is fine, just so long as it isn't shiny.

106. Design your life to work for you

Sometimes it's not the most talented, gifted or exceptional people that reach the top. So, what's stopping us?

Have you ever wondered how boring old Julia got to be company president, yet you're still in the postroom sorting her mail despite the same education, a more charming disposition, more talent at maths and being better looking?

The difference between you and her, my friend, is the way you think. Julia knew what she wanted and was prepared to go for it. But do you know where you're going or are you simply floating around in a small boat without a rudder on the sea of 'I haven't got a clue'?

Sorting you out

When the famous industrialist Andrew Carnegie set Napoleon Hill the task of finding out what made successful people successful, Napoleon found out a few vital top secrets from all the hundreds of successful people he interviewed. One of these jewels was that you have to be definite in your purpose or you don't get to your destination. Definiteness of purpose is just another way of saying goal setting – know where you're going and make a plan to achieve it! In the great man's own words: 'We live in a world of overabundance and everything the heart could desire, with nothing standing between us and our desires, excepting lack of a definite purpose.'

Most people will have heard the story about the Harvard University Class of 1954 where they measured those who had set goals against those who had failed to. Those that had set goals ended up much richer, far happier and with more free time.

Go and get a pen and paper right now and start listing the things you want to do or have. You must be specific when you write down your goals. If, for example, you want a car, then specify what type of car you want or you might end up with an old banger (if that's what you do want, then be my guest). Next, set a time when you want to have achieved each thing by and, finally, make a plan of how you might achieve this. This is natural territory for a life coach – it's powerful stuff but only if you get it off the page and start doing it folks! Having someone to spur you along is a great way of ensuring that goals are ticked off.

Here's an idea for you...

If a goal appears to be too big and intimidating to tackle, resist the temptation to run away and hide and instead try to break it into bite-sized chunks. First look at the whole huge scary dream and do a five-year vision, based on where you dream of being. Do you see yourself in that corner office on Wall Street or relaxing on the beach with your two kids? If you fancy the latter, you'd better get yourself into gear and start earning more money. Ask yourself what you need to do to achieve that. Can you earn more in your present job? Do you need to change jobs? Should you start your own company? Once you've figured out what you need to do to achieve your big goal, list just one thing you could do today to get there, however small.

Visualisation is a powerful way to reinforce goals and it can sometimes produce some astounding results. Many years ago, I was between apartments and wanted somewhere big in a great, central location, with very little rent to pay. Highly unlikely! However, the next day a friend of mine left a message asking whether I knew anyone who wanted to look after a two-bedroom flat right in the part of town I'd had my mind on. I paid very little for it too.

Defining idea...

'What the mind of man can conceive and believe it can achieve.'
NAPOLEON HILL

107. Effortless balance

If you feel you're working your life away, take stock of your life and do things differently.

Life's usual rigmarole involves getting up and dressed, walking to the bus stop, battling through the crowds, working and then reversing the process. Then it's bed at 9.30 p.m. sharp or you're too tired to function properly the next day.

And what is it all for? To be trapped on the mortgage wheel like a hamster? Let's design you a new life.

Make that wheel work for you

Talking of wheels, a great tool to use in starting to create a life of balance is a 'wheel of life' in order to score your life up and see where you might be out of whack. Get a large sheet of paper and draw a big circle. It doesn't have to be too perfect – apparently, a perfect circle is the first sign of madness! Divide the circle up into eight to twelve sections, like the spokes of a wheel. Allot each section an area of your life such as Relationships, Careers, Social, Health, Spiritual, Family, Dreams, Experiences, Aspirations, Leisure & Recreation, Self-development & Education, Attitude and Financial. Choose the ones that grab you! Give the sections a score out of 10 by assuming that 10 is perfect and lies on the outside of the circle and that 0 is a miserably low score and lies in the middle of the circle. (By the way, a great site to find out more about goal setting is www.mindstore.com.) Next join up the dots and your wheel of life should then have an amoeba-shaped splodge in the middle of it. You should now be able to see where your life is out of balance.

Take two or three of the low scorers off and start setting some goals in those areas. However, before you start setting goals, visualise the big picture first and decide where you're heading. What would be the ideal? Working in a farmhouse in the south of France from your laptop? Next, start making a list of goals on your path to achieving this big dream, even if it's only one small goal at a time. Do one thing a day towards your dreams. For example, if the dream was to go and live in France, do your research and get a brochure about houses in the south of France, and use the web to find out about job opportunities out there. You might find out in doing all this that your goals change and evolve but at least you'll know that you've looked into them before rejecting them. The aim of the game is to have no regrets on arrival at the Pearly Gates.

Here's an idea for you...

Designing your dream plan will require a lot of time and thought so book a few days off work to take stock of things. If possible, go somewhere nurturing and restful. If you go on a long walk by the beach (or wherever), then take a pen and paper to take notes. If you have a partner, involve them in your 'Get a life' mini-break and establish whether you share the same dreams. For example, you might have visions of living in New York whereas he wants to be near his parents in England. So, keep your other half fully immersed in this exciting journey.

Defining idea...

'Things do not change; we change.'
HENRY DAVID THOREAU

Before you start anything, however, do your integrity list. An integrity list is really a deck-clearing exercise. Make a list of the day-to-day things that affect your life such as your environment, your health, your emotions, your finances and your personal relationships. Within these sections, make a list of all the outstanding areas that you haven't given attention to and make a timescale to resolve them. For example, do you save 10% of your earnings? Have you made a will? Are you in credit? Have you found a way to get out of debt and made a plan for it? Once you've started through this list and cleared all those annoying areas that hold you back, you're ready to carry out your *big* dream plan.

108. Working your purpose out

My particular purpose in life is lifting your game. What's yours?

You get out of bed, put the cereal in the toaster and the milk on the toast, and pat your husband and kiss the dog as you leave for work. You have a dark suspicion lurking deep within you. Is this it? Is this all I can expect?

You don't have to be a slave to your job. But knowing what you don't want to do is the easy part of the equation. The tough bit is deciding just what would make you happy. Working with a life coach is a great way to force yourself to face these big questions head on.

Coaching is a relatively new concept that has exploded into quite a movement over the last five years, to the point where in certain circles everyone who is anyone is working with a coach. Coaching shouldn't be confused with mentoring. A mentor is someone who is, for example, a leader in your field that will tell you how to avoid pitfalls and to avoid making the same mistakes as they did. A coach, on the other hand, doesn't 'tell' you to do anything. Coaching works by asking you the right questions so that you can find the answer yourself. As the saying goes, 'Give a man a fish he eats for a day but teach him how to fish and you feed him for life.' There's no point in a coach telling you what to do unless you want to live the coach's life

Here's an idea for you...

Ask yourself what you really enjoy doing, and then think about ways to make this activity more central to your life. See how the professionals do this at www.laurabermanfortgang.com and at www.fionaharrold.com.

and not your own. Coaching isn't a counselling process either. It assumes that you're healthy in mind and ready to move on from your past and into your future.

You might think that you have lots of friends who could do the same job as a coach but for free, but remember that all of your friends have a vested interest in keeping you just where you are now. They won't usually want you to move on as they like you just the way you are, plus you might show them up for being stuck where they are. Imagine that you tell your best mate that you're considering starting a new life in Spain. 'Oh', she says, 'I heard a story once about someone moving to Spain that would make your hair curl...' And before you know it you've retreated under your own personal rain cloud.

Laura Berman Fortgang, a coach from the US, talks about finding your essence. Finding your essence means finding a nugget of passion in you that might grow into an ingot of gold. Laura was an actress desperately seeking success. The essence she mined, which ultimately led her to be a professional life coach, was that she loved getting up and performing (which she does now in coaching). Also, she loved understanding people and their motivation (again, she now does this in coaching). Although she wasn't successful as an actress, she found that coaching had many similar roots to acting.

Your clues to your future are in your past. My brother was lucky to find his essence early on. He loved aeroplanes as a kid and would always be scouring the skies identifying types. He was passionate about making model planes from kits and my dad encouraged him all the way. My brother went on to become the aviation editor for a huge specialist magazine and is now a novelist writing about the obvious. You guessed it, planes. Look for your essence in the hobbies and activities that you do in your free time and especially in the careers that you abandoned for being impractical. Start putting together a list of all your passions and establish why you're so enthusiastic about them. Let's say you loved catching bugs and putting them in matchboxes as a child. What turned you on? Was it being outside? Was it collecting something? Was it the intellectual discipline of collecting bugs of one species? Keep digging until you find that nugget. Don't abandon your dream to play a small game. Play a huge game instead. What have you got to lose?

> *Defining* idea...
>
> **'Our deepest fear isn't that we are inadequate. Our deepest fear is that we are powerful beyond measure. It is our light, not our darkness that frightens us.'**
> NELSON MANDELA,
> 1994 inaugural speech

109. Finding work to make your heart sing

What do you do if your job is dragging you down?

It's really, really hard to feel energised when five days out of seven are dedicated to an activity that bores you stupid – or worse, saps your self-esteem. Yup, we're talking about work.

At any one time, forty per cent of us are looking for a new job. If you're one of them, the chances are that your present job is sapping your strength.

Do you basically love your job but need to move on for promotion, more money or simply for a change? Then terrific. It's just a matter of time, sending out enough good quality CVs and brushing up on your interview technique.

But this idea is for those people who know at heart that they are on the wrong track; that changing job may give a temporary fillip to their mood, offer new challenges and a change of environment, but really, deep down, it is going to be more of the same. You're the people who haven't yet found your dream job. You're the ones who fantasise about winning the lottery because it's the only way off the treadmill.

To find work that will energise, excite and stimulate you, you will have to do some soul-searching and perhaps face some hard decisions. Use the five words, often called 'the journalist's best friends', that are the start of any investigation – namely, when, what, why, how and where.

1   When do you lose yourself? Think back to the last time you were so completely engrossed in what you were doing that you didn't notice time passing. Were you painting a room, listening to your friend talk, dancing at a wedding, decorating a cake? Were you driving, shopping, helping your child with their homework, volunteering for your local charity? Write it down. Try to remember a few more occasions. It might help to remember what you used to love as a child. Did you love to wander about the garden examining flowers and rocks? Were you always at the swimming pool? Did you prefer to be alone, or hang out with friends? Search for your passion. Seek out your joy. Look at your list, and mull on it.

2   What do you dream about? Another version of step 1 is to think about what you'd do if you won the lottery and didn't have to work anymore. How would you choose to spend your time? Any clues there?

Here's an idea for you...

Phone a friend – or three. You almost certainly know people who have transferred skills and started working in another career. Pick their brains on how they financed it, got their family onside, garnered the qualifications, coped with problems. Those who have pursued their happiness are going to have more practical advice, on coping with the good and bad, as well as more enthusiasm, than those who haven't taken a similar leap.

3 Why are you scared? Ask why you're not fulfilling your dream. At the root of it will almost certainly be fear. That could be fear of telling your spouse you want to give up your lucrative job to become a windsurf instructor or it could be the fear that giving up a profession into which you've invested a lot of time makes you look a fool. The longer you've studied or worked at a profession, the harder it is to give it up. Think of it this way: you're not giving up, you're transferring skills; you're not wiping years off your CV, you are using past skills to find a parallel career that gives you satisfaction.

4 How much value can you add? It may take a while. In the meantime, try putting your most into the job you've got. Bringing a good attitude to work will almost certainly result in you doing well because most people simply don't – their work is mediocre – and that makes it easy to shine if you put in some effort. Being enthusiastic will energise you.

5 Where are the soulmates? Go back to your step 1 list. While you're looking, or retraining for your dream job, include more of what makes you happy in your life. Pursuing what makes you happy means you'll meet other people who share your interests, and who knows where that will take you? Listen to your instincts. While I was listening to a casual business acquaintance describe the re-training she wanted to pursue, the thought popped into my head: 'I should do that'. Two years later, I did.

110. It takes two to tango

Networking is a two-way street – you have to give to get. Are you a devil of a networker or on the side of the angels? Take our quiz and find out.

Choose answer a), b) or c) for each of the following questions. There are no right or wrong answers – just choose the one that comes closest to your own instinctive response. The results will tell you more about your attitude to networking.

1. When you leave the office at the end of the day, are you most likely to:
   a) say 'good-night' and head off home;
   b) wait for that colleague who lives near you so you can travel home together; or
   c) troop out with the crowd and head round to the local pub for a drink with them?

2. You bump into a co-worker you've had disagreements with in the past. Do you:
   a) take a deep breath, go over to her and make light conversation – perhaps you can be friends, after all;
   b) remind her why you're not talking to her; or
   c) look past her as though you haven't noticed?

3. Your 'ex' tries to contact you via your Facebook entry and asks you to give him a call. Do you:
   a) invite him to Sunday lunch to meet the family;
   b) reply that you really must get together again sometime, while resolving never to be available; or

    c) explain politely but firmly that your relationship was in the past, that you have moved on and hope that he has, too?

4. A friend of a friend asks you to meet her for a drink after work. She wants to pick your brains about opportunities to work in your sector. Do you:
    a) agree to meet but warn her you only have half-an-hour;
    b) say you don't have time to meet but you're happy to have a chat on the phone; or
    c) suggest she sends her CV to your HR department if she's looking for a new job?

5. You arrive at the office Christmas party. Do you:
    a) start talking to other people who are just arriving and join them on the way in;
    b) head straight to the free bar and stay there all evening; or
    c) head off in search of your closest colleagues so you know you'll have fun?

6. Your boss asks you to be his 'friend' on a social networking website. Do you:
    a) agree to give him access to a new page with limited details that you set up specifically for work colleagues;
    b) agree happily to his request, on the basis that there is no distinction between work and play when it comes to social networking;
    c) explain to him that you no longer use social networking sites because they eat into working time.

Scoring

Questions 1, 3 and 5: For every reply a) that you gave, score 1 point; for every reply b), score 3 points; and for every reply c), score 5 points.

Questions 2, 4 and 6: For every reply a) you gave, score 5 points; for every reply b), score 3 points; and for every reply c), score 1 point.

Defining idea...

After first confidences between people moving towards friendship, a rest between exchanges of information somehow hastens, not impedes, the growing trust.
CANDIA MCWILLIAM, Scottish author

The verdict

If you scored 25 or more, you're on the side of the angels and in tune with the true spirit of networking. You understand that it's about forming relationships of trust and mutual support. But you are no soft touch – you have understood that a commitment to mutual support does not mean that you spend time on hopeless cases or lost causes.

If you scored 10–24, your experience of networking seems to have been disappointing. Perhaps you've found that others have let you down or are unwilling to go to any trouble to help you. If so, bad luck. Try lowering your expectations. Just look out for people you get on with and with whom you can have a good relationship; don't just go for those who seem most influential.

If you scored less than 10, you may be a bit of a devil but at least you're honest! You're inclined to disregard the value of networking – it's simply not worth the bother. The very idea of soulmate support probably leaves you muttering about 'do-gooders'. I wouldn't like to be around the next time someone tells you 'life is about give and take'.

111.Soft sell

You don't have to be a pushy salesperson to network successfully but it helps if you like to talk, listen and present yourself well.

Here are some sure-fire ways to market yourself to best advantage.

There is more than one way to sell yourself in a networking situation. You do not have to try to be like that stereotypical, pushy and ambitious salesperson you see in the movies. However, it helps if you like talking to people. And you do need to believe in what you're doing if you want to influence them. If you are not excited about it, why should anyone else be?

You are your number one customer

Of course, there's one person who has to be wholeheartedly convinced that you're worth backing before you try to persuade anybody else – and that's you. If you are less than 100% convinced, people will pick up on your doubts and will be less than convinced themselves.

Tell your story. Show your passion for what you are doing. Give people something to connect with and if it chimes with their own experience they will engage with you. It's your energy and enthusiasm that will carry them along with you and spark their interest in working with you or buying your product or service.

Look the part

Dress as if you are already on the same team as your networking contacts. People relax when they are among their peers and are more likely to open up to someone who is reassuringly like them. If in doubt, opt for a smart outfit. Being female can be an advantage – you can dress to impress so that you stand out against the hordes of men in suits.

Listen to what they want

Ask them what they are currently working on themselves. Show your interest by listening attentively and asking questions that show you understand what they are telling you. When you see the chance, ask questions that allow them to open up on their favourite subject, which in most cases will be themselves. Have some questions ready for a suitable occasion.

Here's an idea for you...

Anticipate people's objections. Think about the reasons that people will be negative about you, your product or your service. Think of all the problems you would face working on a project with someone and how you would overcome them together. Then you will be able to deal with people's objections as your probing questions unearth them. What's more you will feel confident and able to talk with complete conviction.

- ❀ 'How did you get into this type of work?' This invites them to share their story with you, so listen attentively.
- ❀ 'What do you like best about what you do?' This allows them to give a positive response and feel good about themselves.
- ❀ 'In what way are you and your business different from the competition?' This is an open invitation to brag.

357

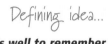

Defining idea...

It is well to remember that the entire population of the universe, with one trifling exception, is composed of others.

ANDREW J. HOLMES, American physician and author of *Wisdom in Small Doses*

❖ 'What's happening in your sector?' This positions them as an expert in their line of business and makes them feel important. You might learn what skills or products will be needed in the future, which might give you a hook for your discussion.

One step at a time

Ask them where they are with their plans and where they want to get to next, such as the next stage on a project or major milestone with a business venture. Listen for any sign that they are looking for help and any buying signal that hints that they would be interested in your help.

Explore their current needs or future plans with them. If you think you can help, make suggestions for how you could work with them to achieve their plans. Focus in on the benefits that working with you or your company will bring them, such as doing things faster, better or cheaper.

Above all, show your enthusiasm for whatever project you're talking about. You have to believe in its value – they won't buy into your story unless you do. Make the running until they start to see the benefits of your proposition, which will spark their imagination and allow you to work jointly to identify the next steps. Logic alone is not enough – work on a blend of reason and emotion.

112. The hallelujah chorus

Don't fancy blowing your own trumpet? Then recruit someone else to sing your praises. Your progress will benefit from a chorus of approval.

Many people are uncomfortable talking about themselves and their achievements. They see any attempt to promote themselves as pushy and vulgar. They believe that their careers should be an apparently effortless progression; a just reward for talent and hard work.

As a blueprint for success, that leaves a lot to chance. For most people, being good at what they do is not enough – they need every advantage to climb the career ladder, including their own PR. Despite this, they still can't bring themselves to push themselves forward.

If it goes against the grain to shout your own worth, you could think about finding help from a professional career coach who can work with you on presenting yourself; or from one of your networking buddies who is a whiz at branding and self-promotion. Ideally, find someone with good contacts in your sector, with an ear to the ground for what's happening and who is recruiting currently.

Here's an idea for you...

Be public spirited. Doing something on top of your work or home life can help you stand out from the competition. Join a public body or become a school governor. The bonus is that public bodies have to be accountable – they have to publish information about their activities and membership. This means that someone doing an online search for background information on you will come across your name in relation to your public duties, which could give you an edge in career situations.

A recommendation carries more weight

Finding people to say nice things about you scores highly, too. What's more, you don't have to spend so much time on your own PR and you can concentrate on your work. A third party's recommendation always seems to carry greater weight than your own efforts. It's a truism that you are more likely to believe something you read in an article in the paper than in the advert alongside it. Similarly, companies looking for staff or clubs looking for members all attach a lot of credibility to other people's recommendations.

The best way to be spotted for a new job is by someone else putting your name forward. While there's nothing to stop you cold-calling an agency or headhunter, it's better by far if someone recommends you. One experienced headhunter explains: 'The bulk of what we do is sourcing. This is where we call people and ask them who they recommend. We keep a large network of informants and we cross-check all the information they supply.'

Tune up the orchestra

Of course, people will only mention your name in glowing terms if they know you are good at what you do. They'll be even more inclined to oblige if they know they can rely on you to do the same for them in similar circumstances.

It's up to you to earn a reputation among your colleagues through your ability and hard work. Then you have to keep everybody up to date on your progress and achievements. Each time you have something to report, such as when you are promoted or complete a successful project, send a customised letter or email message with the good news to each one of your network buddies. Don't overlook friends and acquaintances you have built up over the years – scour those school yearbooks, address books and party invitations for their names.

> *Defining idea...*
>
> **Never look down on anybody unless you're helping him up.**
> JESSE JACKSON, American politician

Turn up the volume

In fields such as writing, sport and showbiz it's customary to have an agent – a good one is worth their weight in gold when it comes to securing a good contract. But whatever your sector, you can probably think of people who would help if only they knew of your ambitions (e.g. satisfied customers who would give you a testimonial to post on your website; or a supplier of products that are complementary to your company's who would pass on sales leads for a commission). You can do something similar outside work, with support from friends, relatives and other people who know you well, such as team mates from your sports club. Sometimes, all it takes is to sit down together to discuss the benefits and spell out any incentive. If you can agree on something that suits you both, suddenly there's a multiplier effect on your own efforts.

113. Someone to watch over me

Look for a mentor or appoint a life-coach to help you achieve your dreams.

Mentoring is a very powerful tool that gives you feedback on your ideas and personal advice on where you're going with your career.

Do you remember a teacher who inspired you at school or college; someone who helped you out when you were struggling with a particularly knotty academic problem or even gave you some advice about your love life?

If you do, then you know what it is to be mentored. We all need someone in our corner from time to time, so we come out for the next round encouraged that we're on the right track or patched up and equipped with some fresh tactics.

Mentoring is a very powerful tool – four out of five successful candidates for promotion have had mentoring from a member of their company's senior management team. A mentor will usually give you feedback on your ideas and – if they know you well enough – personal advice on where you're going with your career.

Young people can no longer count on this kind of advice, which extended family networks used to provide. Women, particularly working mothers, need advice on how to juggle their time without hampering their progress at work. Talk to successful entrepreneurs and you almost always find there's at least one important figure in their lives who has shown belief in their ability.

On the ranch

You can usually find yourself some mentoring in a large company, if you look for it. Certain people will stand out as having a little more experience or knowledge and seem willing to find a bit of time for you now and again. Grab them before someone else does because potential mentors can make all the difference to your career.

The relationship is something like a friendship with a bonus. You can draw on your mentor's experience and understanding of your situation to step back from the daily grind and think about your options. Sometimes you may find it easier if your mentor is slightly outside your own patch at work – for instance, you can enjoy a franker exchange if your mentor knows your boss but has a different reporting line.

Horses for courses

Surprisingly, money rarely changes hands for something so useful. If the mentoring takes place between people who work for the same employer, the mentor is usually happy to give advice for free on company time or over a drink after work.

Here's an idea for you...

If you work for yourself or just want some incognito advice, e-mentoring may be the answer. There are a number of services on the web you can sign up to. It is rather like online dating, only you post your individual business issues and wait for a response from mentors who think they can help. Because both parties remain anonymous, secrets remain secret and if you don't hit it off you can move on without any awkwardness.

At the highest levels, some senior managers and captains of industry pay someone to help them improve their performance at work. They may opt for a business coach to work with them on things like motivation and leadership skills. A good coach knows how to ask the right questions and help their clients find their own answers, so they can move forward with their endeavours. Mentors work more from their own experience.

Michele Jobling, who works as a professional mentor, says that she is most definitely a mentor and not a coach. 'A mentor combines business expertise with coaching attributes while coaches tend to come from a psychology background,' she says. She was previously a retail consultant and is herself a former chief executive. 'We are business people,' she adds. 'We have seen the good, the bad and the ugly, so we can help clients.'

Happy mentoring relationships

Trawl carefully through your own personal network to see who might be the right mentor for you. The key to the relationship is that you get on well together – it should be an enjoyable process for both of you when you meet. Once you've found one, do not take them for granted; your mentor is not at your beck and call and is not a psychotherapist. Listen to their advice but take responsibility for your actions yourself.

Green Goddess

Trend-predictors are very clear. Soon there will be no choice — going green will be the only option. Get ahead by making the changes now that will allow you to sleep with a clear conscience and wake to a healthier bank balance.

Green at heart?

It's estimated that we only use regularly about 20% of our possessions – the rest we never really needed in the first place. There's more to going green than recycling your wine bottles (although we're not knocking that). There's a mindset, too. Have you got it?

1. Your local charity shop is somewhere:
- ☐ a. You can't resist making a purchase every time you drop off donations.
- ☐ b. You enjoy finding what you've been looking for and knowing it's been 'pre-loved'.
- ☐ c. You never visit – not your thing.

2. You have converted to low energy light bulbs:
- ☐ a. In some rooms.
- ☐ b. In every room.
- ☐ c. Not quite yet.

3. When you shop, you think about packaging:
- ☐ a. At the check out when you realise you've forgotten your multi-use bags again.
- ☐ b. When you refuse to buy something that's been way overpackaged.
- ☐ c. Not a lot, really.

4. You love:

- ❑ a. Vintage.
- ❑ b. Rediscovering a much loved outfit you'd forgotten about.
- ❑ c. A brand new outfit bought for the price of a pint.

5. You think twice before:

- ❑ a. Using your credit card to buy a pair of shoes.
- ❑ b. Buying a pair of shoes.
- ❑ c. Buying three pairs of shoes at once.

Mostly 'a's.

Like most of us you are trying to move into a green lifestyle but it's hard, hard, hard when there are so many lovely things you want to buy whether you need them or not. Idea 114 will give you support.

Mostly 'b's.

Your green credentials are strong whether you realise it or not. You have grasped the fact that we can't keep consuming at this present rate and need more making do with what we've got. You may not need any more advice but try idea 126 to improve your quality of life.

Mostly 'c's.

You still shop like global warming never happened. Could you start cutting down a little, gently. No? OK read idea 120 – it might inspire you.

114. It's not easy being green

Peas are green. So is peace.

Green living is not just something that fashionable young
things do to get street cred – this is an issue for us all.

Loving our environment is something that seems to be intuitively right – you don't
need a former Vice-President of one of the most shockingly un-green countries on
the planet to tell you that. You can feel it just by sticking your head out of your car in
rush hour traffic. You'll be choking and spluttering in the space of a few minutes and
so is the planet. If I ruled the world, cars would be banned. Jeremy Clarkson would
be a term of abuse. 'Oh you big Jeremy Clarkson!' kids would yell in the playground
whenever someone let in an own goal. Then they'd get told off by their parents for
using obscenities. Any man who positively encourages us to buy more and more gas-
guzzling leviathan cars deserves to have his name turned into a swear word.

In cities there is absolutely no call for cars. Use the brilliant public transport systems
we have. Oops. Forgot, sorry. The public transport system is a bit creaky at times
and it does get regularly, in fact on a daily basis, shocked that loads of people want
to use it during commuter rush hours. This seems to be the exact time that signals
fail or some passenger decides to dive under the train in order for them to
announce that a 'passenger action' has caused the delay. This sounds almost
accusatory as if to say 'Yes, we know that 99% of the time the delays are our fault

Here's an idea for you...

Join greenmetropolis.com – this is the best idea I've come across in ages. You read a paperback, you then enter its ISBN on the site and they sell it for £3.75, giving you three quid and deducting their fee of 75p. You get an email telling you where to send the book second class. You're probably only making about £2 on each book, when you consider postage, but it's much better than clogging up your home with books you won't ever read again.

but this one is one of you lot actually so don't moan at us'. So public transport sucks but the more you use it, the more people there are who can campaign to have it made good and efficient.

While the companies running our public transport sort themselves out you can help by car pooling. Send an email around the office and find out if some of your colleagues live near you. Then share petrol and a ride in together. This will save the planet much of the aforementioned choking. Get your company to introduce a recycling scheme for paper and plastics. There are several awards out there given to companies who introduce green and ethical practices into their businesses. Convince your boss that a shiny new plaque saying how great the company is at saving the planet will be a real draw for customers and suppliers alike.

Remember small things like not leaving TVs and computers on standby and turning off the tap when you brush your teeth. Switching to energy-saving lightbulbs, insulating your loft and installing double-glazing are all ways that you'll not only save energy but also save on your bills. A double win.

Limit the amount of long-haul journeys you make and always off-set your carbon footprint by purchasing some trees to be planted somewhere suitable. Bear in mind that it's pointless signing up to a pine tree type scheme that some cheeky so-and-sos are passing off as good carbon off-setting schemes. What you need is someone who is planting native trees and retaining bio-diversity. Pine trees are the junk food giants of the carbon neutral movement. Check out a scheme like the Earth C.O.S.T. programme or see if there's a scheme in your local area.

Defining idea...

'Whatever befalls the earth, befalls the people of the earth. Man did not weave the web of life; he is merely a strand in it.'

CHIEF SEATTLE, Native American leader

Above all, as you make greener and greener choices, you must remember not to get smug. Nobody likes a smug environmentalist. No earnestness either, please. Just do your bit and try to convince those in your sphere of influence to do their bits but don't start a witch hunt to see which of your mates forgets to wash out yoghurt cartons and put them in the recycling box. That's a surefire way to get your friends muttering about what a right Jeremy Clarkson you are.

115. Once more with feeling

There really isn't any excuse not to recycle. It's easier than ever, and almost the entire contents of your waste bin can have a second, or even third, life.

I know people who still throw almost all their rubbish away, and I always flinch when I see it. Is it so hard to simply separate waste materials and put the good stuff into different containers?

You wouldn't store fresh and frozen food together, keep the toys in with the cutlery or wash lights and darks together, would you?

Or at least, I hope not. So you are already familiar with the principle of sorting. And recycling works in very much the same way: you sort your waste into three or four different categories, and then pass it to be used again.

It really couldn't be simpler. Local authorities across the world are falling over themselves to encourage us to recycle with kerbside collections, recycling centres here, there and everywhere, and civic amenity sites where you can send everything from aerosols to zinc to be reused. In many countries, individual households recycle at least 60% of their waste and there's no reason why everyone can't aim for this, or even more.

The great thing about recycling is that the effects are immediate. Just think. Your old CDs could be made into designer clocks, coasters or even calendars. Unwanted mobile phones can be reconditioned and donated to charity. Drinks cans can be recycled and the money raised used to plant more trees. Plastic bottles can be converted into fleeces and garden furniture. What could be better than knowing that your unwanted junk can genuinely be put to good use? And it declutters at the same time! Even the smallest change in the way we approach the disposal of our waste would make a big difference if universally adopted.

Recycling helps in many ways: we send less rubbish to landfill or incineration, and we save valuable materials and energy. For example, recycling aluminium cans saves 95% of the energy used in making a new can.

The other great thing is that recycling doesn't cost you a penny, and as you become more aware of the amount of waste you generate, you may even become a more efficient householder along the way.

The three Rs — reduce, reuse, recycle

We would all benefit from:
- ✿ reducing the amount of rubbish we create;
- ✿ reusing stuff we normally throw away; and
- ✿ recycling more.

Here's an idea for you...

If you're not quite wedded to the idea of recycling yet, why not try it for one week? In just seven days you will be astonished (and possibly horrified) to see a small mountain of recyclable newspapers, food packaging, bottles, vegetable peelings and lawn cuttings build up. But recycle and your usual bin-bags will shrink to almost nothing!

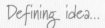

'Garbage is the waste of a throwaway society – ecological societies have never had garbage.'
DR VANDANA SHIVA, campaigner

Reduce

If you opt to buy only the right quantity of what you need, you're not being mean – just eco-savvy.

❀ Choose products with less packaging, and buy second-hand where you can.
❀ Buy more fresh produce or grow your own. This uses less packaging and it's healthy too!
❀ Reduce paper and ink wastage by printing out only what you need, condensing text, reducing print quality and using both sides of paper.
❀ Store food in resealable containers instead of cling film or kitchen foil.
❀ Use rechargeable batteries: although pricier, they will reduce waste and save you money in the long run.
❀ Register with the Mailing Preference Service to stop getting junk mail.

Reuse

Cut down on the amount of rubbish you generate by reusing materials.

❀ Repair broken appliances and shoes or donate them to charity to delay the point where they become waste.
❀ Reuse carrier bags (or better still, buy a durable shopping bag).
❀ Keep scrap paper for telephone messages/lists, etc.
❀ Try to buy products such as milk or cosmetics, that come in refillable packaging. Some specialist retailers such as The Body Shop offer this refill service, as do some delivery services.
❀ Keep worn-out clothing, towels or bed linen to use as household cleaning cloths.

❀ Spruce up old furniture rather than throwing it out.
❀ Choose reusable products over disposable: sponges rather than wipes, tea towels rather than kitchen roll. Opt for cloth nappies, but wash them with an eco-product at a lowish temperature and hang them out rather than tumble dry them.

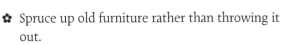

Defining idea...

'Use it up, wear it out, make it do, or do without.'
New England proverb

Recycle

Find out about your neighbourhood's facilities and get going. Recyclable items include: aerosols, batteries, drinks cartons, cans, paper and cardboard, plastic carrier bags/bottles CDs, ink cartridges, computers, some furniture, metal, glass, electrical goods, paint, clothes, textiles, shoes and food packaging.

Other things like toys, household items, bikes, books, bricks and rubble can be sold or given to charity.

❀ Keep separate bins in your house so that you can separate recyclable waste as soon as it's ready.
❀ Start a compost heap. It's simple, cheap and will provide you with free natural fertiliser.
❀ Buy products made from recycled materials whenever possible.
❀ Find out which labels on packaging mean it can be recycled.

116. Clean but green

It's easy to get hooked on the latest domestic products that promise a life of ease and cleanliness, but do you really need them?

Whether you squirt, spray, mousse or wipe, commercial cleaners mean you're adding to the chemical imprint on your home and the environment.

I used to know an elderly lady who kept her coffee cups pristine white with high-strength household bleach. She did in fact live to a ripe old age, but I never felt happy about her cleaning methods and what effect they might be having on her health!

These days there is probably a specialist coffee cup whitener on the market – there is an insatiable demand for 'special' cleaning products. But as fast as these come onto the supermarket shelves, more potentially harmful chemicals appear with them.

It's estimated that fewer than a quarter of the chemicals used in cleaning products have been subjected to a full safety investigation, while others, officially classed as hazardous, are still found as key ingredients.

The overuse of chemical cleaners has also given rise to the so-called 'hygiene hypothesis': sanitation means less exposure to microbes, equals more asthma, allergic disease and multiple sclerosis. Think of the immune system as a noisy, rowdy party, with plenty of bouncers to chuck out unwanted guests. Imagine that if there were no guests the bouncers might turn on each other, which is what happens in these kinds of auto immune diseases.

We don't need to lead a sanitised, germ-free life; we need to be an integrated part of the ecosystem, not eradicate it from our homes!

Softly, softly

Try some of these alternative – and kinder – cleaning materials.

❧ Soda crystals (sodium carbonate), also known as washing soda, used to be the most common household cleaning product. You can use soda crystals for kitchen floors, work surfaces, to clean the draining board, wall tiles and left overnight in the sink they will clear tea stains.

Here's an idea for you...

Make your own household cleaner from less harmful ingredients, which you can buy in large chemists, department stores and hardware shops or even online from eco-suppliers. Mix one teaspoon washing soda, four teaspoons borax and one teaspoon liquid soap or detergent with four cups of hot water in a lidded plastic bottle or old spray container. Shake well to blend and dissolve the minerals. Spray the cleaner onto the surface you're cleaning or apply it with a cloth, wiping it off with a rag as you go. For tougher dirt, leave the mix on for a few minutes before removing. Shake the bottle each time before using. To save time, money and packaging, make your cleaner in advance and buy the ingredients in bulk. Experiment to find a blend that suits you, and maybe add your favourite essential oils or herbs for fragrance.

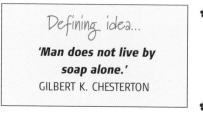

Defining idea...

**'Man does not live by
soap alone.'**
GILBERT K. CHESTERTON

❀ Bicarbonate of soda (baking soda) is also a good cleaner, and if you mix it with water you'll get an alkaline solution that dissolves dirt and grease. Use it dry to lift stains from carpets and marks from surfaces.

❀ Borax is a naturally occurring mineral, soluble in water. It can deodorise, see off mildew and mould, boost the cleaning power of soap or detergent and remove stains.

❀ Cornflour can be used to clean windows, polish furniture, shampoo carpets and rugs, and starch clothes.

❀ Microfibre cloths are made with extra-long fibres that attract dust and remove dirt, cutting down on the need for chemical cleaners.

❀ Olive oil can be used sparingly as furniture polish.

❀ Soap flakes are good for clothes washing and as a general cleaner. Look out for flakes made from natural ingredients that will biodegrade.

❀ Sunlight is a useful free bleach for household linen and all whites.

❀ Tea-tree oil is a strong antiseptic and disinfectant that works on mould and mildew.

❀ White wine vinegar has many uses. It's a surface cleaner, stain remover, limescale descaler, it cuts through grease, deodorises and acts as mild disinfectant. Use half vinegar, half water solution to clean windows, tiles and mirrors.

❀ Lemon juice is good for cleaning chopping boards and wooden surfaces, and can also act as a descaler. Lemon oil makes a good furniture polish.

117. You've got the power

The electricity that powers our homes can be produced by a number of different sources – have you ever thought about where yours comes from?

All utility services are definitely not equal – some are much greener than others!

If every time you switch on a light you feel a pang of guilt, now might be the time to switch your electricity to a 'green' supplier.

When electricity is manufactured conventionally, it produces emissions such as sulphur dioxide and carbon dioxide. These pollutants not only add to global warming but also contribute to acid rain. Electricity produced using renewable energy produces far less environmental damage, and comes from natural resources like water, sun and wind.

Green energy can be loosely defined as energy from renewable or sustainable sources, for instance, wind power, solar energy, biomass energy and hydro power. There are also 'waste to energy' projects where a large proportion of the energy comes from biomass (or plant material), although using waste as a fuel for power generation may not be very sustainable.

Equally, while small scale hydro power is considered renewable, the environmental impacts of large scale hydro make it difficult to exploit in an eco-friendly way.

The information provided by suppliers about these different tariffs is not always transparent and consumers are left confused about their environmental benefits, or even how they add to the renewable energy supplied. At the time of writing there is no scheme in place to verify suppliers' claims about the environmental benefits or 'greenness' of their tariffs.

But just because there is plenty of choice for green electricity it doesn't mean they are all good choices. In fact many of the so-called green electricity offerings do not stand up well to close scrutiny. For example, less money than you might expect is being spent directly on generating extra power from renewable sources on top of that already legally required of the energy firms.

As a result, consumers may not be making the positive contribution they had hoped for. Friends of the Earth has come to a similar conclusion, leading it to withdraw its online rating system for green energy suppliers.

Here's an idea for you...

Getting bogged down by all the confusing deals and information put out by different utility suppliers? You can save yourself a lot of legwork by getting online and accessing one of the websites such as www.uswitch.com that help you switch supplier without having to lift a finger yourself. You can then opt for a supplier that prioritises environmental concerns and offers cleaner energy. The switching service will arrange the transfer free of charge, including severing the link to your existing company, so you can be getting greener power, water, communications or banking within days.

So, at the moment, opting for a green tariff tends to mean one of three things:

✿ 'Green' source electricity: where an energy supplier will guarantee to buy, from a renewable generator, a percentage of electricity to match every unit of electricity used by the customer.

✿ 'Green' fund: tariffs designed to support the building of new renewable sources of electricity generation, environmental causes or new research and development projects.

✿ Carbon offset: tariffs help reduce or offset the carbon dioxide emissions or carbon footprint.

There is very little consensus when it comes to green energy. The best way to judge a supply offer is to ask whether it is using any extra cost paid by consumers to invest in new renewable electricity sources. And what kind of sources is it using?

You can also think about installing your own off-grid power in your own home, for example by installing a photovoltaic (PV) panel. Or you could buy shares in a locally based renewable energy scheme, such as a community wind or hydro project.

You should also remember that even if you are buying green electricity, it is important not to waste power by being as energy efficient as possible – a kilowatt not used is the cleanest kilowatt of all!

Other ways to green power

An ethical power supplier such as Ebico charges all its customers the same price regardless of how they pay. It uses the income generated by direct debit customers to bring down prices for pre-pay and quarterly consumers. Pre-pay customers will see much lower prices, while direct debit payers will still get competitive prices, plus the knowledge they are helping to improve social justice.

Carbon offsetting

Some energy firms (e.g. Ebico) will help you offset the CO_2 produced by your home – and your whole lifestyle. The scheme is designed to help reduce the impact of your home's annual carbon emissions, and is calculated using your home's energy usage as well as the number of flights and car journeys you make per year.

118. Always read the label

If it comes in a box, can, bottle, packet or canister, it'll have a label to go with it. So get informed on what's inside your day-to-day household products.

Are we living with a toxic timebomb? Who really knows, but you can cut back on household chemicals by learning about the worst offenders.

These days we shake our heads over the daft Elizabethan women who cheerfully sported lead-based make-up, the Romans who were poison-metal mad and the Victorians who advocated smoking for health reasons.

But are 21st century lifestyles any better? Research from bodies such as Greenpeace has found high levels of chemicals in all kinds of common products including children's clothes and toys, household paints, cleaners, computers, carpets, PVC products, cosmetics, shampoos, detergents and air fresheners.

Some chemicals have been linked to cancer, liver and kidney damage and reproductive problems, and children and unborn babies are especially vulnerable. But until every single potentially nasty chemical is analysed, we are all playing the guinea pig in a global chemistry experiment.

Here's an idea for you...

Often the garage is a dumping ground for hazardous materials such as old paints, thinners, adhesives, car oil, methylated spirits and car batteries. Get into the habit of having a regular clear out, and go through each tin or bottle to check exactly what it contains. Ask your local authority for advice on disposing of chemical-based products. Ideally the garage should be completely closed off from the rest of the house, but if connected by a door, always keep it shut and the garage well ventilated to release toxic vehicle emissions and chemical off-gassing.

It's up to you how far you go in avoiding substances – it's almost impossible to be 100% green. But the main thing is to be aware, so at least you have the choice. Get into the habit of reading product labels and swapping those that contain toxic stuff for greener alternatives.

Cosmetics and toiletries

Cosmetics and toiletries can contain a variety of hazardous substances, especially in nail polish, perfumes, hair sprays, household cleaners and deodorisers.

Avoid:
✿ Cosmetics, toiletries and perfumes with synthetic fragrances, usually labelled 'parfum' or 'fragrance' on the ingredients list.
✿ Toothpaste, toothbrushes and mouthwashes containing Triclosan.
✿ Long-term use of permanent hair dyes, especially those warning of allergic reactions.

Household goods

Be wary of the these products:

❂ Teflon and other non-stick pans give off toxic fumes if overheated, so use cast-iron or stainless steel pans.

❂ Tinned foods have a lining that contains Bisphenol-A, suspected to interact with our hormone systems.

❂ Products containing Triclosan: certain plastic chopping-boards, washing-up cloths, sponges, liquids, soaps and disinfectants.

❂ Chemical air fresheners, antibacterials or heavily scented cleaning products are also on the hit list.

> ### Defining idea...
>
> **'Feelings are like chemicals, the more you analyse them the worse they smell.'**
> CHARLES KINGSLEY

Plastics

Try to avoid anything made from soft PVC, which is hard to recycle and may contain phthalates, widespread contaminants in the global environment and known to disrupt the endocrine system. Look out for packaging stamped with 'PVC 3', or in the recycling triangle with the numbers 3.

Polycarbonate plastic (PC) contains bisphenol A, which is a hormone disrupting chemical. Polycarbonate plastics can often be identified by looking on the packaging for 'PC7' or looking inside the recycling triangle for the number 7. Decorating materials

Many household paints give off dangerous fumes as they dry. Most paints are now labelled to tell you how many VOCs (fumes) they give off – look for those marked 'low' or 'minimal' VOC content. Use water-based paints where possible.

Worst culprits

✿ Artificial musks are used in many toiletries and cleaning products, usually described as 'parfum' or 'fragrance' on labels. They are bioaccumulative contaminants in the environment.

✿ Bisphenol A is a hormone disrupting chemical found in some polycarbonate plastic, used for baby feeding bottles, refillable water bottles, food containers, CDs and DVDs and electrical appliances.

✿ Brominated flame retardants (BFRs) are found in plastics, textiles, furniture and electrical appliances, and suspected hormone disrupters.

✿ Parabens are preservatives found in most cosmetics. They have also been found to mimic oestrogen, and have been found in breast cancer tumours. They are known skin and eye irritants, and have also been linked to sperm damage in men.

✿ Phthalates are added to PVC plastics to make them pliable, and to a wide range of cosmetics. They are associated with liver, kidney and testicular damage.

✿ Triclosan is a strong antibacterial used in toothpastes, mouthwashes, soaps, deodorants, dish cloths and chopping boards. There are claims that its widespread use is leading to risks to the environment and human health.

119. If in drought ...

Ever stopped to think about how much water you're wasting? Even if you don't live in a drought-ridden area, it's still prudent to cut back on the amount of H2O that goes down the pan.

Some parts of the planet are becoming near deserts, so we must act now to conserve one of life's most essential and precious elements, water.
Water is something that many of us take for granted, not thinking twice before lazing back in a hot bath at the end of a hard day or carelessly leaving the sprinkler on in the garden.

But recent hot summers have left water restrictions in place worldwide, and few have failed to get the message that water is fast becoming a luxury rather than something we take for granted.

Global water consumption has risen almost tenfold in the last century, and UNESCO has predicted that by 2020 water shortage will be a major worldwide problem, bringing with it disease, malnourishment, crop failure and environmental damage. So each and every one of us needs to take responsibility for the amount of water we consume.

Here's an idea for you...

Think before you flush. Toilets use about 30% of the total water used in a household, and the older your cistern the more water you waste, with the worst offenders flushing away a whopping 13 litres of water each time you pull the handle! (Modern dual-flush toilets use six litres for a full flush and four litres with a 'mini' flush.) If your loo is more than a few years old, install a cistern displacement device, which is basically an inflated plastic bag that sits inside the cistern and displaces about one litre of water every time you flush. It doesn't sound like much, but when you think that the average household flushes up to 5000 times per year, that's an awful lot of water!

Saving water in the kitchen and laundry

✿ One of the easiest ways of saving water in the kitchen/laundry is to install a water-efficient dishwasher and washing machine and ensure that you fill them right up each time.

✿ If you wash by hand, use minimum detergent to cut back on rinsing, and use a plugged sink or a bowl of water.

✿ Use only as much water as you need in kettles or saucepans to cut your electricity costs at the same time.

✿ Flow-controlled aerators for taps are simple devices that you fit into existing tap nozzles, and mix air with water under pressure as it emerges from the tap without affecting the flow rate. They can be bought at most DIY and bathroom stores, are inexpensive and can halve water flow.

✿ Try to capture 'warm-up' water for use on plants, rinsing dishes, washing fruit and vegetables, or other cleaning jobs.

✿ Insulate hot water pipes so that you need to run less water before it heats up. Equally, keep a bottle of drinking water in the refrigerator so you don't need to run the tap until the water is cold enough.

- Don't use a garbage-disposal unit. They use about 30 litres of water per day and send a lot of extra rubbish into the sewers. Compost what you can and bin the rest.

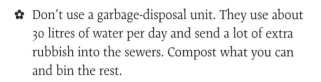

Defining idea...

'The frog does not drink up the pond in which it lives.'
Chinese proverb

Bathroom

- Take showers rather than baths, and keep them short; use a timer if you have a large family. Power showers can use more water than a bath in less than five minutes, though!
- Turn the tap off when brushing your teeth or shaving. A running tap uses about five litres of water per minute.
- Install a water efficient showerhead and toilet cistern.

Outside

- Install a rainwater tank that collects runoff from roofs and gutters for garden use, or ask your local council about getting it connected to the toilet for flushing.
- If you're watering the garden, make sure you only water plants and lawns, not paths, paving and buildings.
- Use a broom or rake to clean outdoor paths and paving instead of hosing them down with water.
- If you have a pool, install a cover to reduce evaporation, and persuade pool users to cut back on over-exuberant splashing.
- Wash your car sparingly, reusing water from inside, or if you don't have to drive too far visit a commercial car wash that recycles wash water.

120. Eco shopping

Ethical shopping – what is it, and how can you do it? The answers are trickling in slower than organic honey.

Local or Fairtrade; organic or free-range; line-caught or netted?
No wonder a trip to the high street gives your conscience a battering. Going eco-shopping means knowing more than just what's on your groceries list.
On the one hand, we're told that we should eat food that is locally produced and not air freighted hundreds of miles; on the other we're under pressure to support producers in far-away developing countries. We're expected to know the difference between organic and free-range foods, stay abreast of flashpoints (palm oil, bluefin tuna, PVC), and only buy goods with certain eco-labels attached.

Confusing? Of course.

Guilt making? You bet.

To me, as the rights and wrongs of living green seem to be shifting faster than the sands in the Sahara, the best starting point is simply to be informed about what you buy. Get to know what's inside the product you're buying; whether it's organic or not; how it is produced, and where; and how it is delivered.

To some extent you have to pick your battles. If your main concern is climate change, then you'll want to know how far your goods have travelled. (Some retailers are now providing point-of-sale freighting information.) If you're worried about chemicals, then you'll go for organic and natural. If you hate the thought of producers getting a raw deal you'll buy Fairtrade. And if you deplore the way that supermarket giants have squeezed supply chains and taken over neighbourhoods then you'll shop at small, local shops instead. One of the main plus-points of 21st century living is that consumers have a choice – so use it wisely.

Here are a few starting tips:

* Only buy what you really need. Make a shopping list and stick to it to ease the temptation of cut-price offers and BOGOFs.
* Cut down on the number of plastic bags you use, bring your own or buy a bag for life.
* Reduce the amount of packaging you use – plastic production uses around 8% of the world's oil supply every year. Buy in bulk or choose loose produce rather than packaged fruit and vegetables.
* Don't waste a car journey – take a friend.

Here's an idea for you...

Try this as an exercise: spend one week shopping only at your neighbourhood's shops and markets, and see how different it makes you feel. Instead of the rushed, anonymous experience of racing round the supermarket aisles with a trolley, enjoy the shopkeeper's personal attention, tried and trusted goods and pride in their stock. Ask to look, feel, taste and smell, too – and leave the car behind if you can or share with a friend. Supermarkets may be cheaper to shop at than local retailers as they can use their mighty buying power, but give the little guys a chance too!

What to look out for

Household products

Many household cleaners, air fresheners, paints,
toiletries and cosmetics contain harmful chemicals
and are manufactured in a wasteful and polluting way.
Opt for eco-friendly goods instead.

Furniture

New furnishings can contain chemicals that release VOCs into the air, so buy
untreated carpets, furniture covers and cushions in natural materials such as wool,
cotton or hessian. If you're buying wood, look out for the FSC logo.

Clothing and textiles

Try to find out how and where your fashion goods are made. Buy organic cotton,
second-hand or from ethical suppliers if you can.

Bottled water

How mad is it to bottle and ship water round the world and pay up to 10,000 times the
price of tap water? Buy bottled water from local sources, or better still use your taps!

Electricals

Buy energy efficient models, and find out about the manufacturer's environmental
policies. Buy models that have an on/off switch rather than a standby-only option.
Greenpeace has a guide to greener mobile phones and PCs. Avoid giant plasma-
screen TVs – they use four times the amount of energy of a normal TV.

Palm oil

Palm oil is very versatile and is used in chocolate bars, ice cream, ready meals, margarine and other products. But as demand for palm oil plantations increases, so does the threat to the habitats and biodiversity of tropical forests. Only buy from members of the Roundtable on Sustainable Palm Oil (RSPO).

Fish

The world's fish stocks are shrinking alarmingly, thanks to over fishing and pollution. Fish such as tuna, swordfish, cod, salmon, halibut and some prawns are all endangered. Check out what's best to buy from the Marine Stewardship Council (www.msc.org).

Meat

Avoid intensively farmed meat – chicken and pork in particular – and buy outdoor reared/free-range and organic when you can.

If this all sounds a bit much, don't worry – just start with one aspect and take it from there. After all, it's better to do something than nothing, so view it as a long term plan and kick off with what fits in best with your lifestyle.

121. Clothes care

By all means stay fresh, but laundering and ironing your clothing with the minimum use of chemicals and energy is the 21st century way to go.

Are you super fussy when it comes to clothes care? If the answer's yes, you could also be using up valuable resources.

We may as well be back in the days when you boiled your whites in a massive pan on the stove – it always surprises me how many people routinely wash their laundry at very high temperatures. What a waste of electricity! It shortens the life of fabric, too.

Modern, highly efficient detergents are designed so you can usually reduce the temperature of your wash to around 30C without compromising on cleanliness, meaning you use a whopping 40% less electricity. You can get away with a shorter wash, too.

Wait until you've got a full load before using your washing machine – using the 'half load' programme does not save you half the energy, water or detergent, and use the economy programme where possible. Combine clothes with the same wash symbol, but if you have to machine wash mixed loads, put them through the most delicate cycle on their labels.

Be kind to your washing machine

Help prolong the life of your washing machine and keep it working efficiently.

✿ Go through all the pockets to check for pens, coins, tissues, etc. – they won't do your machine or wash any favours.
✿ Before loading, shake items out, and load one at a time to reduce tangling, small items first, then large. Don't overfill it.
✿ Clean your washing machine occasionally by clearing out filters and running it empty on a hot cycle with a little white vinegar in the detergent compartment to clear soap deposits.
✿ Buy refill packs of detergents and fabric conditioners. Use correct dosages, don't guess.
✿ Use eco friendly laundry products.

Using a tumble dryer

It's obviously more environmentally friendly to dry laundry outside rather than tumble dry it, but if you must:

✿ Spin dry clothes first unless the label advises not to.
✿ Don't run a tumble drier too long as this wastes energy and over-dries the clothes which makes ironing harder.
✿ Help it work efficiently by leaving plenty of space for clothes to move around.

Here's an idea for you...

Love the idea of never having to buy detergent again? Then suspend your scepticism and give laundry balls a go. These little plastic reusable spheres are used in place of soap, meaning you use less water and less electricity as you bypass the rinse cycle. They work by producing ionised oxygen that naturally activates the water molecules. The balls soften the water so no fabric conditioner is needed and also minimise colour fading. If your clothes are very stained, you can add a little eco-detergent. You can order them online from most green suppliers, and each pack of three should last for 1,000 washes.

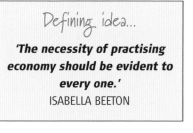

Ironing and drying clothes

❀ Keep ironing to a minimum by hanging up or folding clothes as soon as they come out of the tumble drier.

❀ Iron items that need the coolest setting first, and work up to the hottest setting. Iron in loads, as irons use up a lot of electricity heating up.

❀ Use shiny board covers to reflect heat back onto the clothes and improve efficiency, or place aluminium foil underneath.

Dry cleaning

Dry cleaning has to be one of the most environmentally unsound ways of laundering clothes. The strong smell of chemicals as you step into your local shop is a bit of a giveaway, and the plastic cover and disposable hanger just add to its sins. The solvent used by the vast majority of cleaners is tetrachloroethylene, also known as perchloroethylene, or perc, the latest in a long line of chemicals used to clean delicate textiles.

A number of cleaning firms are now looking for safer alternatives, one being global company GreenEarth, which uses relatively harmless liquid silicon. But if your local dry cleaner is less than green, it's best to simply reduce the amount of 'dry-clean only' clothing you buy. Some items can, with care, be hand washed.

122. Low power dressing

Green is definitely the new black: highly creative eco fashion is flying off the shelves and into wardrobes all over the world.

If it's eco, it's in. More and more fashion brands are jumping on the ethical bandwagon, so there's plenty of choice out there.

If you stand back and examine your wardrobe, you're more likely to be fretting over its shortcomings as a fashion statement than as an eco product.

But behind every garment is a story, and often it's not a good one. Many clothes are made from synthetic materials such as nylon and polyester, which come from highly polluting petrochemicals whose manufacture contributes to climate change. They are also non-biodegradable, which means they are difficult to dispose of. Natural fibres aren't all squeaky clean, either. Cotton uses more pesticide per plant than almost any other crop, causing damage to the environment and the people who farm it. The chemicals used to grow or treat cotton remain in the fabric and are released during the lifetime of the garments so they affect people wearing clothes too.

In many parts of the world, garments are dyed or bleached using chemicals which affect workers and flow into sewers and rivers, damaging local ecosystems.

Virtually all polycotton plus all 'easy care' and 'crease resistant' cotton, are treated with the toxic chemical, formaldehyde.

Here's an idea for you...

Keep tabs on your wardrobe so you don't become a wasteful hoarder. If you haven't worn something for a year, out it should go! But your idea of a designer disaster could be someone else's dress to-die-for, so why not get together with a few friends and host a clothes swap party? If each guest brings along a bag full of wearable but unwanted clothes, chances are between you you'll be able to swap quite a few outfits over a glass of wine or two. Any remaining items can be donated to charity.

But the fashion industry, or parts of it, is one step ahead, and is now turning its attention to producing a new breed of environmentally friendly clothing, or eco fashion. Eco fashion is manufactured using low carbon, non toxic processes, and includes organic clothing, recycled textiles and materials such as plastic drinks bottles. Yes, it does come with a higher price tag, but wouldn't you rather pay a little more knowing that workers aren't being exploited and the planet trashed?

Organics

Organic fashion, where clothes which have been made with a minimum use of chemicals, does the minimum of damage to the environment. For instance, organic cotton is grown without the use of chemical pesticides and insecticides, and organic cotton garments are often also free from chlorine bleaches and synthetic dyes.

Hemp needs few or no agrichemicals to grow, and at the same time it binds and enriches the soil with its deep roots.

Linen is made from flax, another traditional fibre crop which needs few chemical fertilisers, and less pesticide than cotton.

Organic wool is produced using sustainable farming practises and without toxic sheep dips.

Bamboo has recently been developed as a clothing fibre, which is great for eco fashion as it's highly sustainable, and produces clothing that is soft, breathable and fast drying.

Fairtrade and fashion

You can find Fairtrade products by looking out for the logo, which guarantees that that product has been made in line with standards as set out by the Fairtrade Foundation.

Recycling

Take old clothing to charity shops or recycling points, support fashion brands, charity shops and businesses that use second-hand and recycled products or customise your own clothing to extend its life.

Jewellery

Jewellery is not exempt from the ethical minefield, as anyone who has seen the film *Blood Diamond* will know. In fact diamonds have gone from being a girl's best friend to being a downright eco-enemy, linked to arms funding in Africa, child slave labour in India and huge environmental damage. The ethically minded are now only buying certified diamonds, or shunning diamonds in favour of semi precious stones such as agate, jasper, and carnelian. Gold has a tarnished image, too, for similar reasons. Buy from reputable sources, ask to see certification and think about buying recycled precious metals.

123. Your body, your skin

When is natural not natural? When it's a faux 'eco' beauty product that is stuffed full of the usual chemicals.

Pamper yourself by all means, but could your beauty products be doing you – and the planet – more harm than good?

Like many other industries, the world of beauty is undergoing something of a revolution, with manufacturers racing to get new organic or 'ethical' products onto the shelves as fast as they can. Greater consumer savvy about ingredients and sourcing has driven some brands to rethink their whole ethos right down to the packaging they come in and their involvement with the communities they source from.

And perhaps it's just as well.

The average Western bathroom cabinet is a veritable pharmacopoeia of shampoo, soap, mouthwash, toothpaste, shaving gels and hygiene products. These products contain a wide variety of chemical substances, the safety of which remains questionable. There are over 1000 chemicals currently available to manufacturers of cosmetics and toiletries suspected to have harmful effects. Some of these survive the journey through sewage works into the sea.

Our skin soaks up 60% of what we put on it, which ultimately can end up travelling throughout our entire systems. The term 'natural' is now highly dubious – a

product has to have only 1% natural ingredients to earn this moniker!

There are a number of genuinely natural products on the market. The best ones will provide a list of ingredients, and most of these ingredients will have familiar names. (Natural soaps, for instance, will contain coconut, corn, soy or olive oil.)

Look out for the word 'organic' instead, and especially for logos such as the Soil Association's, which will guarantee 95% organic contents.

There are other ways to be ethical. Take a look at the way the manufacturer runs its company. Aside from what it puts into its products, it should have a responsible attitude towards the environment. Ask about company policies on chemical usage, recycling, employment, and health and safety. Support companies whose policies you agree with.

Some of the best companies run initiatives in developing countries, too, although that doesn't necessarily mean that their products don't still contain chemicals such preservatives. (For instance, Body Shop products are based on ingredients from natural sources wherever possible, but may contain synthetic chemicals where they are needed, e.g. for safety, or where no suitable natural alternatives exist.) Body Shop sources cocoa butter for

Here's an idea for you...

If you have a hoard of old cosmetics and toiletries lurking in your make-up bag, chuck them out! Changing legislation is slowly nudging out the most harmful chemicals (although many remain), but the older a product the more likely it is to contain potentially damaging substances that can be absorbed through the skin. Look out especially for synthetic fragrances or musks, dental products containing Triclosan, and permanent hair dyes that carry warnings of possible allergic reactions. Switch to natural products, for example the WWF's range of gentle toiletries and cosmetics, that have the added benefit of not being tested on animals or containing animal materials.

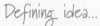

its moisturisers from the Kuapa Kokoo co-operative in Ghana. As well as its non-animal testing policy, the Body Shop is committed to environmental protection and has a large community trade strategy.

Aveda, another ethical company, makes use of wind power, which offsets 100% of the electricity used by its main manufacturing facility. Aveda has raised more than $6 million for environmental causes since 1999 through its Earth Month campaigns.

Other things you can do

✿ Wear less make-up! Try having a day without make-up and see whether people even notice.

✿ Buy cosmetic and beauty products which are simply formulated and as ecologically sound as possible.

✿ Try to avoid synthetic fragrances and perfumes, and opt for diluted essential oils instead.

✿ Don't believe all the hype – watch out for 'greenwash' (bogus or inflated environmental claims) and pseudoscientific claims. Words like 'natural', 'environmentally sound' or 'safe' often can't be substantiated. Read the small print first, and look out for specific information that backs up claims and certification from recognised bodies.

✿ Try to avoid products in unnecessary packaging.

✿ Avoid PVC packaging as it's hard to recycle and toxic to manufacture. PVC is signalled by a recycling triangle with a 3 in the middle of it.

124. Four wheels bad

It's a biggie, but ditching your motor will make you happier, healthier, wealthier and wiser.

If you can't do without your wheels, then at least take action to reduce CO2 emissions.

Cameron Diaz, Leonardo DiCaprio and Thandie Newton all have one thing in common, apart from being famous: they ditched their petrol-guzzling celebmobiles in favour of a low carbon hybrid car, in their case, the Toyota Prius. Other stars, including George Clooney, are going all electric with models such as the Tesla Roadster.

While Hollywood celebs seem to be embracing the new breed of eco cars, the rest of us are rather trailing behind. A hybrid or electric car may be too expensive or not suit our day-to-day needs for various reasons, but there are still things we can look out for when buying a new car.

The most obvious route is to choose the smallest and most fuel-efficient vehicle possible. This will also save money in road tax and other running costs. Look for one with the lowest CO2 emissions of its class and which meets the new Euro IV standard.

Many new car makers are giving plenty of useful information to help you make your choice, such as eco labels that shows its CO2 figure and estimated annual running costs, and possibly even its life cycle assessment, which examines the whole impact of the vehicle from factory to final disposal.

Driving more environmentally friendly vehicles can help reduce emissions, improve people's health and save money.

Manufacturers now produce low-carbon electric, hybrid and dual-fuel vehicles. Some of these low carbon vehicles also have financial benefits such as lower tax, discounts on city congestion charge, cheaper fuel options and lower running and maintenance costs.

Electric vehicles produce no emissions – CO_2 or toxic emissions – but need to be recharged often and can't travel long distances. But they are great in cities, on set routes or for short trips.

Hybrid vehicles switch between petrol (or diesel) and electricity. Because they use far less petrol than traditional vehicles, they produce much lower CO_2 and other emissions. Most big car manufacturers are planning to introduce a hybrid model in the next few years.

LPG vehicles run mainly on LPG (liquid petroleum gas), which produces much lower emissions – about 10% to 15% less CO_2, 75% less carbon monoxide and 85% less hydrocarbons – and is much cheaper than unleaded petrol.

Here's an idea for you...

If you live in a town or city, joining a car club is a brilliant way of cutting down on petrol emissions and will save you loads in running costs as well. You only hire the car when you need it, but this can be by the hour, week, month or longer. Membership gives you access to a pool of cars near your home, which you can book in advance or on the day, and covers road tax, insurance, servicing, maintenance and valeting. Most car clubs are run on very simple lines – you can log in online (or by phone) and reserve your car on the spot. A pin number enables you to drive the car away.

These aren't the only options. More vehicles are being produced that emit less CO_2 and other pollutants. Specialist magazines, websites and Government bodies will have useful comparison data.

> Defining idea...
>
> **'Environmentally friendly cars will soon ... become a necessity.'**
> FUJIO CHO, Toyota Motors

Eco-driving

The way you drive your car also has an impact on the environment. But if you're eco-savvy, emissions and fuel consumption can be reduced by up to 25%.

✿ Drive off straight away rather than leaving the engine to warm up.
✿ When the engine is cold, journeys of less than 2 miles pollute by up to 60% more per mile than a hot engine.
✿ Use higher gears as soon as traffic conditions allow. Minimum emissions happen between 40–60 miles per hour and increase when you drive faster.
✿ Regular maintenance will reduce emissions.
✿ Restarting the engine uses less energy than ten seconds of idling, so switch off if in a long queue.
✿ Hard acceleration and sharp breaking use more fuel as well as being more dangerous.
✿ Plan ahead: choose quiet routes, combine trips and car share.
✿ Don't carry unnecessary weight on the roof or in the boot.
✿ Make sure your tyres are inflated to the right pressure and reduce greenhouse gas emissions by 5%.
✿ Cut back on onboard electrical devices and air conditioning to reduce fuel consumption.

125. Try a low carb diet

We've all got one, and most of us have a bigger one than we ought to. Yes, our carbon footprint is a key indicator of just how green we really are.

So what exactly is this guilt provoking measure, and how can you reduce yours? A couple of years ago few had even heard the phrase 'carbon footprint'. But now we're all fast becoming carbon literate, if not yet neutral.

A carbon footprint is the measure of the total amount of greenhouse gases released into the atmosphere as a result of things we do in our everyday lives such as travel, shopping, washing, even watching TV! Your footprint is made up of two parts: the direct or primary footprint; and the indirect or secondary footprint.

The primary footprint measures our direct emissions of CO_2 from the burning of fossil fuels including domestic energy and transport, e.g. car and plane journeys. The secondary footprint measures indirect CO_2 emissions from the whole lifecycle of products we use from manufacture through to eventual breakdown.

A carbon footprint is measured in tonnes per year, and numerous websites can help you work out yours, such as www.carbonneutral.com and www.carbonfootprint.com.

Given the plight of the planet, if you worked out what might be an acceptable carbon footprint for the entire globe and then divided it by the global population, you might come up with a figure of about one tonne per person.

Oh dear. It goes without saying that in the pampered West our individual carbon footprint is a tad larger. For example, the national average for the UK is around 11 tonnes. The average US carbon footprint is nearly 20 tonnes, while each Chinese person has a footprint of around 3.2 tonnes and the average Indian emits 1 tonne.

It's pretty obvious that the poorer a person is, the less carbon they emit – which doesn't bode well for the future when you consider the rate of economic growth in countries such as China and India!

But everyone can cut their carbon footprint. Although individual actions can't possibly have the impact that reducing aviation fuel use and power station emissions would have, every little helps.

For instance, you could save 2kg of carbon for every journey under three miles where you walk and don't use the car, and 30kg by switching the power off in your house at night.

Here's an idea for you...

Gather together the information you need before you go online to estimate your carbon footprint. You'll need to know how much gas, electricity or other fossil fuels you've used over a year. If you own a car, you'll need to know the mileage and model. Then think back to your holidays, and any regular commutes you do, to roughly work out your year's worth of travel. When you key this information into the calculator it should convert it into a figure that shows your carbon emissions in tonnes per year – your very own dark mark!

How to shrink your primary footprint ...

✿ Don't go by air.
✿ Sign up to a renewable energy provider.
✿ Insulate and install solar water heating.
✿ Use public transport.
✿ Car share.

... and your secondary

Don't buy items that produce high emissions in the manufacture or delivery e.g.:

✿ Bottled water, especially from abroad.
✿ Food and drink from far distances – buy local or grow your own.
✿ Meat, especially red meat.
✿ Clothes from far-off lands.
✿ Highly packaged items.

Carbon offsetting

Carbon offsetting aims to reduce the impact of carbon dioxide emissions from everyday activities such as driving cars, heating homes and flying. A carbon offset provider can calculate the emissions you produce and then pay for them through a donation to a project that reduces carbon by the equivalent amount.

Energy efficiency schemes include installing energy saving devices in houses; renewable energy schemes such as wind farms; or tree-planting schemes that can take carbon dioxide out of the atmosphere.

However, carbon offsetting is not the panacea we'd all like. There is tendency to think that you can simply buy your way out of the problem of rising carbon emissions, and some environmental campaigners are worried that offsetting discourages people from cutting greenhouse gases in the first place.

Still, if you do want to offset – and surely doing something is better than doing nothing – make sure the offset provider conforms to the government's gold standard (www.cdmgoldstandard.org), which adheres to the Kyoto protocol on climate change.

At the time of writing only four companies do: they are Pure (www.puretrust.org.uk); Carbon Offsets (www.carbon-offsets.com); Global Cool (www.global-cool.com) and Equiclimate (www.ebico.co.uk).

Still, offsetting only accounts for a fraction of all emissions produced. Long term we need to radically cut our emissions rather than mitigate them.

126. Mindful eating

What's in your food? Before you push another forkful into your mouth, can you say for sure that there are no nasties lurking in the lettuce or hiding in the hummus?

Here's how to know your enemies.

It seems that with every day's news we hear about more things in our environment that are bad for us – in the air we breathe, the water we drink and most of all in the food we eat.

News reports of alar in apples, GM crops, food irradiation, BSE in beef and dioxins in milk are enough to put you off eating for good. But is it really that bad? Intensive farming methods have been used extensively to maximise production in recent years. This is not because farmers are intrinsically a greedy, profit-focused bunch; it is because it has become increasingly difficult to make a living as a farmer and many businesses – often generations old – have, sadly, failed.

Intensive production relies on the use of herbicides (weedkiller) and pesticides to boost the production of crops. Intensive farming methods are used to increase milk and egg yield, and to promote faster growth of meat animals. Such methods mean that livestock often lives in cramped, stressful conditions. Apart from animal welfare considerations such as the de-beaking of hens to prevent pecking and the docking of tails and trimming of teeth in piglets, cramped conditions make disease more likely to take hold and spread – and this leads to the routine use of antibiotics and other drugs.

Such factors, together with chemicals used to increase shelf life in food, means that we as consumers can end up taking in a cocktail of potentially dangerous chemicals, albeit in small doses, every time we eat a meal. Combined with the pollutants found in our water and air, these chemicals may build up over time and may well have long-term health implications.

Many pesticides and herbicides such as organochlorides (OCs) and organophosphates (OPs) have been linked with the development of diseases and disorders such as cancer, fertility problems, birth defects, immune system deficiencies, nerve damage and ME. And it's not just the chemicals sprayed on the food you actually eat that you need to worry about. As chemicals are sprayed in a fine mist, they travel in the air. This means that they enter the air we breathe, and settle on unsprayed areas. The chemicals are walked into our houses on our feet, and residues may be found on the carpet the family lounges on to watch TV. The chemicals are also leached off into the soil by rain, enter watercourses – and thus also enter our drinking water.

> **Here's an idea for you...**
>
> Find out more about organic producers near you, and if there are any brown box schemes available locally. Don't be afraid to shop around as some are more expensive than others and quality can vary.

Defining idea...

What we don't know can indeed hurt us.

JOSEPH LIEBERMAN, US Senator and campaigner

The chemicals that enter our bodies can stay there in our body fat. The organochloride DDT has been banned for many years (in the US since 1972; in the UK since 1986), but traces are still found in human breast milk, animal milk and in the body fat of Arctic penguins.

And it's not just the dose of pesticide that needs to be considered when we assess danger. The timing of the exposure is crucial. Doses of pesticide seen as safe in a healthy adult will have a different – harsher – effect on more vulnerable people such as babies in the womb, children, teenagers and the elderly.

This all makes frightening reading. What we need to do is to become better informed. We need to read the news reports (even if they scaremonger) and keep up to date with current research into the effects of chemicals on our bodies. Only once we are well informed can we make the choices that affect the health of ourselves and our families.

127. Box clever

Organic box schemes represent quality, locally produced organic food which promotes sustainability and enriches the local economy. It's the ethical ideal.

And you get good value, organic vegetables on your doorstep. Literally.

Veg box, or brown box, schemes were pioneered in the UK by the Soil Association. The idea is simple; people buy organic produce from local producers, fresh from the soil. The scheme helps local producers to find a knowledgeable and consistent market for their crops, which allows them to continue to grow food under organic principles. Under the schemes, the customer knows that food has not been flown or otherwise transported hundreds or thousands of miles before it reaches the kitchen, leaving a large carbon footprint. Food sold as a part of a box scheme also allows consumers to munch happily in the knowledge that their food is fresh. The longer the food is stored, the fewer vitamins it contains – and what's the point of eating fruit and vegetables if they are not brimming with goodness?

Seasonality

In your grandma's era fruit and vegetables arrived in the shops according to season. There was real excitement back then when the summer berries started appearing in the greengrocers' shops. You knew that it was summer, and that afternoons were going to be spent making yourself utterly nauseous with a glut of strawberries. As the fruits faded you knew it was nearly time to go back to school... but the

Here's an idea for you...

Check out box schemes near to your home. In the UK, you can find out by looking at the Soil Association's website. You could also try asking your neighbours, some of whom may already be getting boxes (they could give you useful feedback, too), or type 'organic box scheme' into an Internet search engine. The more local the better; you'll be supporting the local economy as well as cutting down on food miles.

pumpkins would soon appear in the shops, glistening with the promise of Halloween. Today, we can buy strawberries, raspberries, blueberries and a myriad of other soft, all-too-perishable fruits all year round in the supermarkets. The rub is, they don't taste of much (they will likely have been picked when unripe and have ripened in storage) and are incredibly expensive. There is a risk that biodiversity will be decreased as some varieties of fruit and vegetables are found to transport more easily than others, causing localised, more diverse varieties to become 'uneconomic' – at least for the supermarkets. As consumers we end up with less choice and a monoculture of tasteless food stacked up in startlingly uniform displays in the bright, antiseptic supermarket environment.

Organic box schemes, on the other hand, emphasise the seasonality of foods. Over the summer, they may contain peppers, tomatoes and green beans. In the winter, the emphasis is more squarely set on root vegetables – because that is what is in season in your local area. This aspect of box schemes appeal to many people who like to feel the wheel of the year as it turns, keeping rhythm with the seasons. There is also an element of surprise which is fun. Whilst customers are generally encouraged to specify any vegetables they do not like, there are no guarantees about what will appear from week to week – keeping you out of a rut with your cooking. Children, especially, are interested to see the different veggies appearing and may be tempted to try something new when it appears in the weekly box.

Food miles

Ethical consumers worry about food miles, the journey that the food you buy has taken – possibly having flown miles around the world before you pop it into your shopping trolley. Food miles are responsible for a huge amount of pollution. Food transportation and agriculture accounts for 30% of goods transported by road in the UK alone. The CO_2 emissions from food miles are a major contributor to climate change, and that's without the methane production of farmed animals added to the equation (but that's an argument for vegetarianism rather than organics). In the UK, a report by the Department for the Environment, Food and Rural Affairs (Defra) showed that food miles rose by 15% between 1992 and 2002. Air-freighted food is the worst culprit, contributing an amazing thirty-three times more CO_2 than food eaten in the country where it is produced. Perishable fruits and vegetables are also likely to have been treated with pesticides to prevent spoilage of crops in storage.

In contrast, fruit and vegetables bought under a box scheme are likely to have been grown within fifty miles of your home. That means that, if it comes from the supplier, you have cut down dramatically on food miles and thus on pollution. The food's fresh, the food miles are down: it's a win/win situation!

> ## Defining idea...
> *Far from being a quaint throwback to an earlier time, organic agriculture is proving to be a serious contender in modern farming and a more environmentally sustainable system over the long term.*
> DAVID SUZUKI, geneticist and environmental activist

128. Dreadful deodorants

Do you slather your armpits in the hope of avoiding an awful odour? You might want to choose carefully. Find out why conventional deodorant reeks.

Substances applied to your skin are absorbed directly into your bloodstream, so is there anything to worry about?

Newspapers and magazines have been full of reports recently about the possible link between deodorants and breast cancer. There have also been reports that the aluminium in deodorants may contribute to Alzheimer's disease. Are these just scare stories?

People produce between one and two pints of sweat a day. It's amazing, with that statistic, that we don't all stink! The thing is, sweat itself is an odourless liquid; it only begins to smell once bacteria begin to break it down. We sweat to regulate temperature, and to excrete toxins dissolved in liquid from our bodies. Many antiperspirants contain products that block the sweat glands, not allowing this excretion to take place. It has been suggested that fatty breast tissue tends to store toxins (as does all fatty tissue), and that antiperspirants can contribute to this. Other studies have suggested that there may be an increase in breast cancer among women using aluminium-based products because the ingredients actually mimic oestrogen – a known contributory factor in the development of breast cancer. A review published in the Journal of Applied Toxicology has called for further research to evaluate the potential that this could increase the risk of getting breast cancer.

Concerns have also been raised by a study, published in the European Journal of Cancer Prevention, about the fact that the aluminium salts found in antiperspirants and deodorants are applied directly under the arm, adjacent to the breast. If the underarm area is already damaged from shaving, it has been suggested that aluminium may enter the body more readily to affect the lymph nodes nearby.

Here are some ingredients to avoid:

✿ Aluminium chlorohydrate, aluminium zirconium – or any other aluminium compound. Aluminium can be absorbed through the skin and has been linked to Alzheimer's disease as well as breast cancer
✿ Parabens – these are derived from tolulene, which is toxic when inhaled, ingested or in contact with the skin. It may cause reproductive disorders
✿ Triclosan – a skin irritant; may be carcinogenic
✿ Silica – a skin irritant

Here's an idea for you...

Tweak your dietary habits to improve your own smell. It has been claimed that eating a lot of meat is a contributory factor in the development of body odour. Try eating lots of leafy green vegetables, sprouted seeds, nuts and whole grains as an alternative to some of your meat dishes and you'll see a difference. It really works! Alcohol and spicy food don't just give you bad breath; you excrete the smell along with toxins through your skin. Cutting down on these types of food will help to cut the likelihood of B.O., so a trip to the pub followed by a spicy kebab is out, then! Yoghurt can help, as it affects the bacteria within the body, and try a herbal tea – peppermint and sage can help as well.

Defining idea…

Sweat is the cologne of accomplishment.

STEPHANIE PIRO, comic artist

✿ Propylene glycol – absorbed quickly through the skin and enhances penetration of other substances. It's a possible neurotoxin; may cause kidney or liver damage

And now for some gentle alternatives… Well, there are many aluminium-free alternatives to keep you smelling clean and fresh. These work by inhibiting the growth of the bacteria that causes sweat to smell. You can buy a variety of deodorants with ingredients such as lichen, herbal extracts, green tea, aloe vera and essential oils.

The rather literally named Pit-Rok has many devotees. This is a chunk of ammonium alum, a material which has been used cosmetically in Egypt and China for over 2000 years. It works via bacteriostatic action, which means that it inhibits bacterial growth. It allows the excretion of toxins and does not clog pores. You wet the crystal (or use it as you get out of the bath or shower) and rub it in the armpit. It leaves no white marks, doesn't stain clothing and leaves no sticky residue. It's also available as a spray now. Ammonium alum does contain some aluminium, but it is bonded into a molecule that is too large to pass through the skin. Another source of deodorant crystals is Crystal Spring. They really are worth trying, so do some hunting.

129. Green period

With increasing public concern about dioxins in sanitary products, many women are looking for alternatives. How easy is it to find something fitting the 'green' bill which is comfy, secure and convenient?

First on the green agenda is the issue of where all the discarded sanitary towels, tampons and nauseatingly titled panty liners go when they are flushed or discarded. Landfill is increasingly full of them, and they take a l-o-n-g time to biodegrade, with their often plastic backings, and beaches are swamped with them. More than four million tampons and pads are flushed every day in the UK alone, where women buy more than three billion disposable sanitary products every year. A western woman will use around 12,000 tampons or sanitary towels in her lifetime. That's a lot of waste.

Second – but just as important – there's the question of whether the products that we use to mop up our monthlies are actually safe to use. Tampons are usually made from cotton or rayon, and rayon is made from chemically processed wood pulp. Disposable pads and liners are also sometimes made from wood pulp, bleached from natural brown to dazzling white. Until recently, elemental chlorine was used – and this was a source of dioxin which is a known carcinogen. Dioxin builds up cumulatively in the body over time, right from the moment we are born. After campaigns from such groups as the Women's Environmental Network (WEN) manufacturers have moved onto chlorine dioxide or hydrogen peroxide. Think about it though: do these items really need to be white? They are just destined to get messed up anyway. Would it matter if they came out of the packet unbleached?

If we think about the cotton used in the production of sanitary products we meet another dilemma. Cotton production accounts for 10% of the pesticide used in the world today. That means the growers suffer health problems as a result of exposure, and the pesticide is detrimental to wildlife. In addition to this, pesticide residues are found in the cotton produced. Think about this too – your vagina walls are very thin and the mucous membrane remains damp to protect the body from infection. Add a tampon potentially contaminated with pesticide residue and some of that residue may find its way through the damp mucous membrane into the body. There is also, of course, the potential risk from Toxic Shock Syndrome (TSS). This is rare but fatal, and strikes quickly. It has been linked to super-absorbent rayon tampons (rather than 100% cotton) which may encourage the growth of the bacteria staphylococcus aureus.

Now, we all know the adage that you should never put anything in your vagina that you would not put in your mouth. Even with pads, residues such as pesticides and dioxins from the bleaching process are held next to your skin and these chemicals

> *Here's an idea for you...*
>
> **There are reusable devices, such as a Keeper (rubber) or a Mooncup (silicone), designed to be inserted into your vagina like a contraceptive cap. These catch menstrual blood and are rinsed out regularly. Lots of women first come across them when looking for something convenient to use when backpacking, and they're very 'green'; they can last for years if you look after them.**

have been linked to birth defects, reproductive disorders and cancer. Perhaps we should think harder about the risks we take with our bodies when we choose our sanitary protection, in the same way as we think about the food we put into our mouths. And many women suffer unnecessarily from irritation and rashes due to perfumes added to sanitary protection. Nobody wants to smell, but a daily bath would have the same effect. A worrying development has been the introduction of tampons with added lubricants which contain parabens; these chemicals are suspected of being oestrogen mimics which can damage fertility. Some towels contain super-absorbent polyacrylate gel which absorbs moisture. There is a possible danger with these super absorbencies that women will change less regularly and that dangerous levels of bacteria may develop.

Defining idea...

If women are supposed to be less rational and more emotional at the beginning of our menstrual cycle when the female hormone is at its lowest level, then why isn't it logical to say that, in those few days, women behave the most like the way men behave all month long?

GLORIA STEINEM, campaigner

So what can you do about it? Well, sanitary products containing unbleached, organic cotton are available. You could also consider using washable cotton pads and even make them yourself; the Women's Environmental Network provide a pattern on their website. You won't be alone; in 1983, a World Health Organisation survey of women in ten countries around the world found that more than 45% used home-made pads – so finding this idea strange could be a cultural taboo. It may seem like a weird idea, but look at the number of parents turning to washable nappies instead of disposables; nobody thinks that's weird.

130. Make it natural

**A little bit of powder, a little bit of paint...
but at what cost? Look closely at what's
lurking in your make-up bag.**

Do you ever think about what cosmetics you are putting
on your face beyond whether the colour matches your outfit or eyes?

You may be surprised – or even horrified – when you realise what your make-up
contains. Coal tar colours, benzene, even formaldehyde, are just a few of the
synthetic chemicals commonly found in everyday cosmetics. These toxins are, of
course, absorbed into your skin every time you use conventional eye shadow,
foundation, mascara, blusher and lipstick. Although there are only tiny amounts of
these substances applied each time, there is the danger of the 'cocktail effect' when
a variety of substances are used together – they may interact. Using conventional
make-up over the course of decades has a cumulative effect, as well. It has even
been claimed that some of the substances confuse hormone receptors and alter cell
structure. If you avoid unpleasant chemicals in your diet then it makes sense to also
try and avoid them, wherever possible, when you are choosing your make-up.

Think about where and how make-up is applied. Eye shadow, mascara and eye liner
is put on in such a way that some of it can actually enter the eye (as anyone with
contact lenses can attest). This means it can be absorbed by the very sensitive

mucous membranes. Any powders can be inhaled, and they can irritate your lungs. Lipstick disappears off your lips – however thickly it is applied or however many times it is blotted – even long-lasting ones (and ask yourself how they are made to last so long, too). All that lipstick doesn't end up on glasses and napkins either; lots is chewed or licked off and is subsequently swallowed. It is vitally important, therefore, that the make-up you apply is safe, and organic make-up is free from the dangerous chemicals that conventional make-up is filled with.

The alternatives...

There are organic alternatives available for almost anything, and new companies are being set up all the time to fulfil growing demand. A growing number of manufacturers do not use synthetic or petroleum-derived ingredients, GMO ingredients or irradiated products. They use organic ingredients and do not use animal or animal slaughter by-products.

Greenpeople stock a range of certified organic lipsticks, using organic coconut oil, jojoba oil and cupuaçu butter (the produce of a tropical rainforest tree similar to cacao). They are soothing to dry lips, containing organic beeswax, castor oil and myrrh. Nvey Eco UK have a fabulous range of organic make-up with a wide variety of colours. If you carry out an Internet search, you will find many other alternatives available, such as LoveLula, Logona and Suncoat.

Here's an idea for you...

If you find some make-up you think you're interested in, but don't know what colour to go for, ask if they can send samples. This is particularly important when you are buying cosmetics by mail order. It is difficult to get realistic and accurate representations of colours online and you do not want to make expensive mistakes. Some companies will send samples of new products with orders, too – enquire. You won't be the first.

Defining idea...

Beauty is about perception, not about make-up. I think the beginning of all beauty is knowing and liking oneself. You can't put on make-up, or dress yourself, or do your hair with any sort of fun or joy if you're doing it from a position of correction.

KEVYN AUCOIN, make-up artist and author

The problem is that, at present, most of this organic make-up is not available in high-street stores, but actually has to be bought online. That removes the pleasurable buzz of looking at new colours and samples, and makes it harder to choose appropriate colours. Life's hard without a range of testers in front of you! However, it's worth it in the long run to know that you have bought quality make-up containing safe ingredients. I make a point of asking where the organic make-up is in shops so that they know there is a demand for organic products. It hasn't worked yet, but if we all ask, we'll get there!

Me time

We all need me time — time to grow, time to relax, time to contemplate how we're going to take our life to the next level. This section is full of inspiration — dive in and you'll soon be tingling with anticipation. Your new life really does start here...

Time for you – what's stopping you getting it?

You make your plans, they just never happen. Our quiz might help you pinpoint why. Select the answer most likely to be your response.

1. You are watching your favourite TV programme when your partner phones to ask you to pick him up at the station. You say:
- ☐ a. Sure.
- ☐ b. Go to the pub for an hour and I'll pick you up then.

2. When you think of saying 'no' to someone, your first thought is:
- ☐ a. They won't like me.
- ☐ b. They may not help me in future.

3. I have got behind with my own workload because I've been helping out others:
- ☐ a. A lot of the time.
- ☐ b. Occasionally.

If you've answered 'a' to one of these questions, then you may not be able to pursue your dreams because you are too busy keeping other people happy. At the root of your problems are issues with self worth and lack of confidence, turn to idea 132 to start combating them. Idea 138 will help when you can't make up your mind whether you should put yourself first (the answer is almost certainly, yes!).

4. The house is a pit. Not your fault. You end up doing all the tidying:
☐ a. Because you can't be bothered with the arguments.
☐ b. Because you might as well do it properly.

5. You cook a fabulous meal. You:
☐ a. Bask in the glowing compliments.
☐ b. Barely notice compliments.

6. When you have spent a lot of time on a report you find handing it in:
☐ a. A relief – you get it off your desk as soon as you can.
☐ b. Difficult, you can't stop fiddling with it.

If you answered 'b' to just one of these questions, you may be seeking perfection beyond the point where it's helpful. You find it hard to delegate, hard to let go and hard to hear how well you've done, all of which make it hard to stop working and start living. Read idea 150 to remind you of the price you might pay for perfectionism – is it worth it?

131. Sell fish

Being selfish isn't the most terrible thing you can be. In fact, if you're a bit of a doormat it may be the best thing you can do for yourself.

Good boys and girls aren't selfish. Good boys and girls have stress-induced heart attacks before the age of 40 or run off and abandon all the responsibilities they've kept up for years once they hit middle age. Be bad.

Imagine that there's a fisherman who sells his catch off the dock. A pretty girl walks by and asks the fisherman if he'll make a present of a fish to her. The fisherman, being a red-blooded straight male, agrees and gives her two for good measure. While he's busy chatting up the girl, a seagull swoops down and nicks two more of his fish before he can stop it. An old man comes by, criticises the state of the fish and asks for a discount of 50%. As the day is getting on now and the fisherman has yet to sell a fish, he agrees to a 50% sale. The man only buys one small fish. The fisherman doesn't have much of his catch left by now but just as he gets ready to holler out his wares, a man with a knife runs up to the dock, threatens the fisherman and steals the rest of his catch. The fisherman is left with nothing but the pathetic 50% sale of a small fish.

Did you like my metaphor there? Tortured, wasn't it? Well, there's a serious point behind it. While we'd like to believe in the abundance of the universe, the fact is that we are temporal creatures, bound to this space–time continuum, and time is a

Here's an idea for you...

Borrow a film that only you want to watch. Hog the TV and DVD player and watch that film that only you want to watch. If your partner or family protest, stick your fingers in your ears and go 'la-la-la-I'm not listening-la-la-la' until they get fed up and leave.

finite commodity in our world. Your quest for inner peace will be seriously derailed if you let time bandits steal away your catch. Whether you overindulge in socialising (the pretty girl), extra unexpected chores (the seagull), family commitments (the old man) or work (the thief), you leave nothing but a tiny pathetic sliver of time for yourself – most of which you'll spend sleeping.

So what can you do about it? Get selfish. This is almost impossible for some as we've been brought up to believe that only very horrible people put themselves before others. Now I'm not suggesting that you leave for a golfing holiday just as your wife goes into labour or that you choose a spa break over a relative's funeral but I do believe that if you don't factor in some time for yourself, you will explode like a pressure cooker. And nobody wants to clear up that sort of mess.

Women are usually the worst for this one as those evil little pod people, sorry, I mean 'children', can make you feel very selfish if their needs don't come first. Naturally when sprogs are babies, you shouldn't leave them with a dirty nappy and no food while you go get your nails done. I hear that sort of thing is frowned upon. But you should definitely come to an arrangement with the gentleman who provided 23 of those chromosomes that make up your little bundle of joy so that you can both enjoy at least one evening a month away from the demands of the petite dictator. And if you can rope a willing relative into looking after Junior so you can both escape together, so much the better.

Adopt a similar policy with regards to housework. Paid work is harder to get selfish about (unless you're the boss and can delegate things) but you can certainly ensure an equitable division of labour at home. But don't be rigid about it. If you love ironing but hate hoovering and your partner loves hoovering but hates ironing, you have the makings of a beautiful partnership. If you both hate doing everything, spend Junior's college fund on a cleaner. It's not selfish, it's sensible.

Defining idea...

'I am a greedy, selfish bastard. I want the fact that I existed to mean something.'
HARRY CHAPIN, musician and humanitarian philanthropist

132. Guilt be gone

Kick guilt to the kerb.

Guilt exists for one purpose only, to flag up when we've done something wrong that we should feel bad about. It is our moral centre kicking us in the backside for perceived wrong-doing. It is our conscience pricking us to make amends. It exists to ensure we're nicer people who don't treat others in a way that would be considered cruel or hurtful. However, there is another type of guilt that has nothing to do with morality or right and wrong. It's a false guilt that is the result of your inability to forgive yourself for not doing what's expected of you. Do not succumb to that second sort of guilt.

Do you often do things out of a need to avoid feeling guilty? Make phone calls, maintain friendships with people you don't really like, sign up to make charity donations you can't really afford, agree to do things for the Parent Teacher Association because you don't want to seen as not pulling your weight? Such a widespread misuse of guilt has to be halted. We need to appreciate the true reasons for guilt and, as long as you're not a felon, you really don't need to feel half as much guilt as you probably do.

The best way out of having guilt as your motivating factor in doing things is to learn the liberating effect of just saying 'no'. Most children go through a phase, at around the age of two, where they will start yelling 'NO!' in response to just about everything. That's why they call it 'the terrible twos' but psychologists reckon we all go through this phase as this is the first time we start to see ourselves as separate individuals and so we experiment with asserting an independent will. If you are to effectively get rid of guilt, you'll have to revert to this stage for a bit. You also need to experiment to find out what is your true will and what has simply been imposed upon you through an attempt to avoid guilt.

The next time someone asks you to do something, say 'let me check and get back to you'. That way you're buying time to consider whether you do actually want to do it. We often respond to things hurriedly, in a fluster, and then have to cancel afterwards – causing us more guilt for having let someone down. Even if you don't cancel it, having to do something because you couldn't think of a reason/excuse on the spot to say 'no' will only leave you feeling resentful and 'put upon' later. So buy yourself that time to respond.

Here's an idea for you...

Excise the word 'sorry' from your phone conversations for a week. You won't be able to do it because it is actually impossible. Try it and you'll see. Imagine what a conversation without 'sorry' sounds like: 'I couldn't come to your wedding. I hope you had a good time.' Saying that will sound to your ears as if you're calling the mother of the bride a crack ho. The conditioning is very, very strong and you'll be hard pressed not to say the 's' word but try anyway and may the force be with you.

Before you start to feel too guilty about anything, ask yourself whether you could have helped what happened. If you could have, well, it's too late now, it's in the past. All you can do is offer a heartfelt apology and find a way to make amends. Wringing your hands about it won't transport you back to that time when you could have done things differently. So it's now time to move forward.

> Defining idea...
>
> **'Guilt: the gift that keeps on giving.'**
> ERMA BOMBECK, American humorist and columnist

We are often a lot more compassionate toward the guilty feelings of others than those of our own. If a friend feels guilty for letting down a member of her family, we comfort her and tell her to stop beating herself up about it. No such nice words of solace for our own selves. The next time you feel unduly bad about something, think about what you'd say if a friend was in that position. Would you hate her for not being able to do x, y or z? Of course not! So give yourself the same break.

133. Booking in peace

A good book can be a companion that lets you leave the workaday world behind.

Losing yourself in a book is one of the few times you can travel anywhere and not worry about baggage or passports.

Think about the history of the humble book. People have been killed for writing books. Some books themselves have been burned and banned. Despite this being the age of the ghost-written, 12-year-old footballer's autobiography, we still attach a degree of respect to books. We expect books to have substance and be somewhat timeless, in a way that magazines and newspapers aren't.

Worryingly, in the UK today, in some areas one in five children leaving primary school can't read. This is one of the greatest tragedies in our country as reading sets you free. If you're having a bad or boring time of it, picking up a good book is like Alice going down the rabbit hole – you're bound to have an adventure.

However, the sheer number of books that are released each year can make choosing what to read more stressful than it need be. Should you listen to Richard & Judy or will your snobbish friends laugh at you for allowing TV presenters to choose your reading material? Should you ask at the local library what might be good to read?

Here's an idea for you...

Get a day pass for a seriously good library that covers the subjects you're especially interested in. Treat it like an outing and read not for work or study but for pleasure, surfing the books like you do the internet. I am interested in occult subjects and the Harry Price Library of Magical Literature is my library of choice. Find the library considered best for your own interests and immerse yourself in knowledge.

Books can change your life but they require the commitment of time, in both the hunting out of good ones and in the reading of them. So choosing the right book is a bit like choosing the right relationship, you have to like it enough to commit to it. I used to be a bit crab-like in both books and relationships; I'd cling on to the bitter, bitter end instead of abandoning and walking away if things were clearly not going to work out. I couldn't dump a book mid-way through, even if that meant dedicating a day to a book that I was clearly not enjoying. The day this all came to an end was when I spent a whole weekend reading a truly dreadful stream-of-consciousness number about an Indian woman and her Iranian husband. The book rambled on and on like a bad dream until eventually we got some action on – and I kid you not – the last paragraph where after reams and reams of philosophical musings about love, sex, race etc., etc. the husband kills her lover. I cheered and wished that the husband had killed the protagonist too. And the author. And me, for having read it right till the end.

Apart from culling bad books from your life, actively seek out the good ones. Ask your friends for recommendations and note who was most successful in suggesting a book you liked and stick to asking them. Consider joining a book club. This is the age of the funky book club so pick one near you and it will be a chance to meet new people as well as read more widely. Keep a reading diary and note what books you read and when, it becomes like a journal of where you've been in your imagination.

It's a bit sad that everyone on the tube is usually reading the latest big blockbuster and there's very little variety. It feels like being spoon-fed things from the publishing, retail and marketing industries. There is something to be said for safe choices though. I adore self-help books but I'd never read them in public as they have garish covers and titles like 'Feel the pain and rejection of being dumped – and date again anyway' or 'He's just not that into you' (the last one is a real title). Since I'm horribly judgemental about people based on their reading material, I'm careful not to fall on my own sword.

Reading material is also a great way of judging whether you could ever fancy a particular stranger on the train. A man reading Proust is trying too hard to be an intellectual, a man reading Dan Brown is not trying hard enough to be an intellectual and a man who's reading Terry Pratchett will force you to go to role-playing gaming evenings and may disturbingly want you to dress up as Princess Leia on occasion. I want a sexy, Nietzsche-reading superman.

Being able to read is a tremendous blessing and one that we probably overlook when we're thinking of things to be grateful for. Exercise this fabulous skill as often and as passionately as you can.

134. A change of scene

**From the countryside to the coast, a
break is as much of a necessity as food
and a home.**

Having two days away in a completely different setting can make
you feel much, much happier with your daily round once you return.

Sometimes you can feel like a hamster on a wheel, doing the same things over and
over again. Getting up at the same time, going to the same shops, the same desk at
work and the same faces around you all the time. It can make you forget that you're
here to explore and enjoy life rather than wear down the pavement into a rut. One
of the best ways of countering this is to pick a place that is the direct opposite of
your usual abode. If you live in the country, book a couple of days in a bustling city.
Choose to visit during the week rather the weekend as restaurants and exhibitions
are less busy and there's simply nothing more relaxing than walking about at a
leisurely pace while all the busy-bee workers are frenetically going about their
weekday lives.

If, like me, you're a city girl then head for the country or the coast. The change of
pace can be startling and sometimes people suffer from a 'communication neurosis'
whereby they feel the need to have their laptops and mobiles on to feel connected

with world. Here's an idea: make the only blackberries you see on your break the kind you put in jams. Or head to somewhere like the Brecon Beacons where mobile reception is usually pretty bad.

I regularly housesit for a friend of mine in Sussex. The days that I am off house-sitting near the seafront in Newhaven are heavenly. Early morning walks to the beach, lunch at a dockside pub, a stroll through flea markets and then back home to cook the fish I got first thing in the morning at the market off the harbour. As an urban-dweller, I find it amazing that I can go down to the dock and pick up a fish caught that day to cook in the evening. It seems almost unreal to see the catch all lined up on ice instead of covered in cellophane at the supermarket.

Here's an idea for you...

House sit or house swap with a friend. As the holiday season comes upon us many of our friends who live by the coast or in the city (if we're coastal dwellers) are off on holiday, leaving their homes empty. Ask if they want a house sitter and enjoy an almost free holiday. You'll be shopping for groceries in a new town, discovering new walks and maybe even looking after a dog (a pleasant experience if you're not allowed them in your city flat).

One of the big mistakes that people make is to save their money and time up and then blow a substantial amount of money on two weeks somewhere exotic. That's all fine and good, but imagine how much pressure you're putting on yourself to have a great holiday. You've saved up your days and your money for a big break and you expect the pay-off to be a great time, great weather and to come back feeling very rested. However, if the hotel isn't what you expected or the weather turns bad or you have a row with your boyfriend, you could well return stressed, cheated and miserable because it will be a whole year before you can afford another break.

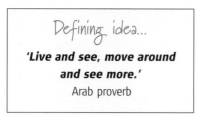

A better idea is to spend little and often. The weekend break can be fantastic with a little planning. Spend a couple of weekends doing extra chores like washing or cleaning out the fridge so that on your weekend away, you're not thinking about housework or what you'll have to do before work on Monday. Before you leave for your break on the Friday, lay out and plan what you'll wear to work on the Monday. Turn off your mobile and give the number of the hotel you're staying in to a family member in case of emergencies. Don't even think about bringing your laptop. Let the office know that you are away for the weekend and so can't be contacted. Then enjoy exploring a completely new place with no worries beyond which restaurant to have dinner in.

135. Switching off

From the internet to mobile phones, we are always switched on and plugged in. Turn it all off and see what happens.

The buzz of electricity is always with us. Try reverting to a slower, more calming time when bleeps and ringtones didn't interrupt your every thought.

I recently arrived from London at a house I was minding for a friend in Sussex to find all the lights out. He has an electricity meter and, while he'd been away, the electricity paid for on his card had run out. As it was 6pm, the shop where you could top up the card was shut. I'd have to spend the night with no TV and no lights. It was winter so it was already pitch black. I lit some candles and discovered that you can singe your eyebrows if you try to read by candlelight. I made a hot drink on the gas stove and then carried it up to bed. Lying in bed I started to feel bored as it was still only about 6.30. Luckily I had a battery-operated radio and I listened to that for an hour. Then I turned in to bed at 7.30pm, the earliest I'd ever gone to bed. The next day I woke up well rested but I virtually ran to the shop to get the electricity back on.

The experience made me think of how things must have been before electricity, when people used the sunset to tell them when to go to bed. The winter must have been a cosy time of rest and relaxation while the summer would have been busy

Here's an idea for you...

If it is at all possible, remove all electricals from your bedroom. Only have low lighting and see how it feels for a while. If you like it, keep it like that; if you don't, ask yourself why you need to be so switched on, even in your room of rest and recuperation.

work all day long. I am a modern enough girl not to hanker back to those times but I do think that switching off some of our gadgets and gizmos is great for the search for inner peace. Try to do it for one day or even a few hours and see what it feels like.

Someone I know once referred to the mobile phone as an electronic leash. The office could call you to heel at any moment. You are always available. Some offices pride themselves on a good work–life balance but this often means blurring the boundaries between work and home life. I think your home life suffers if you're on the laptop or mobile phone when you're with your family. It is far better to be out of the home from 8–6 and completely present with your family when you're back than it is to be doing 'flexi-time' and always be checking mails and taking calls, even through meals.

If there's one thing you should never do it is to take a call during a meal without apologising profusely to the people you're dining with. I once left my boyfriend having a meal by himself in a restaurant because he had spent 40 minutes on the phone to work. I just walked out the restaurant and he didn't even notice. He said later that he thought I'd gone to the loo. I hadn't and he found out that I had left because the waiter told him. He was annoyed at how rude I'd been to do that. I was annoyed at how rude he'd been to invite me to dinner and then spend 40 minutes on the phone. Needless to say, we're exes now.

Another bugbear is the internet. You can spend hours and hours trawling through site after site. Do you remember when we had books? In those funny old-fashioned places called libraries? I say head back there. Oftentimes the information you get on the internet is unregulated and inaccurate. My cousin was described as the daughter rather than stepdaughter of her horrid stepmother on Wikipedia. I was having none of it and changed it to a more accurate description, but it is one small example of how you should take everything you read on the internet with a pinch of salt. Better still, turn it off for a bit and do something quaint like read a book.

Defining idea...

> '**He that can take rest is greater than he that can take cities.**'
> BENJAMIN FRANKLIN, one of the Founding Fathers of the USA

136. A one-minute answer to mid-afternoon slump

Practically every medical system in the world (with the exception of our own) believes that energy flows around the body in channels. Suspend disbelief!

Lack of energy is attributed to a block somewhere in this energy flow. Release the block and you get increased energy.

You can do this by applying needles, fingers or elbows to specific acupuncture points around the body.

True? Or unmitigated waffle? Here we're dealing with acupressure and there isn't scientific evidence that would pass muster with the British Medical Journal when it comes to acupressure and energy. However, there is evidence that acupressure works for helping with post-operative nausea and lower back pain – so working on the principle that if it works for one thing it may work for another, it's worth a try. I have derived benefit from the following facial massage which is specifically for tiredness and mental exhaustion. It was taught to me by a TCM (traditional Chinese medicine) doctor about twenty years ago. There may be a placebo effect going on here, but hey, who cares? Whatever gets you through the night or, in this case, through the afternoon. This is brilliant for mid-afternoon slump. I've since taught it to friends – specifically those who spend a lot of time at their desk– and many use it.

Shiatsu facial massage for instant energy

✿ Lean your elbows on a table and let your face drop into your hands, with your palms cupped over your eyes. Look into the darkness formed by your hands. Stay there for as long as you feel comfortable or until your colleagues start to get worried.

✿ Place your thumbs on the inner end of each eyebrow and use your index fingers to work out along the upper edge of the eyebrow, applying pressure at regular intervals. When your index fingers reach the outer edge of your eyebrow, release all pressure.

✿ Return index finger to the inner end of each brow and work thumbs along to the lower end of the brows in similar fashion. Release as before.

✿ Place thumbs under ear lobes and apply pressure. At the same time, use the index fingers to apply pressure on points on a line from the bridge of the nose under your eyes, along the ridge formed by your eye sockets.

✿ Touch fingertips to fingertips along an imaginary line running up the middle of your forehead from your nose to your hairline (no pressure is necessary). Use thumbs to apply pressure to points fanning out from the outer edge of the eyebrows to hairline. Repeat four times. (Feel for tender points and massage them. I find pressing on my temples when I'm stressed decreases tension in my jaw where, like a lot of people, I hold a lot of tension.)

Here's an idea for you...

If mid-afternoon tiredness gets you down, combine the massage with this energising meditation – or do this instead of it. Empty your brain as far as possible, sit quietly, get an orange and concentrate on peeling it. Look at it first – orange is an energising colour. Smell it – citrus scents such as orange, bergamot and lemon are revitalising. Eat it – vitamin C and fructose make a wicked combination for energy. After your orange, drink a large glass of water. You should feel better in ten minutes.

❂ Use thumbs to apply gentle pressure in the eye sockets under the inner end of the eyebrow where you feel a notch at the ridge of the eye socket. (This is a very delicate spot. I was told by a doctor once that it is the major nerve closest to the surface of the body: I don't know if that's true, but go gently. You can really hurt yourself by pressing this point too hard.)

❂ Use one index finger to work up that imaginary line in your mid-forehead from the nose to your hairline.

❂ Now drop your head forward and, lifting your arms, work thumbs from your spine outwards along the ridge of your skull from the spine out to the point just under your earlobes. Do this four times.

OK, it's a bit of a faff to get the hang of the different points, but once you've practised a couple of times with the instructions, you'll have the hang of it. And it will be a good friend to your energy levels for the rest of your life.

137. Dealing with interruptions

Other people and their agendas – they suck the energy right out of you. But there are ways of dealing with interruptions.

It's been one of those days. This morning I had a clear day to get on with writing this. And then it all went wrong.

I've taken two phone calls and been side-tracked at the school gates by a friend wanting a coffee and a chat. I've agreed to pick up another parent's kid, which shouldn't be a problem but, somehow, now it is. It's now 12.45 pm and I've written 100 words. (That's not good, by the way.)

I'm reminded of the definition of an optimist: someone who believes that today will be better than yesterday. What's the definition of a fantasist? Someone who believes today will be better even if she doesn't make any changes. Sure, I can be an optimist, imagining I'll zip through everything I want to achieve today, but if yesterday was constantly hijacked by other people, and I don't do anything to change that today, I'm living on Fantasy Island if I think I'll get everything done. And that feeling of having wasted time is a total energy bummer. So it's time to start making some plans to ensure that I don't let other people interrupt me. My trigger points will be different from yours – as you've probably guessed, mine is being seduced by my friends into going off-track. Below we explore some possible energy drains, and what hopeless cases – and that means me – can do about it.

You work in an office

The average office worker is interrupted every three minutes, according to research undertaken in California. It's a wonder that we get anything done at all. If you're lucky enough to have your own office space, how about operating a one-hour-door-open, one-hour-door-shut policy, when you can't be interrupted. It's also worth learning some great exit lines for bouncing the interrupter back to the drawing board until it suits you and/or they find someone else to help them. You could try 'Sorry, got to finish this project; can we talk about it tomorrow?' or 'Sorry, this week is impossible; what about next week.'

Your hobby is chatting

Yep, this is me. The answer is simple. Just say no. Personally, knowing how weak I am, I don't engage in conversation. Tomorrow, unlike today, I won't answer the phone but let the machine pick up. I'll check messages for urgency at noon and five o'clock.

You're a 'social emailer'

This tag is the invention of my friend Jane Alexander, a wonderful writer who admits that one of her occupations is 'social emailer'. She lives in the depths of Devon, so for her there's some excuse: email is her window on the world. For the rest of us, it's probably nothing but a huge distraction. One radical idea that works for me is not to look at e-mails first thing in the morning. Instead, spend that first hour doing the most important task of the day. Often that first hour is the calmest you'll get, and what do you spend it doing? 'Chatting' to your friends – it's just that the written word fools you into thinking you're working. Or else you're answering other people's banal requests. Try ignoring your emails until you've done some serious work, and check them no more than three times a day.

> ### Defining idea...
>
> *'I choose to ... live so that which came ... to me as a blossom, goes on as a fruit.'*
> DAWNA MARKOVA, poet

You can't say 'no'

Perhaps you need to look at whether you are just being helpful or are hooked on being needed. Next time, when you're tempted to let yourself be distracted, ask yourself 'if I respond to this distraction, who am I disappointing?' It might be your boss, it might be you, it might be the child that you won't be able to take to the park at the weekend because you'll be making up time on a work project instead. Seeing the human cost of allowing yourself to be interrupted can help you decide if it's worth it or not.

138. Stop dithering, start living

Here's how to make swift, smart decisions.

Learn this vital decision-making formula. You'll free up
your mind from niggling worries in seconds, saving your mental energy.

I've had a bit of a dilemma today. I'm staring at an email advertising a two-day self-development course that I'd love to attend. There's just one problem. The weekend in question is the one (of admittedly many!) on which we will be celebrating my partner's fortieth birthday. I've promised to take him out for dinner that night and since the course is near my home, I could do both – attend the course during the day and take him for dinner that night. But ... but ... I've got that sneaking suspicion that by trying to pack too much in, I'm taking too much on. I'll be rushed and late for dinner.

In the past, this is the sort of dilemma I would have spent time on. I would have weighed up the pros and cons, written lists, talked to my partner about it, talked to friends perhaps, spent valuable time dithering when I could have been getting on with my life.

But that was before I learned the magical qualities of what I call 'the power of 10' question.

When faced with any dilemma simply stop and ask yourself: what will the consequences be in:

10 minutes?
10 months?
10 years?

When you're faced with a problem where there's no win-win situation and someone will end up unhappy, at least in the short term, 'the power of 10' helps you cut through the emotions of the moment and focus on what is really important.

Let's take my present dilemma.

If I decide to go to the self-development course, what will be the repercussions in 10 minutes? None. I'll explain to my partner, he won't really register it – it's down the line and as long as I'm not actually cancelling dinner, he won't care. I'll be happy.

In 10 months? That depends. If there are no mess-ups and I get there on time, probably it will be fine. But if I am late for dinner, in 10 months' time, he'll still be making sarcastic comments.

In 10 years? You know, that's the tricky one. Even if I manage everything, I think he's still going to remember that on the weekend of his fortieth, I wasn't really around. That's the general impression he'll have long after he's forgotten the presents, the party and all the other gestures I'll make to 'big' up his birthday and

> *Here's an idea for you...*
>
> **The very quickest form of this idea is brilliant for procrastinators. Think of a task that you're putting off. Imagine what the consequences will be in one month (or whatever time span is relevant) if you don't act. If the consequences don't frighten you, go to the pub; if they do, get on with it now. Worrying about it even subconsciously is sapping your energy.**

Defining idea...

**'But all will be well, and every
kind of thing will be well.'**
JULIAN OF NORWICH.
Medieval mystic

distract his attention from the fact that I'm not actually there very much. Would I be better off attending the course? I might learn a lot. I might make some lifelong soulmates. But there's no way of knowing if it will be worth it, or not. And there's potentially a lot to lose. So this time, I think I'll have to pass.

It took me as long to make that decision as it took to type it, and now my mind is free to get on with writing this, and everything else I have to do. I won't waste any more time thinking about it.

This is a variation of an old idea – imagining yourself one year, five years, ten years down the road is commonplace. 'What will it matter in twenty years' time?' we say to each other. But I find 'the power of 10' particularly elegant and easy to use. Try it when you're not sure what route to take and know that either will end up making someone unhappy. The three different timescales help you see through the emotional turmoil of yours or somebody else's short-term unhappiness to what the potential benefits could be when disappointment has passed. It helps you cut through the emotional 'fuss' that occurs when your plans are unpopular with some people, and to see clearly if they're worth the grief.

139. Are you getting enough?

Pleasure is what we're talking about. Jumping off the hamster wheel of relentless grind energises you very fast indeed.

Here's a fact: people who enjoy life live a longer, healthier life. The research into why happy *bons viveurs* live longer, in better health, is still in its infancy, but we're learning more every day.

One of the pioneers in what is called 'positive psychology' was a Yugoslav psychologist by the name of Dr Grossarth-Maticek, who did some studies into 3000 elderly Germans. He measured how often they felt pleasure and then followed them up twenty-one years later. The results showed that the 300 with the highest score (who had the most pleasure) were thirty times more likely to be alive, healthy and happy compared with the 200 with the lowest score.

The author of *The Attitude Factor*, Thomas R Blakeslee, has done a lot to publicise this research. 'Many people think [pleasure] is a luxury,' he wrote, ' but it's a vital necessity for good health and long life.'

Blakeslee took the theory further. He reckoned that at around thirty years old, we start to close down to pleasure, partly because we shut out new experiences and are less interested in new things. Basically we allow our ability to be adventurous to atrophy – and that directly impacts on how much pleasure there is in our lives. We stay in our comfort zone, and that comfort zone gets smaller and smaller.

Who cares, you might well be thinking (perhaps a tad defensively)? Who cares if my idea of excitement is a new series of *Celebrity Big Brother*? Big deal. Well, it is actually. If you're a couch potato, you are literally killing yourself. Traditional medics would say that it's because you're getting no exercise. Blakeslee would say it's because you're boring yourself to death.

To get you thinking, this is my much-simplified version of the quiz first given to the Germans and explained in full in Blakeslee's book and on his website. Base your answers on your usual behaviour and feelings in the last year, and pick the answer than is closest for you, even if not absolutely right. Add up your score from the bracketed figures.

1 Imagine you wake up on a beautiful summer morning without a care in the world. You feel happy. How happy?
Slightly (score 1) Moderately (4) Intensely (7)

2 How long do these feelings last?
Seconds (1) Hours (4) All day (7)

3 How often do you take pleasure in simple things such as a good meal or a conversation with a friend?
Almost never (1) Weekly (4) Every day (7)

4 Look at your diary. How many events have you scheduled for the future that are guaranteed to give you pleasure?
None (1) One or two (4) Plenty (7)

5 When you think of the future, how sure are you that you're going to have sensations of sheer pleasure in the future?
Not at all (1) Pretty sure (4) Certain (7)

6 Think about the greatest pleasure you've ever had in your life. Do you think you'll feel that much pleasure again?
Unlikely (1) Perhaps (4) Sure (7)

7 When you feel that all is well with the world, how strongly do you feel it?
Minimally (1) Moderately (4) Intensely (7)

8 How often do you experience this kind of feeling of wellbeing?
Almost never (1) Weekly (4) Many times in a week (7)

9 Think of the best you've ever felt in yourself. Do you think you'll feel that good again?
Unlikely (1) Perhaps (4) Sure (7)

10 After feelings of pleasure and wellbeing, do you get negative feelings such as guilt or depression?
Almost always (1) Sometimes (4) Almost never (7)

Add up your score and divide by ten.

If you scored 1-4. Your pleasure quotient is low, and your chances of being healthy and well in 21 years, are according to this research, lower unless you start planning for pleasure now.

If you scored 4.1–6. This corresponds to the people who had a 45–55% chance of being healthy twenty-one years later. So pretty good, but could do better.

If you scored 6.1-7. Your score on this quiz corresponds to the people who had the most pleasure in their lives, and consequently the healthiest outcome on follow-up.

A two-pronged attack is needed

- ✿ Plan for pleasure. Dedicate time every day to simply enjoying life and planning for fun. Knowing you have something to look forward to, rather than letting life just happen, is a wonderful energiser. Plan something pleasurable for tonight, next Wednesday night, and one weekend in the next six months, just for starters.
- ✿ Bust out of the comfort zone. Why is this so important? Because it's the simplest route to intense pleasure. Anything we have to work for, we appreciate more. Start a conversation with someone interesting in the lunch queue, go to a foreign-language movie, book up to go abseiling. It doesn't matter how much you actually enjoy these things; you'll feel great after doing them just because you pushed yourself.

140. Revamp your 'to do' list

'To do' lists are essential for most of us but they can be a huge drain on energy.

The list that never seems to get any shorter is not so much an aide-memoire as a horrible reminder that we're running fast but getting nowhere. And what could be more dispiriting than that?

The other side, of course, is that 'to do' lists are incredibly useful tools for motivating us and making us more productive. Having a clear plan for the day ahead focuses the mind and puts you in control like nothing else. Whether you're a CEO, freelance, stay-at-home parent or student, the well run 'to do' list will give you a sense of full-capacity living.

But for it to work, you have to have a definite system. Try this one. It is based on the advice given to 1930s magnate Charles Schwabb by a young man he challenged to double his productivity. The young man told him to write down the six most crucial tasks for each day in order of importance and work down the list. Then teach his staff to do the same. After a few weeks, the story goes that Schwabb sent a cheque for £25,000 to he young man, which was a huge sum then.

Here's an idea for you...

Switch off your mobile for as long as you can comfortably get away with, but aim for at least an hour in the morning and an hour in the afternoon. These should be your high productivity times when you aim to really motor through your tasks. The act of switching of your mobile sends an unconscious message to your brain that this is time when your interests are the priority, and it helps to focus your mind on the task at hand.

This idea works on the principle that we put off important stuff (or we work to others' agenda so we don't get round to what's important for us) and keep ourselves busy with lesser tasks to distract ourselves. But if we don't do the one important thing, no matter what we achieve, we'll feel dissatisfied at the end of the day. Instead of an abstract list of things to do that you attack randomly, switch the angle from what you must do to when you are going to do it.

How to revamp your 'to do' list

In your diary or a separate notebook, draw a line down the left hand side of the page to form a column and mark in the working hours of the day. This can be precise (9.30 to 10.30, 10.30 to 11.30) or loose (morning, afternoon). Now you're set to go.

✿ At the end of your working day, brew a cuppa, sit for a second, take a deep breath and gather your thoughts. Pat yourself on the back for what you have achieved today. Now. Swing your mind forward into tomorrow.
✿ Ask yourself what regular scheduled tasks or meetings you have for tomorrow. Block them off on your diary page.
✿ Remember to add in travelling time, lunch and relaxation.

✿ What is your major task? What must you do tomorrow? That gets priority and should be done first thing if possible. Set aside a realistic block of time (err on the side of caution). Be precise.

✿ Put in specific times for phone calls/emails. It is more time effective to do these in two or three blocks rather than breaking concentration and doing it ad hoc during the day.

✿ What's your next most important task? Is there room in your day? If you have time left, you can schedule in other tasks, but be realistic.

✿ For each week have a short list of brief one-off tasks (phone calls, paying bills, birthday cards) and if you have a few down minutes, slot them in.

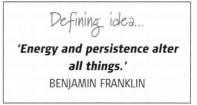

Defining idea...

'Energy and persistence alter all things.'

BENJAMIN FRANKLIN

141. Be irresistible

The ability to draw others towards you effortlessly saves you the sweat of having to go to them. Result!

The secret to magnetism is dead simple – love yourself.
And remember, high self-esteem isn't a constant; it's a work in progress.

Imagine if life just got easier. If the things you wanted in life seemed to flow towards you effortlessly. That's what the father of life coaching, US guru, Thomas Leonard, called 'irresistible attraction'. Which is a fabulous way of saying 'sky-high self-esteem'.

Without self-esteem you feel helpless, depressed, isolated. Life seems difficult and you don't feel other people care about you enough. Needless to say, it's a major bummer and brings your energy levels crashing down.

Fluctuating self-esteem is a major energy drainer without us realising it. We struggle on, feeling rubbish without really knowing why. Which is a shame, because making a few simple steps to feel better about ourselves can boost our energy immediately and that makes us more attractive to others. Life gets easier and we need to expend less energy to get through the day. Keeping a beady eye on our fluctuating self-esteem levels is a win-win situation energetically speaking.

Answer 'yes' or 'no' to these statements based on how you're feeling now, today– not how you felt last week, last year or last millennium.

1 Does life seem unnecessarily complicated?
2 Do all your attempts to make life better seem to get stuck?
3 Do you feel you're at the mercy of your family, job or other people?
4 Are you feeling slightly sick at the thought of all you have to achieve by the end of the week?
5 Do you feel that, if you want something, you can make it happen?
6 Do you feel that you are expressing who you really are through your image, home, work or interests?

Answer 'no' to the first four questions and 'yes' to questions 5 and 6, and you can skip this idea – for now. 'Yes' to the first four questions; 'no' to questions 5 or 6, and your self-esteem could use some work. The good news is you can start right now. You'll have higher self-esteem by the time you go to bed tonight.

Here's an idea for you...

Set aside half an hour and write down every single thing you've been successful at or that you've completed successfully. Put anything on the list as long as it's meaningful to you. Finding a good dentist could be as much of a success as getting a promotion at work. When you run out of steam, look over the list and write down the qualities you needed to achieve each success – perseverance, courage, quick wit. Return to this list until you have at least 100 successes – and then give yourself a really nice reward for being so darn successful.

Make a difference – it makes you gloriously attractive

One characteristic of people with low self-esteem is that, deep down, they don't think it matters if they exist or not. Those with healthy self-esteem know they make a difference to the world. Easiest way of doing it? Pay a genuine compliment and then 'big' it up. Tell the bloke who makes your coffee how good it is, and let his manager overhear. Compliment your assistant on a job well done, then email your boss to let her know about his good work. Paying compliments makes you powerful. You remember the person who gave you a heartfelt compliment for the rest of your life. Don't you want to be that kind of memorable person?

Ditch the martyrdom – it's deeply unattractive

All of us do things we don't want to do, but some of us get caught in a trap of working to other people's agendas too much of the time. And that's majorly exhausting. Think of one chore you really don't want to do: visit your aunt, help at the school fête, paint the bedroom. Now remember – it's optional. Pretty much everything in life is. Cancel it and do something that makes you happy instead. When 'duty' tasks mount up, we feel overwhelmed and out of control. Saying 'no' means you start to question every single time you say 'yes'. Saying 'no' to other people and 'yes' to yourself is very, very energising.

142. Are you sitting comfortably?

Pilates isn't just about classes or mat work. Its principles can be applied to almost any situation, making it possible to do yourself some good wherever you are – in the office, on the bus or down the pub.

Life, I find, has an irritating habit of butting into my schedule of exercise and well-being. In theory I have an eight-hour regime of taking care of myself in the gym and Pilates studio, but in practice little things like work, family and friends tend to get in the way.

One of the beauties of Pilates is that it can be applied to almost any physical activity – or inactivity. You can be working out without anyone knowing. You really can be working out by sitting on your arse.

Sitting isn't as easy as it looks. Most of us manage to put stress on our shoulders, necks and backs just by the way we sit. Pilates posture can help.

First, make sure you're sitting back in your chair with your feet flat on the floor. Imagine that your coccyx (tailbone) is made of lead and pulling straight down into the chair. Make sure your spine is in neutral and you can feel the middle of your back lightly pressed against the seat back. Your shoulders should be relaxed but not slumped. To get a feel for that position try some leg lifts. Lift each knee alternately

Here's an idea for you...

'The lift' is another exercise you can do at your office chair or on the bus. The aim is to work on zipping up from the bottom of the pelvis towards your ribs. While sitting upright, imagine that there is a lift on your pelvic floor. As you breathe out try to take that lift 'up' to the next floor – you should feel your pelvic muscles go taut. As you take the 'lift' further up the floors from 'first' to 'second', you should feel your lower abdominals tighten. Higher than that and you risk the six-pack muscling in on the action.

up, placing it smoothly down again with the foot flat on the floor. You should be totally stable, if you can feel your coccyx moving, then check that you are sitting back and in the neutral position – you may be sitting too far forward with your pelvis tilted. If you're not sure about neutral when sitting, then try lifting the knee right up towards your chest. As you do you'll reach a point where you can feel the pelvis tilt, and the coccyx slides towards the front of the seat. Hopefully that feel for being out of neutral should help you settle into neutral.

With your pelvis and back sorted out, the next issue is your shoulders and the neck strain that all too easily results from tension and poor posture. Hunching your shoulders upwards is a shortcut to tension and trouble as it tightens the trapezius muscle at the top of your back and that transmits its strain into the back of the neck. If you feel tense (and who doesn't at some point in the working day) then try this.

Slide your shoulder blades towards each other and then down and at the same time extend your neck. You should feel an immediate easing of the pressure on your spinal column, shoulders and neck as well as feeling as if you've just grown an inch. Next time you want to shout at someone, try doing that first.

A really great time to try the sitting exercises is on the bus/tube or at the traffic lights on the way home. Because we're tired we're likely to slump and take all that tension back home with us. Try and make it part of your daily routine to ease that pressure out as a way of leaving work behind before you get home. Don't forget that it's just as effective in the pub or sat in front of *Lost*.

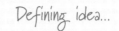

Defining idea...

'The greatest monarch on the proudest throne is obliged to sit upon his own arse.'
BENJAMIN FRANKLIN

Are you sitting comfortably?
Scoop that stomach, park that pelvis and we'll begin.

143. Timesaving exercise tips

Too pressed for time to have time for presses? Try a few of these tips to maximise those fleeting moments in the gym.

Modern life is hectic, no one has enough time, there are a gazillion things demanding your attention and since fitness isn't your profession or your first love it's the gym time that ends up suffering.

This is only natural. We're all forever promising ourselves that we'll do an extra long session next time just as soon as we've finished with this budget/school holiday/international arms deal. Little and often, however, is a much better way to exercise than sporadic blitzing. For a start it means you're less likely to half-cripple yourself by launching an under-prepared body into an overambitious workout. It's also easier mentally to keep up the momentum and the feel-good factor, not least since mega sessions with long gaps in between quickly become daunting and may lead eventually to cancelled gym memberships. Little and often makes it easier to monitor progress – a motivational bonus – plus frequent short spells in the gym will do more to raise your metabolism on a daily basis than a once-a-fortnight gut-wrenching osteopath special.

So how can you make sure you get a decent workout when you only have a few precious minutes to dedicate to the temple of toning?

Try the following:

Have your kit ready, packed up, and by the door

Einstein used to line up seven sets of clothes on the hangers each week so he never wasted precious brainpower deciding what to wear or trying to find it. Take his lead. When you pull stuff out of the dryer, match it up into complete sets of kit, then make sure you have a gym bag ready to go for every day. Leave it sitting by the door like a patient dog hoping to go walkies and it will be both convenient to grab and a helpful reminder to your conscience.

Plan your workout, work your plan

Nobody has enough time at the gym so who are all those people wandering around from cardio room to weights and back? Be clear in advance what your workout goals are. Don't fix on a single machine – it may be in use – but decide in advance how much cardio you're going to do or what weight session you have in mind.

Try going early

What? Like in the morning? Working out before the day gets its claws into you means you start out feeling good and get your metabolism up and running. There are also fewer people and it's hard not to feel virtuous which makes it more likely you'll be back for more tomorrow.

> ### Here's an idea for you...
>
> We spend half our time in the weights room waiting for someone else to get off the machine we want. Meanwhile there's a rack of dumbbells sitting unused in front of a mirror somewhere. Learn the range of dumbbell exercises and you'll be able to get a whole upper-body workout without moving from the spot, or doing the gym 'excuse-me' mamba around the machines.

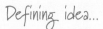

Train with your beloved/kids/mates

Don't force fitness to compete with friendships and lovelife – it will come a sad second and if it doesn't you will become a sad individual. See if you can mix gym/social life by training with friends and family. This may mean thinking a little laterally. You may have trouble getting your spouse to show up to an abs class, for example, but swap it for something more fun like a core class and you can frolic with the whole family.

Don't rest, cross-train

Your gym tells you to spend no more than 20 minutes on a machine? Fine, just leap straight off it and onto another one. Take ten on each if you like. Forty minutes working on a mix of rower/treadmill/bike will give you a more thorough workout than the same time spent plodding away at the same machine. It uses different muscles and psychologically allows you to put more effort because you know you're changing soon.

Don't rest, superset

Normal practice if you're doing weights is to rest at least 30 seconds in between sets. Well don't. Instead switch straight to an exercise that works the opposite set of muscles and cut to and fro between the two with no rest time at all. For example, if you're working biceps, then alternate with a triceps press. Pair chest press exercises with lateral pull downs. Hamstrings with quads, etc.

144. Girls just wanna have fun

Women learn faster when there are no guys around. No wonder women-specific ski and snowboard camps and clinics are becoming big business.

The label 'women-only' doesn't mean a snowsports clinic for lightweights. Today you can find same-sex clinics for every ability. The benefits? More support, more self-confidence and less testosterone!

About half the resorts in the world now offer women-specific ski and snowboard programmes – that's how popular they've become. From novice clinics to gnarly camps, female-focused teaching has exploded.

Let's be clear, this is not about man bashing

There are real differences between the way men and women approach learning, especially when risk is involved. Girl-specific courses aim to use those differences to a woman's advantage.

In the last decade, women's snowsports have been revolutionised by the advent of women-specific gear. For years, girls had to settle for equipment made for men that didn't take our physical differences into account.

Here's an idea for you...

Feeling the fear? Women seem to experience fear more often and more intensely than men. Don't let inappropriate fear paralyse you. Instead, when you feel scared, take five long, deep breaths and repeat to yourself all the reasons why your fear is irrational (for example, the snow is soft and won't hurt, you know how to stop and so on).

Today we understand that physiological differences play a huge role. The 'Q' angle (the angle from our hips to our knees), centre of mass, bone length, foot shape, weight and strength are all different in men and women. All of these factors affect performance on the snow.

Now that manufacturers have run away with the women-specific boom, the girls are back on a more level playing field physically. Women-specific teaching aims to put them on a level playing field psychologically, too.

So why would you abandon your partner to play with the boys while you bond with the girls?

Well, there are many benefits to the single-sex environment. Women are typically less self-conscious when men aren't around. They worry less about making fools of themselves, they are less intimidated to try new things and they are less afraid to fail. Let's face it, boys can be competitive and, if you aren't comfortable with the added pressure of competition, it will sap your confidence. With these obstacles removed, you can focus all your energy on learning and improving.

Women are also thought to favour a different style of learning. Whereas men usually prefer to just get started and figure it out for themselves, women tend to prefer more detailed instruction, support and encouragement.

'Girls tend to be much more relaxed without guys around,' says Elissa Koskinen at Girlie Camps, one of the pioneers of women-specific winter camps across Europe. 'They can progress at their own tempo, without feeling intimidated, and take it easy until they are 100% sure. Girls are also really supportive of each other and push each other in a way guys never would. Guys push each other on a different level and much harder.'

> *Defining idea...*
>
> **'Courage, sacrifice, determination, commitment, toughness, heart, talent, guts. That's what little girls are made of; to hell with sugar and spice.'**
> Anon

It's also about support and camaraderie. Girls tend to thrive in a supportive environment and are more likely to offer support than men. They are also motivated by other women's achievements. 'When the girls see another girl doing a trick, they think "Wow, if she can do it, why not me?",' says Elissa. 'If a guy did the same trick, the girls would just think "Ah, that was a guy, I'll never be able to do anything like that anyway".' When women are surrounded by other women, intimidation gives way to support and encouragement, making it easier to easier to confront self-doubt and fear. And fear is a big issue for most of us.

Girls tend to be more scared of hurting themselves (even though it is said women have higher pain thresholds than men) and so feel more cautious. This is where women-specific teaching comes into its own, as instructors focus on working with their clients' fear, rather than trying to convince them there is no reason to worry. Female-focused teaching builds confidence slowly, rather than urging you to throw yourself over the edge.

145. The scrapbook of your mind

The mind – it's where all ideas begin. But does it sometimes feel like you could use a second mind just to make sense of them all? Keeping a record in words and pictures really works.

When you think about what is going on in your brain at any given moment, it's astonishing that it has time to do any creative thinking at all.

What with maintaining all the bodily functions, helping us go about our daily round of work and social activities, speaking a language, remembering anniversaries, songs, faces and the shopping list, it already has its synapses pretty full.

So if you want to pile onto its workload the non-essential luxury of imaginative thought, it's not unreasonable to come up with a strategy for helping it. (Yes, I know, I don't think it's non-essential either; but I'd be forced to admit that it came behind breathing, eating and perhaps sleeping in the grand order of priorities!) In fact of course there are huge areas of your even huger brain dedicated to analysing incoming data; the occipital lobe is the bit dealing with all things visual, for example. There is an argument that, ironically, the more aids we invent for 'helping' the brain out – handwriting, computers and so on – the less we use our brains. If you write something down, for example, your brain is no longer required to remember it, so it doesn't learn how to do so. But the reality is that we do forget and overlook things!

Selection box

More than that, the fact is, it does help sometimes (especially, I think, in visual matters) to have things laid out in front of you and not just stored away in your memory. By concentrating on a particular set of images or ideas, you're inviting your brain to make connections between them. And the more connections your brain makes, the more chance you have of coming up with a brilliant and beautiful piece of work.

A scrapbook, filled with apparently random ideas, with no immediate connection except that you were drawn to them over a period of time, simply acts as a kind of positive filter. It gives your brain a head start (excuse the expression!), with a selection of things you already know you're interested in – a sort of box of bricks for your brain to play with and make something of. Indeed, your brain may subconsciously have directed you towards those bricks because it is already making connections between them.

Here's an idea for you...

For seven days, try to keep a daily scrapbook diary of images and ideas. It might consist of cuttings from magazines that caught your eye, or photos of objects that appealed to you, or scraps of fabric that tickled your fancy, or just your own handwritten notes about a design or a technique you admired or were curious about. At this stage make a conscious effort not to make connections or analyse what you're putting down on paper. Only at the end of the week, look back and start to allow emerging themes to float to the surface, inspiring your current project or perhaps your next one.

Defining idea...

'Creativity is the power to connect the seemingly unconnected.'
WILLIAM PLOMER (1903–73),
South African novelist

Making choices

This is the great value of a scrapbook or notebook for the artist. It's like taking a few books down from the library shelves instead of trying to look through all of them. With your chosen books spread about you open at the relevant pages, it's a lot easier than starting at the shelf of As and just reading all the way through to the Zs in the hope of stumbling across what you're looking for.

What happens next is up to you. As you fill your scrapbooks you will build a terrific library of images and influences, a sort of visual diary. As you look back, different themes and patterns of interest will speak to you at different times. What your scrapbooks will always have in common is that it was you that filled them; and because of that they will always have a connection with what you are working on at any given moment.

146. A promise, a commitment, a dream

You're a craftsperson! Change 'I'm not' to 'I am', 'I can't' to 'I can' and 'I won't' to 'I will'. Honour your imagination and good intentions with some positive statements, and make something special to embody them.

How many times have you said one or all of the following? 'Oh, I'm not nearly good enough to try that.' 'Of course I'm not a real craftsperson.' 'I never finish anything.' 'It's just a hobby.'

Well, first of all, it makes no difference whether you make a living from craft, are a Week One Day One student of it, or have never made a thing with your hands in your life: your experience and contribution are equally valid. Where would teachers be without students? Makers without collectors? Exhibitions without visitors? Secondly, whatever level you operate at – admiring onlooker, enthusiastic amateur or cynical professional – your progress and pleasure will be immeasurably enhanced with a positive outlook!

There are thousands of self-help books out there saying the same thing, and charging you the price of the raw materials of your next project for the privilege, before rewriting it in a different context and charging you all over again. You know the sort of thing: Find your Positivity and Do It Anyway is followed by Finding your

> ### Here's an idea for you...
>
> **Come up with three say-it-like-you-mean-it declarations, starting 'I am ...', 'I can ...' and 'I will ...'. Enshrine these three statements of belief in a piece of work. You don't need to spell them out – they could be symbolised by significant objects in a painting, or by a particular sequence of colours in beadwork. Or you might embroider them in a sampler, or engrave them in the rim of a set of ceramic bowls. Say them out loud first thing or last thing every day, and keep them somewhere to hand where you can be reminded of them when you need them most.**

Positivity in the Bedroom, Where did you Lose your Positivity? and Always Carry a Spare Positivity. But here and now, folks, you can have this whole idea for free (or at least, for a fraction of the cost of the collection in which you found it).

Get used to it

The first thing anyone says is, 'But I don't feel positive. I really do never finish anything. I really am not good enough to try that.' No argument about the only limits to success being one's certainty of imminent failure will convince someone they're wrong about this!

So all I can say is, 'Get used to it!' Get used to the idea of ability, or confidence, or success, or whatever it is you think you lack, that would make what you do valid or valuable. Get used to hearing it from yourself. Say it even if you don't mean it. It's like positive action in the workplace to overcome wrong thinking such as racism or sexism: it feels strange and uncomfortable at first, but pretty soon everyone gets used to it and wonders why they ever thought or acted differently.

Creative people are particularly in need of this sort of positive self-encouragement. We tend to work alone, without the benefit of the support network that comes with working in a team. What we do is for others to enjoy, so we tend to see success depending on the approval of others, leaving us alone to do all the doubting.

> Defining idea...
>
> **'You got it, any way you want it, any way you want it to be. You can have it, take it from me, 'cos it's waiting for you.'**
> AVERAGE WHITE BAND, Scottish soul music success story

Something as simple as letting the first thing you say out loud each morning be 'Today I wake up refreshed and inspired' can transform your approach to your creative life in a very short space of time. Champion tennis player Martina Navratilova used to write herself notes in the dressing room at Wimbledon: 'I am the best player', 'I will win Wimbledon' and so on. It seems to have worked!

147. In the zone

'I'm going to write my book as soon as I have the time!' But if you really want to be successful, you have to make time and space to write.

It's easier said than done. What with working, dealing with children, partners who might not understand your ambitions – free time is a commodity that you're not even sure exists any more.

No matter how busy you are, however, it's essential that you devote time and energy to your writing every day. I've known people who always wanted to write, who carried an idea in their heads for years, but because they were so busy all the time it just never happened – their ideas faded, their ambition died and what could have been a wonderful book was never written. Don't surrender your stories to limbo – there is always more time in the day than you think.

Time is money

It may be an irritating statement, but in many ways it's true. Like money, you only have so much time, and you have to know how to spend it for maximum effect. And in the same way as you'd save money if you wanted to buy a new television, you have to learn how to reallocate time from various other areas of your life so that you can afford to spend a little of each day writing.

Take a closer look at how and where you spend your time, focusing on those things that aren't absolutely necessary. Do you watch television or play computer games in the evenings? Do you read the paper while eating your breakfast? Do you get out of bed at the last possible minute, or go to bed earlier than you need to?

A stitch in time

The chances are you've answered yes to more than one of these questions, which means that you *do* have time to write. Even if you don't actually sit down at a computer during these short breaks, use the time to write notes and thoughts in a notebook. Play with ideas, work on short sketches, character descriptions or snatches of dialogue. These are a great source of inspiration when you do finally sit down to write. Instead of staring at a cold screen thinking you have to start from scratch, your brain will be warmed up and ready to go.

Even during the times that you can't write things down – when you're walking to work, cleaning the windows, making the dinner – keep thinking about whatever you're working on. Picture your characters, imagine your fictional world, unknot any tricky plot points in your head, and write it all down when you get the chance. This thinking time is almost as important as writing itself.

Here's an idea for you...

It's the most simple, but the most important, thing that any writer must do. Buy a notebook, one small enough to be carried wherever you go. Every time you are inspired with an idea, a character trait, a plot point or an evocative description, write it down. Make yourself a promise – that you'll write something every day, either in your notebook or on your computer. Before you know it you'll be finding time everywhere.

The hours

Snatching bits and pieces of time here and there is great for keeping your passion alive, but if you truly want to be a published author then you have to write for a set amount of time *every day*. Try and give yourself an hour or so which is your own time, a time you can slip into your literary world and just write without distractions, without feeling guilty (make sure it's a time when your mind is at its most alert and creative). Pick a space which is your own, where you feel comfortable and relaxed. Tell friends and family not to disturb you unless the house is on fire, unplug the phone and don't let yourself be sidelined by anything.

Finding this time and space may seem impossible, but there are twenty-four hours in each day and I know you can free up one of them – even if it means getting up an hour earlier each morning or going to bed an hour later. And even if you only manage to squeeze in 200 words during each hour, at the end of a year you could have written a 75,000-word book.

148. Starting off

Writers starting something new can easily feel as daunted as Frodo Baggins embarking on his quest. But overcoming the terror of the blank page is simply a matter of putting pen to paper.

The carte blanche is a writer's worst nightmare because it only exists when you haven't written a single word. It fights a zero sum game with the author – only one of you can win. And it wages a dirty battle of fear and ridicule, telling you it can never be filled, that your book can never match the great classics of literature, that you may as well just give up. But the blank page can be quashed with a simple stroke of your pen.

War of the words

The worst mistake any writer can make is to try and defeat the blank page straight away with a masterpiece. Putting immense pressure on yourself is an easy way to obliterate your self-confidence and give the blank page a smug victory. Starting a book is one of the hardest aspects of writing, and I hear countless stories of people who have been so determined to go for the big one first time – the ultimate opening sentence – that they end up sitting staring at that blank page for the next ten years (I wish I was joking).

Too many first time writers see the blank page as something sacred – a canvas that they only have one shot at filling. The most important thing to do is to get rid of the idea that you are about to start writing a finished piece of work, or type out a first line of unrivalled genius. Instead, see that blank page as a sandbox, one where you are free to play and build and experiment in the knowledge that if you change your mind, you can simply start again.

Doodling

Defeat the blank page with a few simple lines or sketches. These don't have to be related to anything you're planning to write – they can just be random words, short sentences, patches of dialogue you heard on your way home from work, even visual doodles of characters and villains. Once you've made that first strike, the power of the blank page lessens.

The key is not to think too hard about what you are writing. Nobody but you will ever see these sketches and doodles, so you've got nothing to feel embarrassed about. Just keep writing and those random words will grow into sentences, then paragraphs and entire pages. With any luck it will be like a dam breaking. Once you've started off you'll find the words come more and more easily, until you segue into your novel or story so seamlessly you don't even know it's happened. And

---

Here's an idea for you...

If your mind is still blank, then look around your room or out of the window – pick any object and start writing about it. Don't pay too much attention to what you're saying, just keep writing for ten minutes or so, and include as much detail as possible. With any luck you'll find that once you've popped you just can't stop.

when you get to this stage, the only problem you'll have with the blank page is that there aren't enough of them.

A running start

If you're still having cold sweats at the thought of facing the blank page then don't panic. Try writing down a few words based on the following suggestions, using these starting points to inspire your own thoughts and feelings and ease you into the creative flow – write about a wedding you went to, the last argument you had, describe a loved one or somebody you fancy. Another interesting exercise is to describe something (an object or trait) you have inherited from a dead relative, and what it means to you.

The most important thing is to try and write every day without fail. Take a blank sheet of paper and write for a set time every morning or afternoon – even if it's just for a few minutes. If you get used to beating the blank page each and every day then you'll soon start to wonder why you were so intimidated by it in the first place. Most of these sketches you'll discard, but others might find their way into novels and stories. Either way, these sessions will help trigger memories, thoughts and inspirations that mean you're never bothered by the blank page again.

> *Defining idea...*
>
> **'How can one not dream while writing? It is the pen which dreams. The blank page gives the right to dream.'**
> GASTON BACHELARD, French poet

149. Show and tell

From old boxes under the bed to dirt-encrusted suitcases in the attic, we all have collections of memorabilia, ephemera and documents relating to the history of our homes and family.

Building up a full picture of your family's past as you go along is as important as discovering who your ancestors were. It is amazing how much can be found in papers secreted about the house or in the memories of your relatives.

So, start rummaging for family papers and memorabilia, and recording the memories of those who now possess them. What have you and your family got stored away? Start with yourself before moving on to your nearest and dearest – and remember too that it may not be the near or the dear that have the most useful stuff. Go through the trunks in the attic and the boxes under the stairs. Disregard nothing: it may be meaningless now but after a bit of investigation it may hold that vital piece of evidence you need. You are after anything you can find: letters, medals, photographs, a family Bible, birthday books, funeral cards, old postcards, birth, marriage and death certificates, baptism certificates, school reports, newspaper cuttings, details of a family grave – anything. You are after facts and you are after clues.

Your big personal breakthrough will come when you realise that most of the apparently insignificant papers and artefacts collecting dust have, as it were, a life beyond themselves. Every item you will come across is what it is – but almost certainly it will also be a clue or clues to further sources of research. Take First World War campaign medals, for example: these are going to be engraved with the recipient's name, regiment and number – all useful references for getting into army records. And birth, marriage and death certificates will all indicate other family members, occupations and address – so leading to census returns, maps showing where they lived at the time, and possibly records of occupations – as well as giving evidence of migration and mobility.

A trick with elderly relatives is to make them curious rather than suspicious. So try to show some interest in them as individuals – even though it is their possessions you are hoping to see. They need to think they are going to be as interesting to you while they are alive as they will be when they are dead!

Sometimes a 'find' will produce as many questions as it answers so try to get to the bottom of matters as you go along. Birthday books are great because they tell you the date of someone's birthday (but not the year). But if it just says something like '14 May, Maisie' you are not much further forward until you know who Maisie is, or was.

> Here's an idea for you...
>
> **Make sure you look after your family heirlooms by keeping them out of direct sunlight and store them in a cool place away from any potential danger from damp or insect infestation. Try to avoid handling them too much as well. Make copies of documents if you can. There are lots of excellent 'storage solutions' available. Using the proper materials to store your valuable memorabilia won't be cheap but it will undoubtedly be money well spent and you, and your descendants, won't regret it.**

Working with the belongings of members of your family is a very meaningful experience. Talking to those who actually knew those now departed, or have stories to tell about them, is something that can never be replaced by searching the bland lists and indexes to be found in record offices and libraries. But be warned: try to be a little detached as you undertake these investigations or there is the danger that you may be imbued with ideas and thoughts that are a little fanciful.

Every family will be different, but here are a few examples of the things to look out for that may contain some piece of vital information.

Account books • Address books • Awards • Baptism certificates • Birth, marriage and death certificates • Birthday and Christmas cards • Birthday books • Club and society memberships • Deeds • Diaries and journals • Diplomas • Divorce papers • Employment records • Family Bibles • Grave deeds • Insurance papers • Letters • Medical cards • Military records • Newspaper cuttings • Obituaries • Passports • Pension records • Photographs and portraits • Printed announcements • School prize books • School reports • Scrapbooks • Visitors' books • Wedding books • Wills and other probate documents

150. You have one day to live!

We undermine our health every day by not living in the present. Why spend all your time worrying about what might have been or what might happen tomorrow?

Have you ever driven somewhere and simply arrived as if by magic? We can become so engrossed in our thinking that we can unwittingly put the operation of our lives on automatic pilot.

Imagine you're at the doctors waiting for your test results. The door swings opens and the doctor sits you down and says, 'I'm afraid the news is bad – you only have a year to live.' What would you do with that year? Who would you become? Would you go out and help run a soup kitchen? Would you go round the world? Would you spend all your money?

This actually happened to my Uncle Tone who had his fortune told by a gypsy who said he would die when he was forty years old. So, he blew all his money on everything in sight, including a very fetching moleskin suit. However, unfortunately, or should I say fortunately, he survived another twenty years, but with a lot less money.

Mind matters

Mind control is everything. You are who you think you are (it took me a while to work that one out too). A good starting point is to accept that you can't change the past, however much you might want to. You can forgive the past and move on, but I'm afraid that without H. G. Wells and his time machine, you're stuck in the here and now. It might be a New Age trick, but forgiving those who have caused you harm is a place to start. Holding on to resentment and hurt over someone's past deeds is actually causing no damage to them whatsoever. The only person affected by that thinking is you! So stop that right now, forgive them and vow to move on to your future. Talking of the future, that's another favourite place of ours to lurk.

Worrying about it is a great way to freak us out completely. What if we lose our job, don't have enough money to pay the mortgage, get thrown out of our house and have to beg for scraps of food? I personally frequently imagine something terrible happening to some family member and then imagine what I'm going to wear at the funeral. Horrible. And a complete waste of time and a drain on our energy.

Here's an idea for you...

Try living today in the present. This won't be as easy as it sounds because thoughts are like chattering monkeys, jumping around from tree to tree. The only time when there's some respite is when we're asleep. Every time you feel yourself worrying about the future say to yourself, 'I'm not going to think about that now.' How does it feel to be right in the here and now?

Get a strategy

A must-have in your personal-development library is *How to Stop Worrying and Start Living* by Dale Carnegie. He also wrote the best selling *How to Win Friends and Influence People*. His book is really all you need for developing a strategy to cope with worry. Written just after the Second World War, he really must have known what worry was about. We forget what an unbelievably destabilising influence the war must have had on people's worlds. My mother-in-law was a little girl in London during the Blitz and came back from school to find her house had been blown to bits. Luckily, nobody was killed. However, imagine losing everything, including loved ones. One of Carnegie's tactics is to imagine that your worries are in watertight compartments. In the days when he was writing, ships had mechanical bulkheads that were able to section off parts of the hull should one area develop a leak, thus stopping the whole ship from being overwhelmed with water and sinking. Keep your worries behind the bulkhead and don't let them out again. That way they won't overwhelm or sink you.

I have several strategies for dealing with worry. For instance, I keep a pen and some paper by my bed at all times so that if I wake in the night and start to fret, I can jot my worries down so that I can deal with them the following day. Sometimes, by the time it gets to morning they're no longer anything to worry about. This strategy is like a mind dump and stops everything swilling around in your brain.

My other main strategy involves the news. I don't ever watch the news on TV or read a newspaper. I listen to the news once a day on the radio and that's it. We're totally inundated with images of bad news, woe, fear, gossip, disaster, war, politics and, worse still, politicians! It's a small wonder that we're worried about our future!

> Defining idea…
>
> **'The mountain is there, whether the clouds hide it or not.'**
> SUFI SAYING

Where it's at...